Duncan Staff is a leading  has produced a number of successful programmes. His work BBC1, BBC2, Channel 4 and ITV's *World in Action*. He also writes for the national press, principally the *Guardian*.

THE LOST BOY

The definitive story of the Moors
murders and the search for the final
victim

DUNCAN STAFF

BANTAM BOOKS

LONDON • TORONTO • SYDNEY • AUCKLAND • JOHANNESBURG

TRANSWORLD PUBLISHERS
61–63 Uxbridge Road, London W5 5SA
A Random House Group Company
www.rbooks.co.uk

**THE LOST BOY
A BANTAM BOOK: 9780553818079**

First published in Great Britain
in 2007 by Bantam Press
a division of Transworld Publishers
Bantam edition published 2008

Addresses for Random House Group Ltd companies outside the UK
can be found at: www.randomhouse.co.uk
The Random House Group Ltd Reg. No. 954009

The Random House Group Limited makes every effort to ensure that the
papers used in our books are made from trees that have been legally
sourced from well-managed and credibly certified forests. Our paper
procurement policy can be found on www.randomhouse.co.uk

Mixed Sources
Product group from well-managed
forests and other controlled sources
www.fsc.org   Cert no. TT-COC-2139
© 1996 Forest Stewardship Council

FSC

Typeset in 12/15pt Times New Roman by
Falcon Oast Graphic Art Ltd.

Printed in the UK by CPI Cox & Wyman, Reading, RG1 8EX.

4 6 8 10 9 7 5 3

Freedom and power – power above all.

Fyodor Dostoevsky, *Crime and Punishment* (1866)

Contents

Acknowledgements

I could not have written this book without the support of Keith Bennett's family. In order to do justice to their faith I have drawn upon the help of a large number of people. It is not possible to acknowledge everyone who has helped me, and I apologize to those whose names I have omitted.

I would like to thank my wife, Lucy, for her reading, advice and support; my editor, Simon Thorogood, for his skilful, constructive criticism; and my agent, John Saddler, for finding the right publisher for this book. I have also received invaluable assistance from Professor Malcolm MacCulloch, Professor John Hunter, Professor Bruno Frohlich, Detective Chief Superintendent Geoff Knupfer, Detective Chief Superintendent Ivan Montgomery, Detective Chief Superintendent Barrie Simpson, Detective Superintendent Tony Brett, Detective Sergeant Fiona Robertshaw, Detective Constable Gail Jazmik,

Detective Constable Alan Kibble, Detective Constable Andy Meekes, David Astor, Father Michael Teader, Andrew McCooey, Peter Simpson and Trisha Cairns. Finally, I would like to thank a teacher who inspired me, Professor David Blamires of Manchester University.

Introduction

It was a sunny Sunday morning in 1998, Bath's stone lit gold beneath the spring sky. I had my back door open, the newspapers spread out on the breakfast table, a steaming mug of black coffee in my hand. It had been a hard week in London, where I was directing a documentary series for BBC1, and I was looking forward to a day off.

Then, from the basement, came the sound of my office phone ringing. Reluctantly, I got up and ambled down the stairs, half hoping that the answering machine would kick in before I got there. I brushed some toast crumbs off my T-shirt and picked up the receiver.

'Hello, Duncan, it's Myra.'

I paused, startled, then stumbled, 'Hello . . . er, Myra . . . how are you?'

'I'm fine, thank you. I have decided that I will write my story for you.'

'Right . . .'

'A lot of people have asked me to do this, and I have refused. But I am going to trust you. All I ask is that you are fair.'

I put the phone down and sank back in my chair. Myra Hindley was trying to get out of prison, and her case was due before the Court of Appeal. Months earlier I had written to suggest that she give an account of her role in the Moors murders. If she agreed, I would make a BBC documentary examining the case. My film would test the claim that she was bullied into killing five children by her lover, Ian Brady.

The Moors murderers were sentenced to life in 1966 for killing ten-year-old Lesley Ann Downey, twelve-year-old John Kilbride and seventeen-year-old Edward Evans. The trial judge recommended that Myra Hindley serve twenty-six years. By his reckoning she should have been freed in 1992. But the only person who could issue a licence for her release was the Home Secretary, and no politician wanted to be remembered as 'the man who freed Myra Hindley'.

From the day she was sentenced the families of the murdered children waged a campaign with a single aim: her death behind bars. The mother of Lesley Ann Downey, Ann West, was foremost in ensuring that her raw grief formed a part of every story on the Moors murders. Hindley's supporters, in particular Lord Frank Longford, only poured fuel on the fire by proclaiming, within a few years of her conviction, that she was 'a good girl' who should be released. Like many, he was convinced that she had covered up for Ian Brady out of blind love.

The story was a gift for the newspapers. All it took was a fresh line, a quote from a mother, the iconic arrest photograph, and they had a splash. Uniquely, the power of the Moors murders story never faded. Hindley made things worse for herself by maintaining the lie that she was innocent. Only after she had served twenty years did she finally admit her crimes, and confirm that there were another two children buried on Saddleworth Moor: sixteen-year-old Pauline Reade and twelve-year-old Keith Bennett.

The tide of public opinion flowed strongly against her. The best she could hope for was that it might ebb enough for a judge to decide in her favour, and overrule the Home Secretary. Hindley saw writing to me, and the film I would make, as a way of saving herself.

I leant forward, stared at the telephone and swore under my breath. I had not really expected her to agree to my proposal. What had, in theory, seemed like a journalistically sound enterprise suddenly seemed fraught with difficulties. I would have to get very close to her to extract the story. Not only would this be distressing, but I ran the risk of being portrayed as a stooge by the tabloids.

The following Friday the first letter arrived. I slit open the envelope, pulled out eight pages of neatly typed words and began reading. The story felt carefully rehearsed but not fictitious; it had a strong, clear voice. I immediately realized that if she continued like this I would be able to make a very powerful documentary. I resolved to apply myself to the task. On the Sunday, I finished breakfast a little earlier than usual.

'Hello, Duncan. Did you get my letter?' She was standing in a corridor. I could hear the echo of footsteps and the rattle of keys in the background.

'Yes, Myra.'

'What did you think?'

'It was very clear, and the depth of the material was about right. It gives me enough detail to examine the credibility of what you are saying.'

'Good. I'll try to continue in the same way. You must let me know if I start rambling.'

'I don't really want to steer you, Myra. If you fail to address an important question I'll repeat it, but that's all.'

'Fair enough.'

We fell into a rhythm. Every week, when I got back from London, there was a letter lying on my desk. I read it straight away, jotted down notes for the Sunday call, and filed it. If not friends, we became familiar. It is impossible to tell your life story, whatever it may be, to a cold and distant stranger.

Things were going well. She described her childhood in Manchester, her teenage years, and the meeting with Ian Brady. But everything changed when she moved on to the murders. I did not find her explanation of how they came about convincing. The descent into violence seemed both inexplicable and horrific.

The words I read at the weekend began intruding into daily life; over time, they even entered my dreams. I came to question my ability to deal with the material in an even-handed manner, to disentangle truth from fiction. I realized that if I was to continue I would need professional help. A former head of Greater Manchester CID, Geoff Knupfer, pointed me in the direction of the forensic psychiatrist who had advised him. Malcolm MacCulloch has expert knowledge of sexually sadistic serial killers in general and the Moors murderers in particular. As the medical director of Park Lane Hospital on Merseyside he recommended Ian Brady's transfer from prison to psychiatric hospital, and spent a number of years treating him. I outlined the situation to him, and he suggested that we meet.

The following week I crossed the Severn bridge to Wales, where MacCulloch was professor of forensic psychiatry at the University of Cardiff. He also, in his spare time, edited *The British Journal of Forensic Psychiatry*. The door was opened by a small, neat man with receding hair and a pair of half-moon glasses.

'Come in, come in. What have you got there then?'

Malcolm MacCulloch did not bother with a lengthy

social preamble. He communicated through his manner, as much as his words, that he recognized the journalistic tools I had deployed in pursuit of a story, and understood the situation I now found myself in. His directness, and incisiveness, allowed me to relax and be straightforward. He read through the letters and listened to recordings of my conversations with Myra Hindley.

'Why do you tape your calls?' he asked.

'To be sure I don't miss anything.'

'Very good.'

The professor squatted low over the tape recorder, listened to me laughing at one of her jokes. I shifted uncomfortably in my seat.

'She thinks she's got you,' he said.

'That's one of the reasons I'm here.'

'It's OK. It's all right.' He gave me a conspiratorial smile. 'I've questioned a lot of mass murderers. They have to feel that they are in charge or you get nothing.'

'The question is, am I being manipulated?'

'Of course you are, but you're also getting what you want. The trick is to remain alive to what's going on.'

The professor pulled off his half-moon glasses and held me in his gaze. 'You also have to understand that this is a unique, valuable opportunity to understand these crimes. It's a once-in-a-lifetime opportunity.' He added that he would read all future letters, and help me to frame questions that would get at the truth. 'Pro bono publico – it's in the public interest.'

I travelled back to England with my mind at rest; this was an important job that needed to be done properly. Over the coming days the nightmares faded as I took a more dispassionate view of the material. I also resolved to be more calculating in the way I dealt with Myra Hindley. This was easier said than done, as she retained an unnerving ability to catch me off guard.

'Hello, Duncan, it's Myra.'

'Hello, Myra.'

'Duncan, you have children, don't you?'

'Hmm . . .'

'They can be so mean to one another. The other day my nephew put a pillow on his baby cousin's head. Luckily his mother came in in time. It's just jealousy, isn't it? Do your children get jealous of one another?'

Her anecdote was meant to convey empathy and understanding, but there was too much detail; I felt she was enjoying the story. I went on the offensive.

'Myra, are you going to address the murder of Lesley Ann Downey?'

There was silence, then a sigh. 'I keep trying to do it, but every time I sit down at my typewriter I can't get the words out. I just find it so difficult to deal with. To think that I could have been such a cruel, cruel bastard.'

Over the next few months Myra Hindley consistently failed to explain the circumstances surrounding the murder of the ten-year-old girl. I kept on demanding an answer because this was the case that had sealed her fate more than three decades earlier.

On Thursday, 9 December 1965, Myra Hindley and Ian Brady were led up the stone steps from Hyde police station to the town's magistrates' court for their committal hearing. They faced three justices of the peace who would decide whether the case should go to Crown Court. The magistrates had to consider every piece of evidence against the accused. As proceedings opened, the chairman of the bench made a decision that was devastating to the defence: she rejected an application to hold proceedings in camera. The court's narrow wooden benches were crammed with reporters from around the world. As the evidence unfolded over the next eleven days it was laid before their readers.

Central to the prosecution case was an audiotape hidden in a left-luggage office at Manchester Central station by Ian Brady. Rather than rely on the transcript, the magistrates ordered it to be played. Lesley Ann Downey's mother, Ann West, sat across from Myra Hindley as the magnetic strip was looped up on a machine in the middle of the court, and the clerk set it running.

There were some loud clacking sounds – lighting stands going up and down as Ian Brady moved about, photographing the girl in a series of pornographic poses. Myra Hindley could be heard in the background, closing a window so the neighbours wouldn't hear. Lesley Ann refused to put a gag in her mouth, and begged, 'Please don't hurt me, Mam.' Myra Hindley told her to 'shurrup crying'. The tape seemed to go on for ever. When Lesley Ann did finally fall silent the court echoed to the sound of Bing Crosby's warm voice singing 'The Little Drummer Boy'.

Murderers' and victim's words, seared forever into the most hardened reporters' minds, were repeated the following morning in almost every English language newspaper around the world. From that day on, the idea of being able to find twelve unbiased men and women to sit on a jury lacked all credibility. The Crown Court trial, at Chester Assizes in the spring of 1966, provided the stage for a horrific rehearsal of the crimes rather than a process to determine guilt or innocence.

Professor Malcolm MacCulloch viewed Myra Hindley's failure thirty-three years later to deal with the murder of Lesley Ann Downey as highly significant. 'Her case rests on the argument that she was bullied into abducting the children, and that she did not actually carry out the killings,' he pointed out. 'The tape puts her in the room. As these crimes were systematic, and conformed to a pattern, it is highly likely that she was there during all the murders. This is the point at which her story falls apart, and she knows it. The best she can hope for is that you fail to understand the significance of the omission.'

This argument was to form the conclusion to my

documentary. I finished the film, and delivered it to the BBC to await transmission. Although it was a piece of work I could be proud of, there remained a nagging sense of frustration. I might have established that Myra Hindley was lying, but I had not discovered the full truth about the crimes, nor had I explained why they remained part of the fabric of national life. The case also remained open, with a child still missing on Saddleworth Moor.

I had planned to end my working relationship with Myra Hindley once the film was finished, but this felt wrong with so many questions unanswered. The only way to maintain contact was to confront her, face to face, with my conclusions. I spent an uneasy evening in Cambridge before travelling the twenty miles to her prison in Suffolk.

I arrived at a collection of single-storey buildings ranged behind razor wire. But for the sign HMP HIGHPOINT you could have mistaken them for an army barracks. After a short wait in a windswept Nissen hut, a guard waved me through security to a small annexe at the back of the prison. The segregation unit's small visiting room was rectangular and painted glossy beige. In the centre stood a Formica table, on it two vacuum flasks, a plate of biscuits and a small white china bowl for putting used teabags into. I pulled out a chair, faced the door and waited.

A woman's low laugh echoed down the corridor; it was over-loud, an announcement giving me time to prepare myself. I stood up as she shuffled through the door on hospital walking sticks.

'Hello, Duncan.'

'Hello, Myra.'

We held each other's gaze and shook hands. Her eyes were those of the arrest photograph taken at Hyde police station thirty-four years earlier.

'Would you like some tea?' she asked.

'Yes please.'

She wore an immaculate lilac trouser suit over a loose linen shirt. Her auburn hair was newly dyed, and her nails perfectly manicured. Around her neck hung a thin silver ingot engraved with a cross. She had a confident, worldly air; there was no hint of the empty despair that has gripped every other 'lifer' I've met.

As I sipped my tea, I knew I was about to test our relationship to breaking point.

'Myra, the film is finished. I've laid events out as they happened and allowed your words to speak for themselves. The biggest problem for you is the failure to address the killing of Lesley Ann Downey.'

'Right.' Her eyes bored into me.

'I have included an answerphone message in which you say that you find it too difficult to deal with.'

'Well, at least you've told me,' she said in a flat, emotionless voice, without breaking eye contact.

Before long we parted, agreeing to stay in touch, and to meet again. But I left Highpoint wondering how she would feel when her evasion was laid bare on screen.

In order to get the facts right in my documentary I had carried out research interviews with as many people as possible. Most of them did not appear in the finished film, but they had a decisive effect on its tone and accuracy. No one made a deeper impression on me than Keith Bennett's younger brother, Alan, who told me about their life together and how it came to an end.

The boys had beds next to each other in a small terraced house at the end of Eston Street in Longsight. The two scrappy white goal lines they painted on the adjoining redbrick wall are still there. It was an enclosed, secure world. But several nights a week the Bennett children left it to spend the night with their grandmother on the other side of the Stockport Road. It gave their mam a break. They were usually walked there together, but on Thursday, 16 June 1964, Alan and his sister Maggie had gone on ahead. 'When Keith didn't show up we thought he must have changed his mind and decided to stay with our mam,' Alan said.

Like most working-class families, the Bennetts did not have a telephone. It was only the following morning that Keith's gran called at her daughter Winnie's to ask why he had failed to come round. 'We knew straight away something bad had happened,' Alan told me. 'I didn't know what to do. I just went outside and banged a ball against the wall. I stayed there for hours, kicking away.' The police came round, took his step-father in for questioning, and dug up the back yard in the search for a body. The Bennett family was plunged into physical as well as emotional chaos.

The children were forgotten among the grief and confusion. Alan retreated into silence. At night he climbed the stairs to the room he shared with Keith and spent hours staring blankly at his empty bed. 'I used to lie there and talk to him. Where are you, Keith? Come back. He was like a presence who was still with me, but physically he'd gone. And that's never changed. He's been with me all these years.'

Alan only found out for certain what had happened to Keith in the mid-eighties. By then, Myra Hindley had broken off all contact with Ian Brady. In revenge, he told a newspaper that there were another two bodies on Saddleworth Moor. His intention was to extinguish any hope of freedom she had. Brady's 'revelation' led to a firestorm of publicity. The police, under severe pressure from the newspapers, reopened the search for Pauline Reade and Keith Bennett. The senior investigating officer, Peter Topping, and his deputy, Geoff Knupfer, visited Myra Hindley at Cookham Wood prison in Rochester. Cornered, she decided to confess. Over three days she gave the detectives a tape-recorded account of her role in the murders. Peter Topping then led a small team of detectives in a long search of Saddleworth Moor.

After several months, during which their methods were heavily criticized, they found Pauline Reade's remains in a shallow grave on Hollin Brown Knoll. Shortly afterwards, the Chief Constable of Greater Manchester, James Anderton, told Topping to stop looking for Keith. His remains have never been found.

It took the Bennett family some time to realize that the police would only resume work if they got, as one officer put it to me, an 'X marks the spot'. Alan took charge of the search himself. At weekends he and his brothers combed the moor with a small group of volunteers. Over ten years they dug through every patch of peat, until they hit rock, along the banks of Shiny Brook stream.

Alan, who worked in the stockroom at Argos, was painfully aware that he and his team were amateurs. He compensated for this by tracking down and questioning forensic experts. Most were willing to talk; few could offer practical assistance. An exception was the leading forensic archaeologist Professor John Hunter.

Hunter revolutionized the way in which police forces around the world find murder victims and prosecute their killers. He has researched, in minute detail, how bodies are concealed. Most burials conform to well-established patterns; understanding these can lead detectives to a victim far more quickly than traditional search methods. When Hunter does locate a grave he treats it as a source of evidence. He and an assistant dig slowly using three-and-a-half-inch bricklayer's pointing trowels, rather than spades, looking for signs that might trap the killer. 'It's surprising how often you find a footprint at the bottom! But every cut in the earth tells a story: when the grave was dug, what with, and whether the killer was in a frenzied state of mind or calm.'

When they met, the professor revealed to Alan that it was very rare for a murder victim to be hidden more than twenty metres from a road. A body, even that of a child, is very difficult to carry. But Myra Hindley told the police that Keith was more than half a mile from the A635. 'This means that Keith was almost certainly buried in the place he died,' Hunter reasoned. 'Brady must have chosen a concealed location with exposed peat in which to dig the grave.' Hunter carried out a survey of the moorland; in all, there were around ten areas of 'dead ground' – ground that could not be observed from the road – along the banks of Shiny Brook stream. He made a couple of tentative efforts to narrow the search down further with a police body dog, but what he really needed was manpower to strip off the turf covering all his 'target areas'. There were simply too many of them.

One evening I was sipping tea with Alan Bennett in his bedsit close to Eston Street when he said something that confirmed I could not simply walk away from the 'story' of the Moors murders after transmission of my film. 'There are only two people who can tell us where Keith is buried. Brady's not going to help us, so it can only come from her.' In other words, my relationship with Myra Hindley could be used to extract new information.

The BBC held a preview screening of my documentary, *Myra Hindley*, in a large, crescent-shaped conference room at the front of Television Centre. More than twenty reporters from national newspapers attended. Four or five BBC press officers huddled around me, as much to try to ensure that I said the right thing as to protect me. The Corporation's management was extremely nervous about the film, and the chairman of the board of governors, Sir Christopher Bland, had sent for a copy. As I tried to make an escape, Antonella Lazzeri of the *Sun* intercepted me. I was on my guard as her paper had already run a story headlined MYRA GETS HER OWN FILM. She said, in a quiet voice, as if in confidence, 'I've always thought she should be released myself.' I stared at her, said nothing, and walked off to take a seat at the back of the room. As the projector hummed into life over my right shoulder I lost myself, concentrating on technical details rather than the content.

When the film finished, I made my way to a chair by the projection screen to answer questions, trying to hide any nervousness I felt.

'Why did you make the film – doesn't it just give her a platform?' asked a *Daily Mirror* reporter.

'You've seen it,' I replied. 'Do you think it gave her a platform?'

He shrugged, and jabbed at his pad with a biro.

'The case has been on the front pages for more than thirty years,' I continued, 'yet in all that time no one had been able to question her before. As her case for release was coming before the courts it was in the public interest to do so. Where she's refused to answer, or lied, I've included it.'

'All right,' the man from the *Daily Mail* cut in, 'could you pull out the new lines for us?'

The following morning there was nothing in the *Sun*. The paper had decided not to attack me, and it avoids repeating other people's stories. The controller of BBC2, Jane Root, sent me an extravagant bunch of flowers. There was a letter from the chairman of the board of governors saying that his 'trepidation' before watching the film had been 'misplaced'.

That Sunday my office phone rang. I walked slowly down the stairs and lifted the receiver.

'Duncan, it's Myra.'

'Hello, Myra. Did you see the film?'

'Yes.'

'What did you think?'

'It didn't help my cause. But I can't complain. You stuck to the deal.'

I quickly moved the conversation on.

'Myra, you know John Hunter?'

'Yes.'

'Would you be willing to answer some questions about the route you and Ian Brady took with Keith?' MacCulloch had advised me to give her a strong reason to co-operate. I had the follow-up ready. 'It can hardly hurt your case, can it, Myra?'

There was a pause. She read my tactics, but could not argue with the logic.

'All right, I'll do it,' she said.

A few days later I met Professor Hunter in a lecture theatre at Birmingham University. He paced up and down, muttering to himself, as he drew up a list of questions on a whiteboard. 'They have to be simple. Not, "Where is the body?" but, "What could you see, smell, hear?" That way we can narrow down the search area.'

'Sure, but you've got to make the questions direct or she'll think you're playing games and refuse to answer,' I warned him.

'Yes, yes. Well, that's what you're here for.'

We worked together for three hours. He came up with the ideas; I helped shape sentences that might evoke a response.

I sent Hunter's letter off with a handwritten covering note, but there was no reply. The Catholic chaplain of Highpoint, Father Michael Teader, saw her every few days. I called him to ask what was going on. 'I'm afraid she's slipped into a deep depression since her appeal failed,' he said. Father Michael needed little persuasion of the importance of Hunter's endeavour.

He told me, 'That boy needs to be found. It's the only way this whole thing is going to retreat into history.' He agreed to try to persuade Myra Hindley to answer Hunter's questions. 'I'm not going to bully her though. That would backfire. I'll wait until she's in the right frame of mind.'

Over the next six months, working with Father Michael, Myra Hindley drew a series of maps. The first of these described the route she and Ian Brady took the night Keith died. It contained many details: 'I climbed up here, flattish; he and Keith went on, I don't know how far; shale bank, buried spade here'. But the map was drawn in black pen on a plain white sheet of paper, with no distance scale, and was very difficult to use on the ground. Professor Hunter's solution was to send her Ordnance Survey maps divided into different coloured zones, for her to draw on. The tortuous process was lengthened by her poor mental health: she kept slipping in and out of depression, and needed much encouragement.

The professor and his assistant, Detective Chief Superintendent Barrie Simpson, the former head of the West Midlands Police murder squad, returned to the moor and used the maps to narrow down the previously identified areas of dead ground. They were assisted by staff and students from the archaeology department at Birmingham University. On a couple of occasions forensic archaeologists on leave from exhuming mass graves in Bosnia came along too. With the help of aerial photographs the archaeologists identified which of the concealed patches of moorland had exposed areas of peat in 1964. They also surveyed the ground using specialist equipment to see if any were deep enough to conceal a body. Hunter's search narrowed down the possible places Keith could be buried to just a few gullies. But, once again, the only way to complete his work was to dig the moorland. He presented his results to the police but, as there was still no 'X marks the spot', they listened politely and took no further action. There was little more Hunter could do.

Myra Hindley's willingness to help Hunter may have been influenced by a recent seismic shift in the legal landscape: the United Kingdom's adoption of the European Convention on Human Rights. The power to decide how long a lifer served could now be taken away from politicians and handed to the judiciary. If this happened, the decision about her future would become legal rather than political. It was the best chance of freedom Myra Hindley had ever had. Helping to find Keith Bennett's body, and closing the case, could only help.

Hindley's legal team, led by Edward Fitzgerald QC, put her case to nine of the country's most senior judges over two weeks in the autumn of 2002. There was a sense of history in the making as distinguished lawyers, many of whom had no direct interest in the proceedings, gathered in committee room 9 of the

House of Lords to hear the arguments. Fitzgerald was skilful and confident in his submissions. The judges listened carefully as he outlined how the life sentence system should now work. Only when he attempted to deploy an analogy drawn from Wittgenstein's *Tractatus* did Lord Chief Justice Woolf scold him: 'Stick to the point, Mr Fitzgerald.'

While he was deferential in front of the bench, and cautious when he thought there was a reporter nearby, in private Fitzgerald allowed his optimism to shine through. He rang Myra Hindley regularly; 'I'm going to get you out,' he told her. An acknowledgement of the Home Secretary's plight was written on the face of his aptly named counsel, David Pannick QC. Even so, I was surprised when I learned that the embattled David Blunkett had instructed Greater Manchester Police to see whether they could come up with fresh charges to keep her inside. The chief constable told one of his most trusted detectives, Superintendent Tony Brett, to assemble a team and re-examine the case.

Officially, the Moors murder inquiry had never been closed. But for the past fifteen years there had been just two officers assigned to it. As these were Special Branch 'spooks' and the IRA was active in Manchester, the case was not a priority. In private the detectives acknowledged that their job was to 'manage' the families and members of the public who came forward with suggestions and offers of help.

They would act if new information came to light, but they weren't out looking for it.

Brett's team were specialist murder squad officers. He gave each an area of responsibility and told them to become experts in it. DC Dave Warren mapped the moor and carried out an audit of all the searches for bodies; DC Gail Jazmik studied Brady's photographs; DC Andy Meekes read every word that had been written on the case; DS Fiona Robertshaw gathered intelligence; DC Phil Steele checked that nothing was missed. Their purpose was clear: to make sure Myra Hindley was never released. If they found Keith Bennett along the way all well and good, but that was not their primary purpose.

Tony Brett thought he might be able to charge Myra Hindley with the murders she had never been tried for. The statement she had given to his predecessor, Peter Topping, early in 1987 was an unequivocal admission of guilt. The new investigating team met government lawyers but were warned that laying new charges was likely to be ruled an 'abuse of process' because of a decision taken fifteen years earlier. After Myra Hindley confessed, the families of Keith Bennett and Pauline Reade had sought a new trial. The Director of Public Prosecutions had opposed them on the grounds that, as there was no prospect of release, a lengthy court case would be a waste of taxpayers' money. The courts agreed. Tony Brett was told by the government lawyers that this decision could not be reversed.

Greater Manchester Police let David Blunkett know the bad news: he was at the mercy of the Law Lords.

The phone call to his office from the Home Office Lifer Unit on Friday, 15 November 2002 must therefore have come as a welcome relief: Myra Hindley was dead. Father Michael Teader asked if I would like to attend the funeral; I declined and watched it on the TV news instead. Cameras crowded the pavement outside Cambridge crematorium. As the coffin was carried in a young blonde woman delivered a carefully rehearsed piece to camera. None of Myra Hindley's family went to her funeral either. It's not that they didn't care – she spoke to her mother every day for news of what was going on 'at home' – but they still live in Manchester under different names, and need anonymity to have any hope of a normal life. Father Michael, who had held her hand as she lay dying, did his best to deliver a dignified service for the six anonymous people who did attend. But the atmosphere was tense.

After the funeral Father Michael packaged up Myra Hindley's ashes and posted them to a former lover of hers. The woman drove the remains, which were contained in what looked like a sweet jar, to a stretch of moor east of Saddleworth. It was a sunny day and she walked slowly along a high path scattering the ash into the air as she went. The walk took her half an hour.

Once she had completed her task she made a decision: she would release Myra Hindley's papers to me. They comprised part of an unpublished autobiography, thousands of letters and hundreds of photographs taken during the period of the Moors murders. She hoped the documents might contribute to an understanding of the case and help the search for Keith Bennett.

I travelled north with mixed feelings. Even though Hindley was dead I was being sucked back into the world of the Moors murderers. I was shown into a small, dark room at the back of a remote cottage and told to take everything I thought might be relevant. I gathered up the lot, drove home to Somerset and spent the next few months reading and cataloguing what I had been given.

As I studied the documents I realized that they began to explain what made Myra Hindley the woman she was, and the true nature of the relationship between her and Ian Brady. It might now be possible to understand why the Moors murders case had remained open, and a part of the fabric of national life, for so long. I decided to investigate the story they told.

Book One
Manchester

'I am a child of Gorton in Manchester. Infamous, I have become disowned, but I am one of your own.'

Chapter One

Myra Hindley lived the first twenty-three years of her life as a free woman; of these, twenty-two were spent in the tightly packed grid of terraced houses that is Gorton, close to the heart of Manchester. In order to understand the forces that shaped her I began my search there.

I left Manchester city centre and drove east along the Hyde Road, past the Apollo Theatre, a boarded-up Victorian school and a succession of abandoned warehouses. On the passenger seat lay a map marked with my destination. After what must have been two miles I came to a cluster of shops and a Kentucky Fried Chicken outlet. I swung left, opposite Chloe's Beauty and Tanning Centre, and looped round the back of KwikSave, past the Pineapple pub and into Taylor Street. The sight that confronted me was a surprise. The terrace she grew up in had been ripped down and replaced with mock Tudor four-bedroom houses. Each had a carefully trimmed square of grass, a car parking bay out the front and a satellite dish. They looked incongruous, and were surrounded by terraces Myra Hindley would have recognized as the homes of her friends and relations.

Towering over the end of Taylor Street stood a Gothic church with the dimensions of a cathedral. Looking down was a pale stone carving of Christ on the cross. The building was abandoned; a buddleia flowered from a flying buttress; pigeons flapped behind stained glass. In the church's shadow a rusting archway to an abandoned garden bore the name 'Monastery of St Francis'. A brightly coloured, thirty-metre-long hoarding around the perimeter revealed that the building had been acquired by a charitable trust. The top half predicted a proud future; the bottom half bore a legend that summarized Gorton's past: 610, colonized by the Saxons; 1555, families survived Great Famine by eating seeds; 1742, stocks erected opposite the George and Dragon; 1792, Gorton has eight 'boggerts', or evil spirits; 1819, Peterloo Massacre; 1846, Gaol built; 1957, 'Monkey-rama' opens at Belle Vue. There was no mention of Myra Hindley or the fact that this was the place where she took her First Communion.

For the rest of the day I wandered around, trying to make sense of Gorton's geography and falling into conversation with its people. The place had a strong sense of identity but did not feel closed. It was easy to talk to complete strangers. 'Ask people here where they're from and they'll say West Gorton, not Manchester,' an elderly lady sitting on a bench in Sunny Brow Park told me. 'It's like a big village really.' I passed the schools Myra Hindley attended; the railway embankments she played on; the pubs she and Ian Brady drank in. Many of the place names spoke of the countryside: Lower Cat's Knowle, Daisy Bank, Sunnyside, Ryder Brow. I wondered how Gorton had been transformed from pastoral idyll to industrial crucible, and whether this might inform me about the people who lived there.

I sought an answer in Manchester's oldest building, Chetham's College of Music, and library. The building stands in the centre of the city, a few minutes' walk from Victoria station. Its honey-coloured walls lend it the appearance of an Oxford college. Inside, across a neatly trimmed quadrangle, choirs competed with orchestras. I made my way across the imposing space, and down a dark corridor. At the end I came to a small oak door set into a stone wall and hesitated, not sure I had the right place. In the end, reasoning that all I risked was disturbing someone's work, I tugged on what appeared to be a bell pull. Far above I heard a high ringing and, after a delay of half a minute or more, the sound of leather-soled shoes descending a wooden staircase.

'Can I help?'

'I was hoping to visit the reading room.'

The archivist, a small, smartly dressed woman with long red hair, nodded, turned and led me upstairs.

As we emerged from the dingy staircase I had to squint to adjust to the bright light. Sunshine flooded through leaded windows onto a polished oak table. Beyond it, stretching into the darkness, I could see shelf upon shelf of ancient volumes. In the corner of the room stood a wooden case containing two rows of dusty tethered texts – a 'chained library' donated to the parish of Gorton by Sir Thomas Chetham four hundred years earlier. The contents did not look like easy reading; there seemed to be a lot of Calvin. A sign revealed that until 1974 it had stood in the corner of St James's Protestant Church. This was where Ian Brady and Myra Hindley attended midnight communion.

The archivist informed me, with a hint of pride in her voice, that this was the oldest library in the English-speaking world, and that the table set into an alcove was where Friedrich Engels had researched a book that changed the course of world history: *The Condition of the Working Class in England*. Engels travelled to Manchester for the same reason as thousands of other young men: it was the most vibrant, fastest-growing city in the world. The difference was that Engels, under the cover of working for his father's textile business, came here to study the effect of capitalism on ordinary people. His book, a cornerstone of communist doctrine, had a profound effect on his friend Karl Marx and the shape of his masterwork, *Das Kapital*. It is unmistakably the work of a radical young idealist, and strays into polemic, but it does paint a vivid picture of working-class life during Manchester's formative years: 'Everywhere before the doors refuse and offal; that any sort of pavement lay underneath could not be seen but only felt, here and there, with the feet.' Living conditions in central Manchester were so bad that even Engels, with his vivid powers of description, found it a struggle 'to convey a true impression of the filth, ruin and uninhabitableness, the defiance of all considerations of cleanliness, ventilation, and health which characterize the construction of this single district, containing at least twenty to thirty thousand inhabitants. And such a district exists in the heart of the second city of England, the first manufacturing city of the world. If anyone wishes to see in how little space a human being can move, how little air – and *such* air! – he can breathe, how little of civilization he may share and yet live, it is only necessary to travel hither.'

I spread a large, yellowed map onto the wooden table. The hand-drawn document showed what Gorton looked like in the eighteenth century, before the Industrial Revolution. It was a mass of fields with a few rows of cottages, and a church. The parish, I read, had been reclaimed from the moor and turned to pasture five hundred years earlier. It turned out that one of the poet Byron's ancestors once bought it as 'an investment'. I pulled out a second map, drawn a hundred years later. I stood and stared in wonder at the human endeavour represented by the mass of tiny rectangles that had replaced the fields. It was almost impossible to imagine that this mass of factories and terraces was once the edge of the moor that stretched east, over the Pennines, towards Sheffield.

The Gorton that shaped Myra Hindley had a distinctive set of rhythms. The time people got up, the paths they took to work, the sounds that came from the factories were repeated day in, day out. This imbued its people with common characteristics, and a strong sense of identity. The nature of this identity owed much to the arrival in Manchester of Karl Beyer, a young German from a far humbler background than Engels', in 1834.

The son of a poor weaver from Saxony, the bright young engineer had worked his way through Dresden Polytechnic, existing on just twenty pounds a year. His original plan, laid down by his sponsors, was that he would study the new textile machinery in England and return home with the secrets of its success. But Karl, who soon changed his name to Charles, had no intention of going back to Saxony. He had come to Manchester to make his fortune.

Charles got a job in the drawing office of Sharp Roberts & Company, a firm of textile engineers, and stood out immediately. When the business diversified into the manufacture of steam locomotives Charles was assigned to the new design office. Six years later, at the age of just twenty-five, he was made chief engineer. Over the next ten years he drove the business with bold projects completed on time and on budget. Charles was recognized as one of the brightest engineers in the manufacturing capital of the world, and he expected to be rewarded with a share in the business he had built, not with a wage. His employer, Richard Roberts, saw things differently and refused the young German both a partnership and, it is rumoured, his daughter's hand in marriage.

Charles found a way forward when he met a young railway manager, Richard Peacock, supervising the construction of 'Gorton Tank' to the north of Taylor Street. The vast complex of railway sheds, workshops and lines would bind Gorton to Manchester, transforming it for ever from a village into part of the city. Charles was struck by the ambition and efficiency of the operation, and he closely questioned the Yorkshireman, who turned out to be two years younger than him, about his background. Richard told Charles that he had left Leeds Grammar School at the age of fourteen, seduced by the 'exciting' prospect of working with trains. Within four years he was made superintendent of the Leeds and Selby Railway. He took charge of the larger Manchester and Sheffield line at twenty-one. Richard Peacock, it became clear, was every bit as ambitious as Charles Beyer.

Peacock would visit the design office to place orders with Sharp Roberts, and he and Beyer developed a close relationship. They soon came to realize that a combination of their talents could form the basis of a formidable business, and resolved to set up Beyer Peacock Engineering – 'train builders to the world'. But though the two young men had plenty of ambition, they lacked money. They found a third partner, Henry Robertson, to invest in the business. Although just two years older than Charles, Henry had already amassed a fortune building railways and a famous nineteen-arch bridge over the River Dee at Ruabon in North Wales. He was looking for a new challenge.

The partners bought a field for their new factory across the tracks from Gorton Tank. The trains would be able to roll straight onto the new lines laid by Richard Peacock and, because much of Gorton remained untouched, they could shape it in their image as the business expanded. The new firm's first big order, from the East Indian Railway, was in the bag before a brick had been laid. This was a significant breakthrough. Beyer was able to poach the best of Sharp Roberts' workforce and guarantee them a future, and he created a design and production process that could deliver high-quality engines faster and more cheaply than his stunned former employer.

The three partners enjoyed their new-found status and wealth. A photograph of 1860 shows Peacock smiling, looking regal in furs and surrounded by packing cases and servants, ready for 'an expedition' to Russia. He was travelling, in style, to sell Beyer Peacock's 'magnificent' trains to yet another new market.

The business challenged, and eventually overtook, the importance of the mills to West Gorton. Former weavers found themselves riveting and hammering engines that helped to power the empire. The work was regular, and for the forgemen there was a perk no mill worker had ever enjoyed: beer to 'quench their thirst'. By the time the owners of Beyer Peacock realized the folly of this practice and offered lemon barley water instead, it had become ingrained. They decided to avoid a confrontation. Men might be getting injured, but the trains were still being built.

Beyer Peacock won orders in South Africa, New South Wales, Caracas and, of course, Manchester. Increasing numbers of men were required for Gorton Foundry, and their families needed houses. The new streets were given names that reflected what Gorton had become. Railway View, later home to Myra Hindley's Auntie Anne, stood so close to the Sheffield and Midland line that the gardens were black with soot and cups shook in their saucers whenever a train went by.

Manchester's reputation as a vibrant, immoral place spread throughout the world. In 1861 seven Belgian monks led by Father Emmanuel Kenners

abandoned their monastery in Cornwall and travelled
north to establish a 'mission'. Their strategy was
simple: they would offer moral encouragement alongside practical help. They bought Bankside cottage, a
small house with some land on Gorton Lane, and
quickly built a combined school and chapel. Their first
mass was held in the new building, amid great excitement, on Christmas Day.

The monks also planned a magnificent church to
demonstrate their faith, and determination to stay,
to the people of Gorton. Father Kenners hired
twenty-four-year-old Edward Welby Pugin – whose
father, August, had designed the interior of the Palace
of Westminster – to come up with a plan. The High
Gothic, cathedral-like building he proposed was both
outrageously ambitious and expensive. He told the
monks that he wanted to create a church that was 184
feet long, 98 feet wide and 100 feet tall. Light would
pour through the stained glass onto a ceiling-high
Bath-stone altar designed by his brother Paul, and
elaborate, gilded carvings of saints would gaze down
on the parishioners as they filed into one of thirteen
confessionals that ran from front to back. These were
of an ingenious design, with two doors each, so that
one penitent could wait in privacy while another un-
burdened his soul to a priest. Father Michael Teader,
Myra Hindley's priest and final confessor, explained
the Franciscans' aim to me: 'They were creating a
piece of heaven on earth, to lift the people from their

surroundings, give them hope.' Because Manchester is flat, Pugin enthused, you would be able to see the church over the roofs of the packed terraces from miles away.

The monks were inspired by the young man's grand vision, but had just £2,500 to spend. They would have to build the church themselves. The job fell to their clerk of works, Brother Patrick Dalton, from County Kerry in south-west Ireland. Over the next eight years he led a gang of volunteers made up of parishioners in his monumental task. First, he ripped down Bankside cottage and replaced it with a friary. Once he had put a roof over his comrades' heads he started work on the church while the other monks fell to work in the parish, opening a soup kitchen for the destitute alongside their school for the poor. Because bricks were expensive and clay was free, Brother Patrick got his gang to build firing kilns in the monastery grounds. While the parishioners worked under the supervision of his deputy, Father Peter Hickey, he fixed a nag to a cart and rode into Manchester. His tall figure, with its closely cropped head, long silver beard and flowing brown robe, stalked the city's construction sites in search of free materials. He relied heavily on a disarming smile and the cross at his waist.

Over the weeks and months St Francis' walls crept higher and higher, first over the terraces of Taylor Street, then over the neighbouring foundry. People across east Manchester stopped and stared in amazement. Until then, the city's grand designs had been wrought to reflect distinctly earthly rather than spiritual values.

Just eight years after starting work Father Patrick nailed the last tile on the roof of the monastery church of St Francis. Every bishop in the country was invited to the grand opening. The rain that lashed priests and parishioners as they arrived only heightened the sense of refuge to be found within its magnificent walls. The bishop of Manchester described it as 'the finest and most beautiful church in the north of England'.

When Myra's great great grandfather, William Lewis, arrived in Gorton the monastery dominated the skyline. He had come to start work as a bricklayer. For years, William resisted the gravitational pull of industrial expansion, but a lack of work finally forced him to leave the small Cheshire town of Warrington. The 1901 census, and Myra Hindley's private papers, reveal that William's circumstances were unusual: his dependants included a wife, Eliza, who was six years older than him, and her young granddaughter Ellen. The bond between the women was unusually strong: both were illegitimate. Eliza and William took the girl in because there was no one else to look after her. Ellen grew up proud of having survived the challenge of illegitimacy. At the heart of this pride lay a belief in the value of family loyalty. But the Lewis family struggled to make ends meet in Gorton, and Eliza was forced to look for work outside Manchester. She took a job as a maid at Newbury Rectory in Berkshire. Ellen, at the age of just nine, went with her.

The experience had a profound effect on the young girl and it is described in detail in Myra Hindley's autobiography, written in the mid-eighties to try to improve her case for freedom. It is a rambling work that was abandoned when her supporters read it, and judged it unhelpful. 'It was a disaster,' David Astor, the former editor of the *Observer*, told me when I visited him at his house in St John's Wood. He funded Myra Hindley's legal campaign and visited her over more than thirty years. 'There was plenty of accurate detail but it added up to self-justification. Not a single mention of bodies. It went from I-was-a-poor-child-in-Manchester to I'm-in-prison without any mention of what happened in between. I told her not to continue. It would have damaged her case for release.'

'Why did you support her?' I asked.

'Everyone deserves the chance of redemption,' he replied.

Myra Hindley did not make another attempt to tell her story until she wrote to me well over a decade later. Both accounts, although very different, were written in order to help her campaign for freedom. Neither succeeded in this aim, but they do have a real value because, while it may be easy to lie, it is almost impossible to lie consistently. She retold her story from different points in time, with shifts of emphasis and changes in content. Setting these accounts against her police confession and interviews with those who knew or loved her yields a new understanding of what really happened.

Myra's grandmother, Ellen, had had no experience of wealth when she moved south to work alongside her own grandmother, Eliza. The closest she had come was the sight of rich people's carriages rolling through the dirty streets. Like all children, she had marvelled at the plumage Richard Peacock's coachmen wore in their hats. On Sundays he threw coins out of his carriage window to the running gaggle. But at Newbury Rectory she was on the inside. She remembered living in the grand old house as a 'golden time', marred only by one incident that gave her 'the fright of her life' (it is recorded in Myra's autobiography). One night, as she was drifting off to sleep in her attic bedroom, Ellen saw 'an apparition' dressed in hunting clothes standing at the foot of her bed. She jumped up and ran downstairs screaming. Rather than scold her for being silly, the rector was 'very kind' and explained that the 'ghost' was a former squire of Newbury who died in a hunting accident. He came back 'to visit' because he could not bear to be parted from his home. The rector did not explain why the ghostly squire preferred the servants' quarters to the drawing room.

While Ellen was better fed and clothed at the rectory than she had ever been, she missed the north and returned to Manchester in her mid-teens. She got a job in the mills, but her pleasure at being 'home' in West Gorton soon faded. She got up for work at four in the morning and collapsed, exhausted, into her bed fifteen hours later. Her boyfriend Pete Burns, an engineers' labourer, lived two doors down from her on Blair Street. He had to support his mother as his father, a fish-hawker, had died. Despite pride in her own background, Ellen did not want to inflict the stigma of illegitimacy on her own children, so she got married to Pete Burns, at the age of twenty-one. Ellen concealed her background from the registrar and told him that she was the daughter of Charles Silgram, general labourer. Soon after the wedding Ellen fell pregnant. When her son, Jim, was born she had to keep up the punishing hours in order to survive. She miscarried several times before giving birth to a second child, a beautiful baby girl called Louie.

At the outbreak of war, in 1914, Pete volunteered. He posed for a photograph, stern-faced in his uniform, before embarking for France. Ellen kept it in a frame on the mantelpiece. As the need for weapons grew, Ellen got a job in a TNT factory. The hours weren't as bad as in the mills; the War Ministry might have wanted explosive, but it didn't want tired women making it. There was also the sense of togetherness that came from all the men being away. Then Pete was killed, and Ellen's world fell apart.

After the war, when her wounds had begun to heal,

Ellen did find a man willing to 'take on' her children –
a coal carter, Bert Maybury. Like Ellen's family, Bert's
had come to Manchester from the Cheshire countryside in the 1890s in search of work. They married and
set up home at 24 Beasley Street, West Gorton. Many
of her comrades from the TNT factory were less for-
tunate: there was a severe shortage of bachelors in
their twenties and thirties. Ellen wanted a large family
but she suffered for her dream. She had ten mis-
carriages and a further three children: Anne, Bert and
Myra's mother, Nellie. The trauma of pregnancy was
compounded by the death of her eldest daughter,
Louie, from a sudden infection. Pete Burns' daughter
had been a favourite child. Ellen never really got over
his death at the front.

In his history of the monastery, Father Aidan reported
that 975 of St Francis' pupils left to fight in the Great
War. Of these, 159 never came home. Four old boys
were awarded the Distinguished Conduct Medal and
nine the Military Medal. The sacrifice of the fallen,
and the debt owed to those who had survived, was
drummed into succeeding generations of schoolboys.
They and the monastery that had shaped them were
something to be proud of.

Listening to these tales of heroism, young Bob
Hindley, whose father worked at the foundry, found
something to inspire him. He was not academically
gifted but he was good at sport and brave. He left St

Francis' school, with his teachers' encouragement, to join the army. Bob found a sense of purpose in the Parachute Regiment and achieved real status. He won the regimental boxing championship and wore the battered nose this cost him as a badge of pride for the rest of his life.

At home on leave, Bob cut a dashing figure. He was pursued by many girls, but one stood out, as much for her strong will as her good looks – an eighteen-year-old machinist called Nellie Maybury. They fell 'head over heels' in love and married. Any notion that the union of two volatile, opinionated characters might lead to trouble was lost in the excitement of the moment. And anyway, Bob was going off to war with the Paras; he might not come back. Seven months after he left, Nellie stopped work to have a child, a daughter she called Myra.

Myra Hindley records in her autobiography that she was born 'an ordinary baby' at Crumpsall Hospital on Thursday, 23 July 1942. The occupants of a very crowded 24 Beasley Street were relieved to discover that she was an easy infant. The tiny terrace stood tucked down a dead end behind Taylor Street. The official tenant was Ellen, long widowed, who now became 'Gran'. Her children Anne and Jim had left home, but Bert remained, with his girlfriend Kath. This type of arrangement was so common, with men away fighting, that landlords could do little about it.

Three weeks after the birth Nellie went to register

Myra; the certificate records the baby's father as Private Hindley No. 3853894. Myra told me in a letter that her father was determined she should be baptized a Catholic at St Francis'. But Nellie was suspicious of religion, and only agreed on condition that Myra would not go to a Catholic school. She raged that all the monks taught was the catechism. It was the first time she and Bob had a 'proper' argument. On 16 August 1942, Myra was baptized at the monastery church of St Francis; Kath stood godmother. Bob could not attend, as he was away fighting with the Paras.

The monastery stood next to one of the Luftwaffe's prime targets in Manchester, Beyer Peacock Engineering. When the German bombers came the vaults beneath St Francis provided a shelter for the inhabitants of the surrounding streets. The worst attacks came during December 1940 when incendiaries rained down on West Gorton. There was a tremendous crashing as the boys' and girls' schools in the monastery grounds were hit. Inside St Francis, the priests and parishioners caught their breath as a third device hit the roof high above them. Luckily the tiles held, and the incendiary rolled down and burned itself out in the gutter. Such attacks went on throughout the war. A map taken from an enemy pilot in Holland in 1945 shows Gorton foundry marked out by a thick black line. There is a scale along the bottom and a caption which reveals that it was drawn in October

1939. The crew that used this map was over Manchester on 9 January 1941. The monastery and streets are so tightly packed around Beyer Peacock that it would have been impossible for even the most discriminating bomb aimer to hit his target every time.

Nellie, Ellen, Bert, Kath and Myra did have an Anderson bomb shelter in the back yard but they felt safer in the company of others. If there was time they would run to the communal shelter built at the end of their street by the War Ministry. Officials paid particular attention to the number and quality of shelters in West Gorton; they wanted its occupants back at work, in the foundry, the following morning, not dead, or mourning loved ones.

Like all families, the occupants of 24 Beasley Street had an 'air-raid routine'. When the sirens sounded Kath and Ellen made straight for the shelter while Bert waited inside the front door. Nellie got Myra out of bed, wrapped her up, and tossed her down the stairs to him. They got quicker and quicker at this, but one night either Nellie misjudged her throw or Bert fumbled the catch, and Myra was dropped. They sprinted to the shelter in a panic, but the baby was fine: she had been saved by landing in a tub of washing. After that, Nellie ran down the stairs holding Myra tightly.

Myra spent the first few years of her life in a world run by women. Her uncle Bert may have resembled a father figure, but he did not carry the financial and moral responsibilities of parenthood. She described him in her autobiography as a gentle figure who loved to play games and never lost his temper.

Because the kitchen ceiling was unsafe, Bert helped Gran hang her long clothes dryer, made of wood and steel, in the front room. It was so close to the front door that adult heads brushed against the damp cotton as they came in and out. This made Myra laugh. Bert, to show his niece what she was missing, would grab her by the arms and toss her high into the air. She'd scream with delight as her blonde curls got lost among the shirts and drawers, before plunging back into her uncle's safe hands.

In 1945, Myra's father returned from the war to his first experience of family life. But the Bob Hindley who came back was very different from the one who had left, newly married, five years earlier. Myra recorded Bob's struggle to adjust to civilian life in various drafts of her autobiography, in her confession to the police, and in her letters to me. With each new version she polished the image of herself as a victim of circumstance. The last, and most refined, account was written to me; by far the most revealing, and unguarded, description of her childhood was to be found in the first version of her autobiography.

Myra's father not only had to get used to family life, he also had to get a job. He ended up at Beyer Peacock, labouring; at least it was a man's world where his physical strength and war record – he served in

North Africa, Cyprus and Italy, and the Paras endured some of the heaviest and most prolonged fighting of the war – were appreciated. But stories of glory are not the same as the thing itself, and a bitterness settled over him.

Myra recorded that Bob and Nellie made a stab at happiness when they secured a new house to live in, 'as a family', at 20 Eaton Street. Myra knew something was up when, one morning, her mam climbed out of bed and pulled on a new red dress. At first she accepted, even believed, that 'a move' was the beginning of a bright new future. But as she sat down to breakfast with Bert, Gran, Nellie and Kath for the last time it sank in that the life they had shared at Beasley Street was coming to an end. It did not matter that their new home was just a minute's walk away. She screamed the place down, and blamed her dad for the calamity.

Bob tried to placate his daughter over the next few weeks by taking her out with him. He refused to let Myra cover her blonde curls with a hat as he enjoyed the compliments they attracted. Although Bob could not yet hope to supplant Bert in his daughter's affections, he did begin to earn her trust. They were in town together once, she recorded in her autobiography, when a manager at Lewis's department store, on Piccadilly Gardens, told her she would have to go into the ladies' lavatory alone. Frightened by the 'posh' surroundings and the idea of performing a private act while surrounded by strangers, she burst into tears. Bob insisted that she be allowed to come into the gents' with him. In the face of his determination the manager relented. Myra was proud of the way her dad stuck up for her. On another day out, at Belle Vue, they had a picture taken together. I found it among her papers. Bob holds a chimpanzee in his right arm and Myra in his left. She appears distracted, but he is grinning into the camera with a father's undisguised delight.

Eaton Street was newer than Beasley Street. It had electricity and a tiled fireplace, but that was as far as the improvements went. The house was inundated with cockroaches which scuttled for cover whenever a light was switched on. There were two rooms on the ground floor: the front opened on to the street, the rear on to the yard, and a damp privy. The house was built to such a poor standard that the back bedroom, which was to be Myra's, had been condemned before they moved in. The ceiling leaked and the floorboards were unsafe to walk on. The Hindleys had to share the one remaining bedroom at the front of the house. Myra slept in a single bed next to her parents' double.

Despite this uncomfortable arrangement, and the frequent rows it gave rise to, Nellie got pregnant. A cot was put up in the corner of the bedroom and, on 21 August 1946, Maureen was born. The new baby was quite different from the first, and frequently cried through the night. Myra lay in bed, listened to her wailing and wished that life could go back to how it had been at Gran's. She sensed that things were only going to get worse. Her mam was so tense that she shouted if Myra so much as stood next to, never mind sat in, the only piece of comfortable furniture in the house – 'Dad's chair'.

But Bob rarely spent the evening sitting at home. His way of 'coping' was to get blind drunk, almost every night, at one of the many pubs dotted around West Gorton: the Bessemer (Bessie), Shakespeare (Shakie), or his favourite, the Steelworks (Steelie). Increasingly often, at around ten o'clock in the evening, a neighbour would burst through the front door shouting that Bob was 'fightin' agen', and that Nellie had best 'come and bring him home'. Bob had been known as a 'hard man' in the army, and needed to be the same as a civilian. To begin with, Nellie pulled him out of the pub, covered in blood and bruises, raging about how 'the other bloke' had come off far worse than him, and dragged him home. She told herself it was 'the war'. Eventually, she tired of this routine. When the door flew open she responded to news of the latest brawl with a shrug, and carried on with whatever she was doing. But Myra's duty remained the same, irrespective of her mam's reaction: to retrieve Bob's jacket. He always took it off before a 'scrap', no matter how drunk he was, so that it wouldn't get ripped. After a fight, the drinkers came to expect the girl with blonde curls. As she ducked into the smoke of the bar a hand would hold the precious jacket out to her.

Professor Malcolm MacCulloch studied the different accounts of Myra Hindley's childhood and asked to see what other material I had.

'He looks a bruiser, doesn't he?'

The professor was stooped over the picture of Bob Hindley, his battered scowl glowering out from beneath a cocked hat, on the benches of the Steelworks Tavern. He was not so much looking at the camera as challenging it. The two men either side of him looked like rogues.

'How useful are the details of her early years?' I asked.

'Invaluable. Most of our flaws and strengths are forged before we reach adulthood. The key to understanding her personality lies here.'

Although Myra Hindley wrote several accounts of her childhood, she discussed it openly with just two people: Ian Brady and the woman who replaced him in her affections, Patricia Cairns. Myra met the former Carmelite nun at Holloway prison, where she was a warder, in 1970. Their relationship endured until Myra's death thirty-two years later. But Patricia Cairns was in no way an acolyte of Myra Hindley's. She does not deny Myra's role in the murders or the lies she told about them. And she was instrumental in persuading her to help in the search for Keith Bennett. Whenever Myra was slow to respond to a question from Professor John Hunter, because she was 'depressed' or 'preoccupied', Cairns put her under powerful pressure. This assistance was on strict condition of anonymity. Her importance to Myra Hindley was such that I had to ask her to tell her story for this book. She, perhaps better than anyone, understood Myra because they had talked about every aspect of her life. I explained that it was impossible to fully understand why the Moors murders have remained in the public eye, and unsolved, without hearing from her. After careful consideration she agreed. 'It's time for the truth to come out,' she said.

Myra Hindley and Patricia Cairns had a lot in common. Both women were Mancunian, Catholic and working class with alcoholic fathers. But Cairns says that, while she was also hit regularly, the violence Myra endured was more extreme; it was at the centre of her day-to-day existence. Bob Hindley was the main source of the beatings, but Nellie was far from blameless.

'Her mum was cruel to her when she was little. She didn't protect her and beat her herself. She hit her about the head. I remember Myra telling me that she made her ears bleed.'

'How come there's no mention of Nellie hitting her in the autobiography?' I asked.

'I think when Myra wrote about that time she made

excuses for her mum. She wanted her to be something that she wasn't. She wanted to have a good mum, so she portrayed her as she would have liked her to be.'

It soon became clear to Bob and Nellie that, while they might be physically attracted to each other, they were ill matched. Arguments soon became part of the daily routine. Bob started hitting Nellie and Myra when he got back from the pub. If he had already been in a scrap, or they didn't talk, there was a chance of making it to bed without an argument. But, often as not, one of them would seek out trouble. Nellie goaded Bob about the amount he spent on beer, asking him if there was anything left for food; he rose to the bait, and threatened to hit her. Back and forth they went until the inevitable explosion of violence. Myra said in her letters to me that she and Gran would wait outside as the voices got louder. When her mum started yelping with pain they would open the door and rush in. Gran would hit Bob with a rolled-up copy of the *Manchester Evening News* while Myra grabbed his legs and pummelled them.

The scenes at 20 Eaton Street did not attract the attention of the authorities as domestic violence was part of life. Friday night was known by the kids as 'wife beating night'. The women had different ways of dealing with it. Nellie acted as though it wasn't happening and kept everything 'within doors'. Mrs Harding, who lived across the street, did the opposite.

She was married to a small man who worked hard all week and went mad at the end of it. When he hit her she ran into the road and danced around, dodging his drunken punches, until he retreated, exhausted, to sleep it off. Uncle Bert tired of this weekly ritual and tried to cut it short by 'having a word' as Mr Harding returned from the pub. But Mr Harding was not in the mood for listening, and took a swing at him. It was an unwise move as Bert was both far stronger and sober. In his anger, Myra's uncle misjudged the strength of his punch. Mr Harding was knocked out cold and collapsed prone into the gutter. Kath called an ambulance, and sat with her arm round his wife while they waited. Mr Harding made a speedy physical recovery but the sting of humiliation endured. For a while the beating stopped, but the small man 'could not help himself' and soon resumed his former habit. Bert did not intervene again.

The contrast between her father and uncle became increasingly sharp to Myra. She began answering back, and refused to do as she was told. This infuriated Bob. Not only did he have a strong-willed wife who 'griped' at him all the time, but now his daughter was turning out even worse. As the tension rose at Eaton Street the number of fights increased. Violence could swirl out of the calmest of circumstances. Every week they had a bath, taking turns in the tin tub which stood in front of the open fire. Nellie topped it up with hot water from a pan on the stove.

At the age of five, Myra was waiting her turn when she spotted Bob's shaving things in front of the mirror on the hearth. Myra smeared shaving soap on her face, stood on tip-toes on the tiled fender and scraped at her smooth skin with a table knife. Bob appeared behind her, asked what she thought she was doing, and cracked her round the head, spraying the mirror with flecks of foam. But Myra refused to cry. Physical punishment was a challenge she squared up to.

'Myra was always a strong character when she was little,' Patricia Cairns told me. 'But they didn't just fight because of their differences. I think there were a lot of similarities between them. They both recognized this and neither of them liked it. And she looked like him, didn't she?'

The thought had never struck me before. I pulled out my laptop and opened pictures of father and daughter. The faces staring out of her arrest photograph and from the bench of the Steelworks are surprisingly similar. I clicked on a file marked 'Maureen: 17'. She had the same heavy jaw and was recognizably from the same family, but her stare was moody rather than combative.

'He never hit Maureen,' Patricia said.

'Why not?'

'She was a lot softer and, frankly, not as intelligent.'

Bob gave Maureen a nickname, Moby. The whole family used it. But Myra was just Myra.

The tension was exacerbated by the fact that six

days out of seven a night broken by Maureen's crying was followed by an early morning. The Hindleys' house stood at the end of Eaton Street, next to an alleyway, or 'ginnel', that led to Beyer Peacock's. First, a solitary pair of clogs rang out on the cobbles, followed by the repeated tapping of a long pole on window panes – the 'knocker-up' waking the early shift. It was a ritual repeated across the working-class districts of Manchester. Although the rapping of the pole stirred Myra she was able to roll over, and Maureen usually stayed asleep. But twenty minutes later the tramp, tramp of massed feet bounced off the thin brick walls and into the family's bedroom, waking Maureen. This was the cue for Bob to yell at Nellie about the 'bloody baby', and Nellie to yell at Bob about his 'bloody hangover'. Myra would pretend to be asleep, but there was only so much squabbling she could take. When she did get up the anger was inevitably deflected in her direction. She was told to stop 'slopping about' and look after her sister while her parents struggled into their clothes. At breakfast, Nellie sat and glowered at Bob over her cup of tea until the inevitable, often deliberately misplaced word sparked the first row of the day. If they did appear to be managing a peaceful breakfast Myra would start something off, while Maureen sat there meekly.

Like Myra, Nellie remembered what things had been like during the war and resented her present circumstances. It couldn't go on like this, but rather than leave Bob, she waited until they were alone and made a suggestion: what if Myra went to stay with Gran? Bob did not argue.

Chapter Two

Myra was five years old when she was moved back to her gran's, and while she was glad to be 'home' again there was a lurking sense of rejection. There had never been any question of Moby being the one to go. Gran, sensing that she needed protection, gave Myra the front bedroom; she would be 'fine', herself, sleeping next to the stove downstairs. It was what she'd done when Bert and Kath lived there. In truth, Ellen saw the new arrangement as 'making the best of a bad job'. She hoped that it might reduce the fighting between Nellie and Bob. There was little shame attached to a girl moving in with her grandmother, even when the parents lived less than a minute's walk away. So many of the houses in West Gorton were overcrowded, and dilapidated, that children were often spread among the extended family. The nature of the Hindleys' problems was far from unique.

Myra's new bedroom was sparse. Standing next to

the window was a rickety marble-topped chest of drawers and a straight-backed wooden chair. A grubby door led to a built-in wardrobe. The floorboards were covered in lino that lifted at the edges, barely disguised by a rag-peg rug. There was an old double bed with a lumpy flock mattress and piles of old coats for blankets. Gran told Myra that the fading jumble was 'cheaper as well as warmer' than blankets. A bolster ran along the base of the headboard, just like in her parents' house, covered in a row of saggy old pillows. There was a fireplace, but it didn't work because it was blocked up with soot.

The back bedroom was empty, but it became part of Myra's small domain. It was completely bare, not even used for junk. All she found when she looked in the built-in wardrobe was a couple of old gas masks. There was no lino in the room to bind the floorboards together, which tipped up dangerously when you put your weight on them. The rear window looked out over the other houses' yards. At the end of each cobbled rectangle stood a small wooden hut. Myra remembered watching men stagger out to relieve themselves, muzzy with sleep, first thing in the morning and again, sedated by beer, just before bed.

At night, Gran heated bricks in the stove, wrapped them in blankets and put them into the bed to warm it. When the weather got really cold and ice formed on the inside of the window, Myra made a nest in the cupboard and crawled inside, curling round the heated bricks to keep herself warm. Sometimes, Gran let her share her bed downstairs, but not often: Myra wriggled too much.

There is no criticism in anything Myra Hindley wrote of her mother for sending her away. But Patricia Cairns says that resentment at being rejected by Nellie endured long into her imprisonment. The two women discussed it at length, shortly after they fell in love in the early 1970s. 'She always said in public that being sent to live with her gran was a good thing. While she was happy to criticize her father she did not want to upset her mother. In reality, it was the most hurtful thing that could have happened to her. It was the first time in her life that she was made to feel the outsider. That lasted for the rest of her life.'

Gran supplemented her pension by taking in washing from families who did not have the time to do their own, or the money to afford a laundry. The clothes were scrubbed in the sink and boiled in a large tin tub on the stove, the whites with 'dolly blue' powder added to make them gleam. Between each pair of houses along Beasley Street was fixed a large iron arm. Gran and her neighbour, Hettie Rafferty, shared one. On fine days, the clothes were hoisted up, like sails, using a rope. When the wind blew, the street looked like Nelson's fleet sailing into battle. But if it rained, which was often, the parlour was filled with dripping sheets, shirts and underwear. Gran tested the iron by rubbing it against a bar of laundry soap. When it was hot enough for cotton there was a loud hissing, and green gobbets of soap danced onto the stone below. Myra and Gran scrubbed the floor with brown chalk, and swabbed it down. The front step, and the stones around it, got the same treatment. Nobody was going to take their laundry to be washed in a dirty house. When ready, the clothes were neatly stacked on a dresser behind the front door, and scented with small bunches of lavender. These came from gypsies who sold door to door. Gran never refused to buy for fear of being 'cursed' – unless, that is, she thought they hadn't noticed she was inside.

Gran listened to Valentine Dyall's *Workers' Playtime* as she pressed the cotton. The radio was powered by two large glass accumulator bottles which had to be charged in turn. Myra recalled an occasion when one of the accumulator bottles went. Ellen handed her the discharged glass and a clutch of coins. In order to save time on her way to the radio shop Myra cut across a piece of waste land that separated the back doors of Taylor and Casson Streets. It was covered with bits of broken furniture and discarded bathroom fittings. Unsighted by the large glass bottle she tripped, smashed it, and burned her legs with acid. It took an effort for Gran not to belt her. The accumulator bottle represented a lot of washing.

Despite having sent her to stay at Gran's, Bob insisted that Myra return home for most meals. Breakfast was fine – just a few barked orders to her,

Maureen or Mam before he ducked out the door clutching a greaseproof packet of butties. The trouble came at tea time. He'd have had one pint on the way back from work with his mates and would be wanting to get down to the Steelworks for a few more. The 'need of a drink' made him belligerent.

He would tell Myra she should 'stick up' for herself, take rubbish from no one. He showed her how to throw punches: hooks, jabs, head-shots, gut-shots. Myra recalled Bob's instruction in her autobiography: 'Don't put both hands up! If you can't deflect the first punch with one arm keep the other one ready to protect your stomach.'

West Gorton was so tightly packed with families and kids that friendships and enmities came along in equal measure. Kenny Holden did not like Myra, and found a nasty way of showing it: he walked straight up to her in the street, rested the nails of each hand against her cheeks, and raked them down, leaving behind eight bloody tramlines. Myra burst out crying, and ran into the house. Bob demanded to know who had done it. 'Kenny,' she replied, hoping that he'd march round to Alice Holden's to demand justice. Instead, Myra recorded, he grabbed her by the wrist, opened the door and said, 'Go and punch him, because if you don't I'll leather you. It's either him or you!' Myra heard the bolt slam home behind her. Kenny came down the street towards her, his fingers curled, ready to scratch again. Myra, mindful of Bob's words, threw her left fist at his head. Kenny brought up both hands, leaving his stomach unprotected. She delivered a hard right to the exposed area and, as he doubled up in agony, slammed her left into Kenny's temple. He slumped to the ground, crying. Myra wrote, 'I stood looking down at him triumphantly. At eight years old I'd scored my first victory.' Bob ruffled her hair when she came in for tea. That made her feel good. News of what she'd done to Kenny got around. It didn't do her any harm, just marked her out as someone not to mess with.

I discussed the account of this fight, and Bob's role in it, with Professor Malcolm MacCulloch. He told me that they were key pieces of evidence in trying to understand Myra Hindley. 'The relationship with her father brutalized her,' he commented. 'She was not only used to violence in the home but rewarded for practising it outside. When this happens at a young age it can distort a person's reaction to such situations for life.'

'Hardly an excuse though, is it?' I replied.

'We're not looking for excuses, we're looking for explanations.'

I asked Patricia Cairns whether she agreed with MacCulloch's assessment.

'Yes, absolutely. She was brought up in an aggressive, violent atmosphere. It would have an effect on any child. And she was a strong child . . .'

Increasingly, Myra retreated into her own world.

She ate at Gran's whenever she could. Bob and Nellie sometimes let her go – she was 'a right pain' when she was at home, her complaints like a drumbeat. Myra recounted in her autobiography how these confrontations would go.

'I don't like stew and dumpling / fish / hotpot / soup.'

'Eat it or I'll give you a smack.'

She was at her most annoying when she compared Mam's food to Gran's.

'Your rice pudding's not the same. It's not lovely and brown on top like hers.'

'You ungrateful little . . .'

A belt round the head made no difference. Myra was too strong to be bothered, and just sat there staring at Nellie. If Bob wasn't there to give her a hiding, Nellie would try, 'Just wait 'til your father gets home.' If that failed she'd say, 'You not only look like your father. You act like him too.' This infuriated Myra, she admitted in her autobiography, because she knew it was true. She also recognized that her personality was moulded in Bob's image. One letter to her mother from prison reveals that when she had to have plastic surgery following a beating by a fellow inmate, she asked the surgeon to remove all the shared characteristics he could.

Gran's rice pudding was better because she made it in the cast-iron oven on top of the fireplace, rather than on the stove she used for boiling up the washing.

There was always a lovely skin on it, which Myra peeled off and ate before mixing in seedless bramble jam. Another of Myra's childhood favourites was steamed prunes. They ate these at the table by the window, looking out on to the street, chatting as they shared their meal. The dark, tasselled table cloth was covered by a smaller white one made of linen. Everything was just so: a tall, thin bottle of sterilized milk, a loaf of 'shop bought' bread, a jar of jam, a quarter-pound of margarine on a saucer, a bottle of HP Sauce and, every now and then, a jar of Camp coffee. Pride of place went to the tin of condensed milk which Myra poured onto her prunes – and, if Gran's back was turned, straight into her mouth.

Nellie thought Gran was far too 'soft', but she was tired of fighting with her wilful daughter. She reached an unspoken compromise: whatever she, Bob and Maureen were eating was accompanied by a 'side' dish of chips which, in reality, were just for Myra. But Nellie couldn't resist a dig. 'If you eat any more chips you'll be called Chippy, just like the Athertons.' Myra ignored her. The family she had referred to were particularly poor and notorious for existing on a diet of almost nothing but deep-fried potatoes.

Myra's triumph over Kenny Holden won her respect from the other Taylor Street kids. Fights, says Patricia Cairns, were a way of establishing a pecking order. 'Like me, she was a tomboy and she stuck up for herself, and for Maureen. If anybody gave them trouble she'd fight. She was always tough. That's how it was on the streets in those days: you either stuck up for yourself or you got picked on. And people were on top of one another in Gorton. There were no gardens. I lived in a working-class area and we had a garden front and back, but there it was all streets and alleyways. There was no place to hide. We used to call Gorton "town". I went to Mrs Moulton's house, where she grew up, later on. It was grotty.'

Like many children from unhappy families, Myra found a retreat in the world of books. Late in the evenings she retreated to her bedroom in Beasley Street. She sat on the bed, a couple of old cushions propped up on the bolster behind her head, and read. She liked Beatrix Potter and Enid Blyton for the same reason: they were a complete world into which she could escape. She imagined that she was George, the tomboy in the Famous Five. When it got dark, because there was no gaslight upstairs, she had to use a candle. The ability to derive nourishment from literature, to realize that there were other worlds than the one she found herself trapped in, was to prove a common bond with Ian Brady.

Opposite the foundry on Gorton Lane stands what was Peacock Street Primary, a brick building painted with murals in bold colours. As I walked towards it I realized that I was looking at self-portraits of children at the 'Buzz pupil referral unit'. Beneath a large planet Saturn, circled with black rings, played a girl with blue hair called Kai, another in a pink top and yellow spotty skirt, and two boys with the Nike 'swoosh' on their jumpers. While the murals were new, the building itself belonged unmistakably to another era. Running up the side of the wall was a heavy cast-iron drainpipe, its dark red shape softened by the contours of eighty years' repainting. The tungsten light shining weakly through the window, mixing with the winter sunset, illuminated a stark classroom.

All the kids from the Taylor Street area came here. Myra's favourite lesson was English. They took it in turns to read out passages from a book. The class sat obediently through Frances Hodgson Burnett's *The Secret Garden*: 'She felt there was no knowing what might happen in a house with a hundred rooms nearly all shut up – a house standing on the edge of a moor.' The book, with its image of beauty hidden in a bleak landscape, captivated Myra. She kept a copy all her life and re-read it at times of stress.

Another favourite was Arthur Ransome's *Swallows and Amazons*. She imagined herself sailing in the Lake District, like the 'posh' children in the book. They had different-sounding names from the Peacock Street kids. Myra enjoyed listening to this book but hated reading it out loud herself. All the boys held their breath when, scanning ahead, they saw their favourite girl's name and fell about laughing as she read out

'Titty'. It didn't matter how often the teacher batted them round the head, they just couldn't help themselves.

After school, Myra mucked about on Gorton Lane with Joyce Hardy, who lived on Beyer Street, next to Peacock Street. Her friend had a mischievous temperament and short blonde hair that made her look like an urchin. They stood in the doorway of the dry cleaner's and stuck their arms and legs out so that, reflected in the window, they doubled up. If they had the cash they bought sweets from the old-fashioned herbalist's. It sold 'halfpenny Spanish', or real liquorice, pear drops, and lemon drops with sherbet inside. If they were 'rich' they got a glass of sarsaparilla, sat at the high glass counter and watched the traffic go by outside.

The school came up in conversation as I sat having a cup of tea with Alan Bennett. Life was going well for him: he'd escaped the job in the stock-room at Argos and started work as a classroom assistant in Moss Side. It was a deprived area, but he felt he was doing something that mattered.

'A strange thing happened . . .' he said.

'What?'

'The local education authority sent me to Peacock Street for a special needs course. One of the people who runs it said, "You'll never guess what. This is where Myra Hindley went to school."'

'What did you say?'

'Nothing. Bit of a conversation stopper, telling them she murdered my brother.'

Myra, emboldened by her triumph over Kenny Holden, did not intend to 'take grief' from anyone. But, over time, some of the boys, like Eddie Hogan, came to imagine that the fight might have been a one-off, or that Kenny was 'soft'. They were looking for an excuse to provoke her. Providence granted Eddie his wish when Myra got nits. Gran kept her inside, raked her hair with a steel comb, picked at her scalp until it ached and poured on 'some awful-smelling liquid'. Only when Gran was sure that she had killed all the insects did she allow Myra out. Eddie was waiting, and chanted, 'Nitty Nora, Nitty Nora.' Myra couldn't believe what she was hearing, and stood there while the words sank in.

Suddenly, she leapt at him. They fell to the ground, lashing out at each other and rolling over and over on the cobbles. A crowd of kids gathered round them and began to cheer. Myra's problem was Eddie's weight. When they reached the kerb at the edge of the road, he pinned her down and climbed on top. This was the point at which etiquette demanded one of two outcomes: either she would submit and lose the fight, or she would refuse and they would get to their feet and start all over again. Eddie broke the rules: when Myra refused to give in, instead of letting her go, he punched her in the face. But as Eddie's fist connected his weight shifted, and Myra was able to twist herself free. Once she was on top he was helpless. Her feet and fists flew into him so that he squealed in agony.

Alerted by the commotion, Gran entered the fray. She tried to prise Myra off with one arm and used the other to beat Eddie with a rolled-up copy of the *Manchester Evening News*. Myra enjoyed the exchange that followed, and recorded it in her autobiography.

'Please, missus, it's not me, it's her. She's mad, gerrer off me!'

'Do you submit?' Myra asked him.

'Yes, let me up!'

Eddie scrambled to his feet and shuffled down the street, bent over with pain. Gran retrieved her *Evening News*, bashed Myra on the shoulder, and told her to get in the house. Myra recorded, 'Eddie never called me Nitty Nora again.'

The first draft of Myra Hindley's autobiography contains many detailed descriptions of fights. Later accounts, like the letters she wrote to me, hardly mention them. It was as if she came to understand that these incidents revealed there was a flaw in her long before she met Ian Brady.

While it is clear from the various different accounts of Myra Hindley's childhood that she was tough, it is just as clear that she was not delinquent. One story in her autobiography, vividly related and convincing, describes how she played an important, if legally dubious, economic role in Gran's business.

The laundry work quickly consumed the hundredweight of coal and half-hundredweight of slack (smaller pieces of coal) that Gran bought off the back of the horse-drawn delivery cart each week. Myra made up the deficit. She wandered round the corner to the wash-house and pushed open the door. Steam enveloped her face, and she had to pause, peering into the darkness, while she got used to the change in atmosphere. She made out four or five figures in the large, dark space. A woman in her forties, her dress covered by a cotton 'day coat', stood in the centre stirring a huge boiling vat of clothes; two others stooped over piles of damp cotton at the long wooden draining boards that ran down either side of the room. They wrung out each skirt, shirt, blouse and sock, then carefully spread them on a large drying rack. When this was full they pushed it into a specially heated room off to one side; to the other side Myra could see more women working mangles, and ironing. This was why families were willing to pay Gran to do the work for them. Ignoring the women, Myra made her way towards a pram that stood close to the boiling vat. It was used for transporting dirty clothes. The woman working there turned to her and told her to make sure she washed it down properly before she brought it back. Myra promised that she would.

As she shoved the pram ahead of her down Taylor Street, Myra kept an eye out for the police. If they saw her they would know she was on her way to steal coal off the railway. The train company had nailed up large wooden boards right through Gorton in order to try to stop people breaking in. All they succeeded in doing was creating a new expression: 'going over the boards'. Myra parked the pram next to a hand-sized gap in the fence and scrambled up. She hooked her fingers through whatever holes she could find, braced her feet against the wood and pulled herself up. Out of breath as she dropped over the other side, she lost her balance and tumbled a few feet down the steep embankment. But there was no pain, only pleasure as she felt chunks of coal digging through her cotton dress. They had fallen off the freight wagons as they rounded the bend – large, beautiful chunks of the best-quality coal. Not the gritty slack that other people trudged to the yard for when they had run out. The best, heaviest chunks had rolled to the bottom of the embankment onto the track. She ran up and down the slope, gathering the pieces into an old pillowcase before emptying them, one by one, through the gap in the fence into the pram. She kept listening for trains, and looking out for bobbies. She'd been caught stealing before and been dragged back to Gran's for a telling-off. As it was Gran who had sent her the reprimand was never very severe. On the way back she threw the pillowcase on top of the large pile of coal. That way a passing constable might just think it was slack.

The only adult who showed real signs of concern about Myra's moral development was Auntie Kath,

who had never had any children with Bert. On
Sundays she took Myra to mass. They met at the
junction of Beasley and Bannock Streets, and walked
hand in hand towards the monastery. Because of
Nellie's hostility towards the Catholic Church there
were no plans for Myra to be confirmed, but, like
Kath, she still fasted before mass. Myra loved her and
wanted to be like her.

Sunday, Myra recorded in her autobiography, was
the only time when unfamiliar faces appeared on the
streets of Gorton. People came from all over east
Manchester to worship at St Francis'. The ritual of
going to mass removed all barriers and people talked
easily as they made their way into the cavernous
church. At the door, women pulled their scarves tight
over their heads and men took off their hats and caps;
inside, many paused to pray before a statue of a
favourite saint. The 'head of the family' usually put a
coin in the collection tray or poor box, with a studied
lack of ostentation, before taking his seat. Myra
positioned herself at the end of a pew so that she was
sprinkled with incense by the passing priest. She didn't
understand a word of the mass – it was conducted in
Latin – but the ritual offered a soothing escape.

She was ten when she first came back here during
the week. There was something about the empty space,
with its memories of Sunday, that allowed her to lose
herself. The red carpet and gold paint mixed with the
afternoon light streaming through the stained glass

gave the space a warm glow. She sat at the back and watched the monks, floating in their brown robes, as they came and went through the side door to the monastery. Many fell briefly to their knees in front of the Calvary scene before returning to work.

The woman scrubbing the floor did not look up as Myra made her way between the aisles. She genuflected as she crossed the carpet that ran down the centre of the church, and walked down the side aisle towards the altar of St Anthony. She dropped a penny into the box for a candle and knelt down to place it as close to the saint as possible. As her fingers stretched out they brushed against a small pile of folded papers – petitions to the saint. In her auto-biography, Myra described how she read these messages. 'For Catherine, who has pneumonia, that she'll be made well through your prayers.' She refolded each petition and dropped it back in its place before picking up another. 'For Ted, that he might, through your intercession, stop drinking for the sake of his health, and so that we'll have more money for food.'

Myra's affection for the monastery never faded, according to Patricia Cairns. 'Myra had a lot of photos of St Francis'. I went and took them for her on a visit north. It had a wonderful atmosphere with the stained glass and beautiful, beautiful altars. There was no place like it. I used to cycle from Denton to go there.'

After church, on the street, Myra's behaviour

remained unchanged; she kept her reputation for being tough. At the bottom of a box of personal effects from her cell I found a small collection of childhood pictures. There was one of her in close-up, grinning, with two bottom teeth missing. It was obviously a cold day as she was wearing an old polo neck beneath a knitted cardigan, and her hair looked like she'd just been playing a rough game. Her head was tipped to one side. She looked self-confident, as if she'd just given the photographer a good ragging.

Beneath this picture were images recording a highlight of Gorton life: the communal trip to the seaside. Two or three times a year the people of Beasley Street, Bannock Street and Taylor Street got together to hire a bus, or 'sharrer', to take them somewhere special – Blackpool, Southport or New Brighton. One trip, recorded in her autobiography, shows that she fitted into these outings like the other children, bowing to the authority of adults.

They were in the sea at New Brighton, being washed back and forth by the surf. The adults, some of them holding bottles of beer, took little notice of what was going on. Until, that is, a boy called Eric, who had polio, lost his footing and went under. When he came up his shorts had disappeared. Eric's mother wrapped the shivering child in her cardigan, but it was no good. He had no pants on; they couldn't go about like that all day. Nellie had a solution – her daughter's knickers. Myra protested at the shame of it, pointing out that

Gran wouldn't let her out of the house with snapped knicker elastic 'in case she was run over'. And here they were suggesting she should walk around in nothing but a skirt? Besides, her knickers were wet. But Nellie stood firm. Myra followed Eric round for the rest of the day, trying to ignore the shame of seeing her damp underwear clinging to his wet skin.

Back at school, Myra stood out as one of the brighter children, and at the age of eleven she was chosen to 'have a go' at the eleven plus. The girls sitting for grammar school left Peacock Street in a small group, with their teacher, and caught a bus to Levenshulme High. They were led up a grand staircase to the examination room. Myra was overwhelmed by the strangeness of it all. There were 'real' paintings on the walls; the girls who rushed past them wore smart uniforms, and carried leather satchels. In the examination hall she sat down at a desk covered with blotting paper and got out her ruler, pencil and pen. Then she froze. It was madness to think she could come here. Where would the money for clothes, never mind the bus fare, come from? She failed the paper.

Myra and Nellie fought about where she should go to secondary school. Like all arguments in the Hindley household it raged back and forth. Myra wanted to attend St Francis'; Nellie wanted her to go to a new mixed-faith school. Myra said she wanted to be with her friends; Nellie replied that all the monks taught was the catechism, and a fat lot of good it had done Dad. Bob became involved, said he'd prefer the Catholic school. But Nellie reminded him of the deal they'd made when Myra was baptized a Catholic, and her argument clinched it. Myra was enrolled at Ryder Brow Secondary Modern, on the other side of the Hyde Road, where she would never quite lose the feeling of being an outsider. It was a decision that would affect the rest of her life.

Chapter Three

I walked out of Piccadilly station and headed down the concrete apron that leads to the centre of Manchester. Ahead of me was a tall, overweight man wearing a faded sweatshirt and a pair of baggy track-suit bottoms. At his side was a similarly dressed boy of about eight. They both carried notebooks, and wore binoculars – trainspotters. But there was something odd about them: they were *leaving* the station with a real sense of purpose, excitement even. Intrigued, I watched where they were going. Five minutes later we were standing next to one another in trainspotting heaven – a shop stuffed with implausible titles like *Diesels of Spain* and *The Great British Traction Engine*. I pretended to be interested while I observed the odd couple.

There was something touching about their absorption, and I had decided to leave them to it when a title caught my eye, *Images of England: Gorton*. I pulled the book off the shelf and looked at the front cover. It showed a sepia-tinted photograph of an extraordinary scene. A terraced street had been closed to traffic, bunting strung across it every few yards, garlands hung above windows and doors. Running down the centre of the road was a long line of kitchen tables jammed end to end, covered in linen and decorated with flower-filled vases. Plates were heaped with carefully cut triangular white sandwiches; biscuits were presented above them on glass stands, covered in crocheted doilies. But the most striking thing was the dense crowd of people staring intently into the lens. The children sat; the parents, some in paper hats, stood behind them. They were impeccably dressed. Everyone looked happy, but there was hardly a smile to be seen. This was a serious endeavour, a demonstration of self-respect, and they wanted it recorded as such. I flipped open the cover: King George V Silver Jubilee party in Henry Street, West Gorton, 1935.

I leafed through the pages – schools, churches, marching bands, the arrival of a new car. Every shot recorded something people had reason to be proud of. Then I came to page 83, Pupils of Ryder Brow in the 1950s. There, carefully captioned, were Myra's friends Jean Hicks and Linda McGurk, and the head boy she fancied, Ronnie Woodcock. At the end of the back row, smiling openly just like everyone else, was a girl in a stripy cardigan, her shoulder-length hair carefully brushed – Myra Hindley. The author must have realized who the girl was but chose to ignore her presence. This story repeated itself across Manchester: there was almost no written record of the city's most infamous daughter.

Myra Hindley described in her autobiography how, soon after starting at Ryder Brow, she began truanting. She used to bully Nellie and Gran into letting her stay at home and writing a letter to the teacher: Myra had a 'bad period', a 'headache', 'the 'flu'. When they refused, she wrote the note herself.

Myra and Pat Jepson, who lived opposite, often walked to school together. If they were bunking off without consent they waited in Sunny Brow Park before looping back to Beasley Street. Once Mam had gone to work, they sloped off down the ginnel that ran behind Eaton Street and in through the back door for a second breakfast. Myra was confident she knew Mam's habits, knew exactly how long she would have the house to herself. But one day she was frying bacon in the kitchen and Pat was buttering bread in the lounge when there was the sound of feet stopping by the front door and a hand on the knob. Pat was first out the back door; Myra followed in her footsteps, still carrying the pan. She jammed it into the narrow space behind the privy and sprinted down the ginnel. It was only when they got to the road that they realized the person at the door was Gran. If they'd stayed they could have talked their way out of it. As it was, flight was a clear admission of guilt. It was one thing to slope off with permission, quite another to do so without it.

They decided to throw themselves on the mercy of Myra's other grandmother, 'Nanna' Hindley. It was a decision made in the heat of the moment, and one Myra regretted as soon as the door cracked open to reveal the grim countenance that had given birth to her father. Myra's grandmothers could not have been more different. Gran used nothing more than Pears soap on her straight white hair; Nanna's 'styled' curls were dyed a frightening shade of orange. Gran did not wear make-up; Nanna never left the house without her lipstick on. Gran was soft and malleable; Nanna was fearsome and opinionated. But, much to Myra's surprise, she invited the girls in and remained quite calm during the long, detailed confession. She told them to make her a cup of tea, and themselves the second breakfast they'd been denied. Myra glanced round as she cooked. Pat, pale-faced with worry, watched as Nanna took out her pin curls and smeared on lipstick. It was the same shade as her hair. She always looked nice for work on 'The Twister' helter-skelter at Belle Vue, and the married lover Nellie unkindly referred to as her 'fancy man'. Nanna then made the girls wash up and walked them back to Beasley Street.

Pat and Myra didn't exchange a word but they were

convinced that Gran would shop them and pack them off to Ryder Brow. But Gran was so astonished to hear Nanna argue leniency for a 'first offence' that she accepted her suggestion: the girls should spend the day cleaning the houses at Eaton and Beasley Streets. But, even as she agreed, Myra could see Gran work out the intended slight: Nanna's house, where she lived alone, was spotless. Nanna departed and, with a cheery wave, told the girls not to do it again. Myra simply resolved never to get caught again.

While the girls worked, Ellen continued with her washing. She had to decide whether to let their parents know what had happened. She turned the handle of the mangle and streams of cold water sprang from the linen into a white basin at her feet. If she told Nellie there would be a row, and Bob would find out. It was easier to let it go; arguments between Myra and Bob almost always turned into full-blown fights. And Gran was not happy about her own daughter's role in this conflict. Too often she had heard Nellie trampling Myra's feelings, transferring the anger she felt at Bob on to her daughter.

But, according to Patricia Cairns, it was difficult for Gran to protect Myra. 'I don't know how much her gran was able to intervene, but she was the only source of kindness to Myra,' she said. 'She was always gentle. Her house was a place of refuge and warmth.'

I was puzzled. 'If her gran was like that, how come Nellie was so violent and malicious towards her?'

'There's no reason for it in her background. Ellen was born out of wedlock, so I have no idea who her father was. Perhaps there's some explanation for it there. I don't know.'

'Do you think that the violence at home affected the way she disciplined Myra?' I asked.

'She was soft. Too soft probably. What Myra needed was a firm guiding hand, and that wasn't there.'

The teachers at school were not fooled by Myra's sick-notes. She remembered how one day, after taking the register, Mr Lloyd-Jones laid down his pencil, leaned back, peered through his thick-rimmed glasses and ordered the class to 'give her a round of applause'. It was the first time she had called out 'present' for five consecutive days. Her truanting had denied her class any chance of victory in the school's attendance competition.

Mr Lloyd-Jones was a patient teacher, but even he found it difficult to endure the quality of Myra's efforts at art, and he expressed his exasperation. Myra replied that while she might not be able to draw, she could write. Taking her at her word, the head-master got her to keep an 'official' class diary. He noted, with satisfaction, that she concentrated and wrote reasonably well. After a few weeks, worried that the task was becoming boring for her, he suggested that she write a story for a classmate to illustrate. Myra threw herself into the task and, after discarding a couple of ideas, came up with *Adventure at Four*

Oaks Farm. The story, which borrowed heavily from Enid Blyton, described how a group of children captured a 'sinister' man who had threatened them in the cellar of a remote farmhouse. A character modelled on George of the Famous Five played a leading role in the adventure. Jean Hicks, the best artist in the class, illustrated it. Mr Lloyd-Jones was delighted; he had it bound 'like a proper book' and put in the school library.

Myra stood out at sport, too. The Ryder Brow rounders team was well drilled, and it competed successfully against other Manchester schools. Myra acquired the nickname 'Monkey' for the speed with which she once climbed over a fence to retrieve a ball and run out an opponent. Many of the children at Ryder Brow came from the surrounding 1920s estate; their homes were semi-detached, and they had gardens. As Myra walked to school she saw men leaving the houses wearing suits. Even the kids who walked the short distance from West Gorton were mainly Anglican. When they played matches Myra found herself copying her team-mates' superior attitude to kids from 'rough' schools, like Spurley Hay. But she felt uncomfortable doing this, as none of them was poorer than the kids of West Gorton. The pretence increased her feeling of being an 'outsider'.

Bob continued to drink heavily throughout Myra's teenage years, and to batter Nellie. The only time they united was to attack their daughter for her behaviour.

Things only got worse as Myra grew bigger and became more able to fight her corner, verbally as well as physically. Once, in the middle of an argument, she used a line she'd learned at school.

'You've only got one bad habit, Dad.'

'Only one? What is it?'

'Breathing.'

Bob was so upset he marched out of the house and slammed the front door. For once, even Nellie was silenced.

Myra hated it when people compared her to Bob, which happened often. It was inevitable, as she had followed in his footsteps by maintaining a reputation as a 'scrapper'. Myra used the excuse of 'defending' other children as a way of getting into fights. Maureen was always being picked on; she lacked the strength, and wit, to look after herself. Myra also 'looked out' for her sister's friend Pauline Reade, the first victim of the Moors murderers, and her brother Paul. When someone wanted to prove themselves hard they came looking for Myra Hindley.

Early one New Year, Myra wrote in her auto-biography, she was making her way down a ginnel when a voice called out from a back yard. It was a boy called Eric Goodwin asking her to guess what he'd got for Christmas. He was standing there with his hands tucked behind his back. She waited, in silence, knowing he'd tell her anyway. He brought his hands to the front to reveal two pairs of brown leather boxing gloves, their long white laces swaying gently in the breeze. Myra looked at them, then at Eric's legs. One was strong and healthy, the other thin and crippled. Surely he couldn't be serious?

It took Myra a while to tie the laces, which she eventually managed with the help of her teeth. Her hands felt big and clumsy. Eric stood there in a crouch, his fists held up in front of his skinny face. She laughed at him: he looked ridiculous. Eric responded by unleashing a stinging combination that sent Myra careering backwards into the yard wall. Her shoulder bashed against a wash tub balanced on top, and it came crashing down on her head. Stars, she recalled, swirled in front of her eyes, accompanied by the ringing of Eric's laughter. She lay there, careful not to get up before she had collected her senses, then charged at Eric. She rammed him with her shoulder. Her knee crashed into his head as he went down; he had no chance to recover. When she had finished he lay on the floor, whimpering.

She was about to untie the gloves when Albert Goodwin appeared, filling the entrance to the back yard, glaring at her. He asked Myra if she would like to fight someone her own size. She could not refuse, and stood there while he gently unlaced the gloves from his brother's hands and pulled them onto his own. Myra worked out her strategy as she waited. She reckoned she'd got the hang of fighting with gloves on, but she was wrong. Albert knew what he was doing, and he drove her around the back yard at will. He was careful not to finish her off too quickly, and jabbed at her face until she could feel it swelling. When she did finally fall he continued to hit her for a long time after she went still.

Two days later Myra bumped into Albert at the top of Taylor Street. There was only a narrow stretch of pavement as the road was blocked by a large puddle. Albert filled it, and clearly had no intention of moving. Myra's right eye was still puffy from the beating he'd given her. Albert smiled, admiring his handiwork. Without warning, Myra grabbed him by the lapels, tucked her right leg behind his, and tipped him over. She went down on top of him, grabbed his hair and slammed his head into the puddle. Stunned by the cold, wet stone against his skull Albert didn't stand a chance. She continued to hammer his head into the ground until a couple of his mates dragged her off. She knew Gran would be furious with her but she didn't care.

In Myra Hindley's autobiography it is striking how accounts of violence are juxtaposed with stories that illustrate her ability to form close personal relationships. One boy she never fought was Michael Higgins, who lived on Taylor Street. He was two years younger than Myra. The age difference meant that they had never been in the same class, and did not wear the shackles of a shared history. They spent hours together, roaming West Gorton and getting into scrapes. There was no question of romance; they were 'mates'.

Myra and Michael enjoyed swimming, and on summer evenings they went to Mellands Field reservoir. Although in the middle of Gorton the reservoir is surrounded by allotments and tall trees, and the shoreline is ringed by thick green reeds that flower a vibrant yellow in summer. They spent hours mucking about here, either on their own or with friends, secure in the knowledge that they would not be disturbed by adults.

In the city's Central library I flicked through pictures of all Manchester's reservoirs looking for an image of Mellings Field in the 1950s. The mundane municipal title does not do the grand circular building justice. The Central library was built as a symbol of Manchester's wealth and sophistication. Its domed roof and Ionic columns dominate St Peter's Square. Even the magnificent town hall bends around its contours. Its local studies section is the largest and most comprehensive I have seen. At one end of the room stands a line of computers on which members of the public can do picture research. Every photograph in the city's vast collection has been scanned, and many more have been supplied by individuals and local history groups.

I typed in the name of another of Myra and Michael's favourite places: 'Belle Vue'. The screen filled with a list of entries. There was an aerial shot that showed the 'pleasure gardens' lying next to the streets of Gorton – a world of escape that constantly beckoned people as they went about their daily lives. The permanent attractions included a zoo, a wrestling ring, bars, fairground rides and a speedway track. There were also occasional 'spectaculars': amazing fireworks displays and title fights.

Myra and Michael loved the speedway, but did not always have the funds to pay for a ticket. The solution was simple: they would break in through a secret entrance. The more adventurous children of Gorton got to know every ginnel, scrap of waste land and deserted building. They could slip, seemingly invisible, from Far Lane to 'the tank' and back again. It was a world closed to adults by the demands of dignity and respect for the law. Myra and Michael scrambled up the fence, dropped down the railway embankment and crossed the railway line towards the pleasure gardens. As they ducked and weaved their way across Gorton they saw adults taking more conventional routes for a night out. They did not hang about on the edge of Belle Vue. The trick was to get in quickly, without being spotted. Myra scrambled up the wall, Michael close behind her. She dropped down and rolled a couple of feet, to give him room to land. Without looking around they jumped up and ran into the crowd streaming towards the stands. None of the staff had seen them, and no one else was bothered.

Before they took their place in the stands, Michael

bought a programme; he collected them. The speed-way stadium had the feel, and appearance, of a Roman circus: high, banked stands around a circular dirt track full of expectation. The crowd roared as the riders shot out from the side, blipping their throttles theatrically. They lined up by the starting tape in team colours, shoulders hunched to absorb the force of rising handlebars, and blasted into the first corner. As the bikes tipped sideways, spitting dirt from their rear wheels, and as those who had overdone it spilled into the hoardings, the crowd stood as one and roared. Scarves waved and rattles chattered as though the noise would make a difference to the outcome. It was an intoxicating atmosphere.

Myra recorded in her autobiography that she and Michael made use of Nanna Hindley's name to get into the riders' enclosure between races. All she said to the guard at the gate was, 'Kitty Hindley sent me!' It always worked; Kitty was the sort to repay a favour. The riders stood around, sweating and smoking. The bikes made a ticking sound as the engines cooled, and mechanics checked them before the next race. Michael walked up to the riders, holding out his programme and a pen. The men affected indifference to flattery as Myra and Michael made their way round, gathering autographs, before heading back to Taylor Street.

The Hindleys' home life remained uneasy. Fights between Nellie, Bob and Myra usually ended with one of them storming out, Myra to Beasley Street, Bob to the pub. If one of their preferred escape routes disappeared the pressure might become unbearable. In Myra's mind, the winter of 1954 threatened exactly that.

Gran was upset. Jim, her daughter Louie's widower, had called round for tea. She was pleased to see him, but as she listened to his soft Irish voice her eyes had inevitably been drawn to the large sepia-tinted picture above the mantelpiece. It showed her and Louie in matching dresses and long, flowing brown locks, looking happy and confident. Just a few months after it was taken Louie lay dead, carried away by peritonitis. Gran told Myra that her hair had turned grey 'overnight', and she'd attempted suicide by taking an overdose. Of course she was glad she hadn't died, but Jim just brought it all back to her. Gran's misery was compounded by the fact that she could no longer even see the picture of Louie clearly. Myra told her to go to the doctor. It turned out to be the beginnings of cataracts. She needed an operation, and a date was set for her to go into the eye hospital.

Myra did not know anyone who had had an operation; she did, however, know that there was always a chance of death. As the day of Gran's surgery got closer and closer Myra became increasingly frightened, and fixated by the idea of mortality. What would happen to her if Gran was gone and Beasley Street was no longer there for her? On the day of Gran's admission Myra sat silently through tea and pretended to read one of Bob's Zane Grey cowboy

stories. The thought of having to move back perma-
nently to her parents' house was crushing. At bedtime
she wandered round to Beasley Street, pushed open
the front door, pulled Gran's old black coat off its
hook and put it on. Enveloped in her smell, she lay
down on the bed, by the extinguished fire, and fell
asleep.

The hospital would not let anyone under sixteen
onto the wards. But Myra was so unhappy that Nellie
agreed to try to smuggle her in. It would do them all
good to be together, confirm that things were going to
get back to normal. Mam lent Myra some stockings
and a pair of shoes with a small heel. She made her
comb the tangles out of her hair and put on a light
pink shade of lipstick. They caught the number 53
down to Oxford Road. No one challenged them as
they made their way onto the ward. Ellen could not
see them approaching as her head was wrapped in
bandages. Myra, upset at finding her so helpless,
began to weep. A hand reached out and gripped her.
Gran told her not to cry, she'd be home soon.

Galvanized by the possibility of loss, Myra set
about smartening up Beasley Street for Gran's return.
She got hold of a tin of maroon paint to do the wood-
work, so that it matched the flowers in the wallpaper,
and leaded the black grate until it shone. Auntie Anne
and Mam joined in; they hung bunting around the
room, and shook out the rag-peg rug. When they had
finished they prepared a special tea for Gran's return.

I asked Professor Malcolm MacCulloch what he thought about Myra Hindley's extreme reaction to her gran's illness. He paused before replying: 'There are a lot of mentions of death, or the proximity of death, in her recollections.'

'Is that significant?' I asked.

'It can be the sign of a personality which has been altered by circumstances,' he replied. 'It's certainly not normal.'

'Have you seen it before?'

'In adult serial killers, certainly. But what is special about this material is that it offers an insight into the formation of Myra Hindley's mind as a child. It's quite unprecedented in cases of this kind.'

Myra Hindley mentioned in her autobiography that a frequent visitor of Gran's was Hettie Rafferty, who lived opposite. The old woman had a lined face which screwed up 'like an irate monkey' when she laughed, which was often. A favourite topic of conversation was their own mortality. It was seen as a matter of great importance to prepare for death. Even the poorest person took out 'funeral insurance', paid in weekly instalments, to cover the cost of a 'proper burial' in consecrated ground. This ensured a dignified departure and protected relatives from the sudden expense of a funeral. For some, this cover extended no further than a wooden box. These families relied on women like Gran and Hettie to help 'lay out' the deceased in their best clothes. It was vital to do this properly, as friends and neighbours would come to say goodbye to the body before the burial. Hettie and Gran used to tease each other about who would be the first to go, who would get to lay the other one out. But when a friend approached death with no funeral insurance it was no laughing matter.

'Old Pebby', a friend of Ellen's, lay critically ill in the workhouse. His health had been slipping away for years, reducing him to the occasional labouring job and forcing him to accept 'charity'. A poor, lapsed Catholic, he faced burial in a pauper's grave. When Ellen went to visit him he whispered, 'If there is a God, I ask him to forgive me and save my soul from hell.' This gave Ellen some hope of laying her friend to rest in consecrated ground. If she could raise the money for a coffin, she could tell the monks he had repented. The only solution, Gran told Hettie, was for her to cash in some of her own funeral insurance.

The first thing Myra noticed as she came through the back door at Beasley Street was the smell of carnations – embalming fluid. Old Pebby's coffin stood on a couple of chairs under the front-room window; a beam of light cut across the middle and illuminated a pair of crossed white hands. Myra stood rooted to the spot in the doorway. Gran told her not to be 'feart', it was only Old Pebby. Hettie Rafferty was sitting with her. How long was he staying for, asked Myra. Only till tomorrow, said Gran; she couldn't leave him 'without a home to be sent off from'. Myra glanced at Gran's bed, just yards from the coffin. Where was she going to sleep? In bed, as usual, replied the old lady. It was not the dead you had to fear but the living. Myra stepped forwards. She noticed how strong Pebby's hands looked. She started as Gran lifted up the hanky covering his face. Myra reached out and touched Pebby's hand. It wasn't cold, as she'd expected, but 'cool and firm'. Gran put the hanky back in place. Myra noticed how still it was. They sat up next to the coffin all evening. When she came back from school the next day Pebby had gone, the chairs were back in their place, and the house smelt normal.

The dark content of this story does not stand out in her autobiography: death keeps reappearing as a theme in her description of everyday events. The decapitated Jack Russell, called Timmy, she found by the railway line; the boy she saw bleed to death after being crushed by a lorry on the Hyde Road; the cat torn in half by two dogs. And the time when she feared she might die herself.

Eddie Hogan did not give Myra any trouble now, and she had come to like him because he had 'nerve'. Myra, Eddie and Michael Higgins had a scam they worked in a corner shop. Myra went in, bought something small and got the shopkeeper chatting while the boys, all innocent smiles, stuffed things into their pockets. Often it was just rubbish, like string or potatoes, which they had to swap or sell. When they got lucky, with sweets, they ate them in secret to prevent awkward questions. Myra recorded that a favourite place was 'over the loco' – Gorton Tank railway yard. She and Michael would climb the boards and wander about among the trains. The risk of it was exciting. They knew the best times to break in without being discovered. But they didn't always get it right.

One day, Michael was in a train driver's cab, playing with the controls, when they were startled by a shout. Two railway workers in blue boiler suits were hurrying towards them. Michael jumped down, they raced towards the boards, scrambled over the top and headed for the allotments. They didn't want the men to get a good look at them. All of a sudden, Myra's leg stopped moving and a searing pain shot up from her ankle. It felt as though her foot had been trapped in a ferocious set of jaws. She lay on the ground and looked at the blood slowly trickling into the teeth of a 'man-trap'. Michael helped Myra to her feet and she tried to stagger on, the iron contraption swinging from her leg, but the pain was too much, and she collapsed. Michael left her and ran off to get help.

Bert and a neighbour, Mr Richards, carried Myra back to Beasley Street. They laid her on the sofa and tried to prise the jaws of the man-trap open. Bert sent Michael for Dr Chadwick; he returned a few minutes later to say that the elderly GP was on his way. Myra lay on the sofa, groaning, and tried not to writhe; every time she moved the teeth sank further into her ankle. Myra later wrote that she asked Michael, 'I'm not going to die, am I?' He replied, 'Course you won't die! You're too young!'

Like the tales of her fighting, almost all of the incidents concerning death were excised from later accounts of Myra's life. But the one story allowed to remain is, probably, the most telling.

As well as baptizing, educating, marrying and burying the people of Gorton, the church organized rituals that brought a sense of occasion and meaning to the passing seasons. The grandest of these were the annual Whit parades. Across Manchester long lines of people, dressed in their finest clothes, walked behind banners that proclaimed the name of their community. St Francis' schoolchildren walked on Whit Friday, the 'scholars' of the monastery on Sunday. The climax was the breathtaking Italian march in the centre of town on a Monday. The women dressed, like marionettes, in layer upon layer of multi-coloured petticoats and flared skirts.

The vaults of the North-West film archive, close to Piccadilly coach station, are filled with 8mm images of Whit parades. The dyes have faded, some colours more quickly than others, leaving bright reds and brilliant whites. Young Catholic girls walk in confirmation dresses, each clutching a posy in snowy-gloved hands with a crown of plaited flowers in her hair. The shots are held for a long time, to capture each passing face. The effort that went into putting on, and recording, the parades speaks of real pride.

For weeks beforehand small family groups boarded the bus from Gorton to 'town'. The parents looked nervous and the children excited. From pants and socks to white dresses and grey suits, everything had to be new. Coyne's on Cross Street did the whole lot 'on tick' for a very reasonable rate. Bob Hindley did not go into town with his wife and daughters in the early summer of 1955, but Nellie was still determined to be careful: it would be her name on the hire-purchase agreement. She was delighted with the special offer: a free pleated skirt with each two-piece suit. She bought Myra and Maureen one each. The children were proud of their outfits; the Whit marches were something to be enjoyed rather than sneered at. Michael's mother bought him a new pair of long trousers, a blazer, a tie and a pullover. He had been chosen to take a leading role in the procession.

There were a couple of photographs of Michael among Myra Hindley's possessions. Looking at them, I found it hard to imagine him in his Whit clothes: they were street pictures, showing him the way he was when he played with Myra. In one, a plaid shirt undone almost to the waist; in another, trousers tucked into heavy woollen socks to stop them from getting fouled in his bicycle chain.

Myra watched the 'Franners' parade on a hot Friday in June with her close friends Pat and Barbara Jepson. The smallest girls, at the head of the procession, wore their white confirmation dresses. They were followed by the older boys. Michael walked alongside Eddie, carrying a large embroidered banner. He disappeared as the Children of Mary, League of Mary and a succession of bands marched past. After the parade the girls caught the 109 to Reddish for a 'posh' afternoon tea with the Jepsons' aunt and uncle. They had scones, cream, sandwiches and chocolate biscuits on proper china. On the way back they rode on the rear platform to get some air. They planned to jump off when the bus slowed for the corner with the Bessamer pub.

As the driver applied the brakes a bicycle, being ridden frantically, appeared at the rear platform. It was Wally, a kid from Taylor Street. He drew up behind them and shouted out that Mike was dead, Mike had drowned. Myra jumped off the bus, skidded to a standstill outside the Bessie and grabbed Wally's handlebars. She asked him what he was on about. He told her that after the parade they'd gone for a swim in the Mellands Field reservoir. Halfway across Mike started shouting he'd got cramp. By the time they got to him he'd disappeared underwater.

Myra started to run, down Taylor Street heading for Mount Road; Pat chased after her. They were full from their tea and still in their best Whit clothes, but did not stop. They tore across the playing fields at the back of the reservoir and down the sandy path to the water where they met a crowd of gloomy-looking boys and girls coming in the opposite direction. Michael's body had been found, they said. The ambulance people tried to pump his lungs, give him the kiss of life, but it was no good. They'd taken him away. His mum had gone with him.

Myra climbed onto the crossbar of a friend's bike and sat there, in silence, as it juddered down the track back to Taylor Street. Everywhere she looked there were groups of adults and children, huddled in stunned silence. Pat's mum, 'Chief' Jepson, had taken refuge in her living room. In the stillness of the house Myra sat down and dissolved into tears, rocking back and forth in Chief's arms.

That night she climbed into bed with Gran and dreamed of Michael. She was diving underwater towards him and trying to grab his hair to pull him to the surface, but it was too short. Then she, too, was sinking into the deep, gulping lungfuls of water. She woke to find Gran stroking her head.

Patricia Cairns says that Myra Hindley felt responsible for the death of Michael Higgins. 'She didn't like to talk about it. She felt very distressed about his death and said she was to blame.'

'How could she be?' I asked. 'She'd just gone off for tea.'

'She felt that if she'd been there it wouldn't have happened. She was a very strong swimmer, and would have been able to save him. But she didn't talk about it at length. You know what Myra's like when she's upset. She just pulls the shutters down and blocks everything out. You can't get through. She couldn't cope with what happened to Mike.'

Mrs Higgins gave Myra Michael's speedway programmes and comb. Myra went door to door collecting money for a wreath, wearing a black armband Gran had made from an old coat. The day before the funeral Michael was laid out in the Higginses' front room. Mrs Higgins ushered Myra in and told her to take a look, otherwise she wouldn't be able to accept he was dead. Michael lay there in his altar boy's clothes. In the autobiography Myra goes into great detail about her best friend's appearance: his lips were slightly parted, and his eyes hadn't been fully closed – Myra could see a thin sliver of blue reflected in the light. Before the coffin lid was fixed in place Mrs Higgins pulled the rosary from Michael's stiff fingers and handed it to Myra.

The monks said a requiem mass for Michael at St Francis'. The coffin was placed in front of the main altar and a choir made up of his schoolmates sang. After the service Myra turned down the offer of a lift to the cemetery with Mrs Higgins and walked with Pat Jepson. She could not face watching the burial and sat, with her back turned, by the canal at the edge of the cemetery. Pat crouched next to her, watched what was going on and commentated in a low whisper: they are at the graveside; his mam has just thrown soil on the coffin; the mourners are moving away; they are filling in the grave.

After the funeral Michael's family and other friends got on with their lives. But Myra remained fixated by grief. She returned every day to sit by the mound of freshly dug earth with a new offering. At first she brought flowers she'd paid for, then flowers she'd nicked from parks and traffic islands. A few weeks after the tragedy Mrs Higgins bumped into her in the cemetery. Michael's mother said she was worried about Myra and suggested they go to church together. It might help.

Attending St Francis' with Mrs Higgins was a way of staying close to Michael. There was comfort to be derived from having his mother kneel next to her as the monks swung incense and intoned Latin in front of the grand Gothic altar. Myra also got fewer comments from people; they seemed to accept her spending hours on her knees in church rather than crouched by a graveside. The only frustration was that she couldn't take Holy Communion. Mrs Higgins suggested she get confirmed.

Her teacher was Father Theodore, who'd gone to school with Bob. They sat in a side room of St Francis' where there were just a few books, a crucifix and a statue of 'Our Lady', and learned the catechism by rote.

'Who made you?'

'God made me.'

Caught up in the excitement of the new, she did not hold up Father Theodore's pronouncements on the sanctity of marriage against her own personal experience. She also did not fully understand the doctrine to which she was swearing allegiance.

Myra chose Therese as her confirmation name. She was anointed by the bishop of Salford. The whole family, including Nellie, came to watch. Auntie Kath sponsored her, and gave her a pocket prayer book as a present. I found it among her belongings, in a frayed white envelope, with a bright picture of Jesus offering benediction on the cover.

Myra did not forget Michael. One evening, she was sitting in the Jepsons' front room listening to music, and watching rain run down the window, when she noticed a shimmering between the thick rivulets of water. It was Michael, sheltering in the fire escape of the Plaza cinema. His wet hair was plastered to his head, he was wearing his old overcoat, and he was staring at her. She ran to the door and pulled it open, but he had gone.

'The obsession with death in her autobiography is quite striking, and very unusual.'

Malcolm MacCulloch put his coffee cup down, pushed the half-moon glasses up so that they rested on his forehead, and clasped his hands.

'In what way?'

'Do you thread stories of death through your entire childhood?'

'Well, no.'

'Exactly! It's a sign of a personality that has been brutalized by personal experience.'

'But what is the significance of an obsession with death?'

'You have to look at the details. There is a constant backdrop of violence here – she experienced it on a daily basis. That led to a distorted personality. The obsession with death is a manifestation of that distortion.'

It does not feel, when reading the earliest version of Myra Hindley's autobiography, as though she had any idea that the frequent, graphic references to death were unusual. The text has no structure, just words poured onto the page from a fast-flowing stream of consciousness. As we know, her supporters, like David Astor, were dismayed by the results and advised her to make changes before suggesting she abandon it altogether. The later version, and the letters to me, are more tightly written, if self-serving. Incidents that hint at a damaged personality have been cut. An exception, the story of Michael Higgins, was so well known it could not go. The purpose of the more refined versions, of course, was to portray herself as a victim, and Ian Brady as the manipulator.

Chapter Four

When Detective Superintendent Tony Brett was appointed to run the Moors murder inquiry, and told to ensure that Myra Hindley died behind bars, I got a request to meet Greater Manchester Police detectives. This made me nervous. I was willing to do anything that might lead to the recovery of Keith Bennett, but I did not want to become embroiled in a highly charged political dispute. I agreed to meet the detectives with Professor John Hunter and his assistant, the former head of the West Midlands Police murder squad Detective Chief Superintendent Barrie Simpson, who were working with the family of Keith Bennett to try to recover his body. I was questioning Myra Hindley on their behalf.

'They are going to push you, you know.'

Barrie Simpson looked hard at me to make sure his comment had sunk in. We were waiting in Professor John Hunter's office at Birmingham University.

'Great. So what do I do?'

'Be open, but make it clear that you are helping them because you want Keith Bennett to be found,' replied Simpson.

'But are *they* interested in finding him?' I asked. 'They've hardly done anything for years!'

Hunter stopped battering away at his email and looked round. 'They've got to! The police can't assign a load of officers to keep her inside and ignore the fact that there's still a child missing!'

There was a knock at the door.

I was surprised at the appearance of DC Andy Meekes, DC Dave Warren and DC Gail Jazmik. They looked like bank managers. They were the smartest-looking bunch of detectives I'd ever met. I was to discover that all members of Greater Manchester Police's FMIT (Force Major Incident Team) dress the same way. I wondered whether this was to mark them out as the elite.

'Sorry we're a bit late, the traffic was awful!' exclaimed Jazmik as she brushed raindrops from her brow. They had obviously hurried up the stairs.

The detectives made small talk as they settled round the table and got their notepads out. I noticed that Barrie Simpson took care not to draw attention to his former, very senior, rank. But he did use the same language as them.

'As you know,' said Jazmik, 'we were assigned to the

case to see if there is a way of keeping Myra Hindley in prison.'

I was surprised by her openness. It would have been easy to fudge.

Meekes added, in a matter-of-fact way, 'We have read every book on the case, and been through the files. There has never been a better briefed team of officers.'

'And Keith Bennett?' asked Hunter.

'Of course if we can find him we will. It's what we all want,' replied Jazmik.

Hunter nodded and began to describe his work on the case.

Many of the decisions Hunter had taken about how to search for Keith Bennett were founded on a detailed understanding of events and how the Moors murderers were likely to have behaved. This knowledge was based both on published information and what I had learned. The officers were thorough in their questioning; they probed Hunter's logic at every turn. When it became clear that he was relying on a piece of information that had come from me, they tested its quality. The questioning went on all morning. I was grilled on my involvement with Myra Hindley, my motives and my opinions. Did I want her to get out? Who were her friends? Who were my sources? I did my best to help, without betraying any confidences. It was a draining experience.

'The more we know the better we can judge

anything new that comes along,' Dave Warren explained as he folded his notepad. 'So you'll make sure you keep us informed of your work, won't you? We all want the same thing, don't we?'

I certainly wanted Keith Bennett to be found, and knew that I had to trust in the detectives' good faith.

When she finished secondary school Myra was offered a place at Didsbury teacher training college. But she'd decided she wanted to 'get on with' her life; she hadn't left one educational institution only to walk straight into another, and spend the rest of her life with kids. She got a job as a typist at Lawrence Scott Electromotors, but had to wait a few weeks, until she was fifteen, before she could start. The three years between leaving school and meeting Ian Brady are described in her autobiography with longing, as though for an opportunity missed. But this description also explains why she was ready to fall into his arms.

Kath 'sorted out' a few weeks' work at a catalogue company in the centre of town. They knew Myra was underage but bent the rules because they were short-staffed. She spent her days packing shoes for sales reps and running errands to buy them muffins or sand-wiches. It was a strange environment: wall-to-wall fitted carpets, heating, soft lighting, and cubicles for customers to get changed in. She got £3 a week tax free, ten shillings more than her new job was going to pay. But she was looking forward to leaving. The city centre was far too busy, with so many people on the pavements that you had to weave in and out of them on the way to and from the bus stop.

When she started work at Lawrence Scott's Myra wanted to show that she had grown up, that she was no longer a schoolgirl. They talked about it for weeks in the canteen before Myra finally plucked up the courage – she was going to go blonde. Her friend Margie said she could do it at her flat after work.

Myra rinsed her head under the tap, pulled a towel from round her shoulders and stood up to scrunch her hair dry. An empty L'Oreal bleach bottle lay on the edge of the sink. The face that stared back at her in the mirror looked older, more sexual. She dipped her chin, tilted her head left and right. Margie said her mam was going to kill her; Myra replied that she didn't care.

She went straight round to Eaton Street, walked into the front room without knocking, and stood there with her arms crossed. The silence seemed to go on for ever, then came the inevitable explosion. Dad said she looked like a whore; Mum raged that she wasn't too old for 'a good hiding', stepped forward and belted her round the head. Eventually the fury subsided. Myra had been expecting an order to 'go down the shops for a bottle of tint', but it never came. Perhaps they were so angry it didn't occur to them. Or they realized that now she'd started work, what little control they'd had over her was gone.

Lawrence Scott's was within walking distance of home. The day she came in 'a blonde' there was a noticeable drop in volume as she crossed the shop floor to her office. She enjoyed that. Her boss, Bill Cockburn, laid a handwritten sheet on her desk to type up but didn't say anything about her hair. He was far too much of a 'gentleman'. Myra sat down and started hammering away at the keys of the ancient machine. By the time she crossed the shop floor on the morning toast run the older men had grown accustomed to her new look and managed to disguise any heightened interest. But a couple of the apprentices, who had to move coils of wire and tools so she could pass, couldn't help themselves. They were teased loudly for stealing an extra glance.

The 'association room' at Lawrence Scott's was large, with ranks of table tennis tables for the workers to relax at. There was also a record player with a stack of old favourites. As Myra walked in, 'At the Hop' by Danny and the Juniors was playing. One of the older men, Keith, called over and asked if she'd ever had a go at table tennis. She hesitated; he was obviously just being friendly. If it had been one of the younger boys she would have walked on by. He stood behind her, moved her hand into position and swung it, by the wrist, to serve. Ernie, on the other side of the table, gently returned the ball. She knew that normally he would have smashed such a slow shot.

Myra found that she had a knack for table tennis,

and she soon began to beat the men. She recorded in her autobiography that Keith said she had a 'killer serve', and she was asked to join the factory team. They travelled across the city, playing other large companies like Oldham Batteries. Afterwards, they went drinking together. Myra was advised by the older secretaries to have a glass of milk before going to the pub, and to stick to shandies.

Every week Myra paid into a social fund that financed works parties. Her first was at the Levenshulme Palais. She bought a blue woollen dress, matching heels and a bag for the occasion. A bus picked them up at the factory for the short journey there. One of the older women told her to watch out how much she drank; Myra said she'd be fine. But it was a long evening, and everyone was having a good time. She ended up in the arms of a welder called Ray. He had thick blond hair cut in a DA, a wavy lock lying on his forehead and fashionable sideburns. She let him walk her home.

Ray took her for long rides on his motorbike, and on evenings out with his mates. Myra looked good on his arm, but they parted when she refused to have sex with him. She did not want a reputation for being 'loose'. Nor did she intend to end up like her friend Dodo, who got pregnant by a 'flash Ted' called Eric, always moaning about how boring her life had become.

On Friday and Saturday nights Myra and Pat

Jepson went to the Ashton Palais, which was 'glamorous', or Chick Hibbert's bar, which was rough. Things often got out of hand between rival gangs, and they fought with motorcycle chains. The bouncers helped the police by turning fire hoses on the scrapping 'bikers' while everyone else fled down the back steps.

Myra took care of her hair. At first she let her mam touch up the roots, but soon decided it would be better to get it done professionally. Every night she washed it and put in rollers. The following morning she lacquered the curls, brushed out the hardness and dressed for work. Her clothes and make-up were immaculate, if a little brash.

One day Myra got home to find Gran in high spirits. They were on the move! Gran told her that Bert and Kath had got a new bungalow in Reddish and had given her the rent book to their place. It had 'all the mod cons!' When Myra walked through the front door of 7 Bannock Street she switched the light on and ignored the cockroaches scuttling for cover. She went from room to room flicking every switch and smiling to herself. The house not only had electricity, but a tiled fireplace and a hot water geyser. Gran told her she wasn't going to sleep in front of the fire any more; she fancied a room upstairs, felt she deserved it after all these years. Myra agreed. It felt like they'd really gone up in the world. They did not have the money, like their new neighbours, to redecorate the whole house, so they contented themselves with hanging a new, warm red wallpaper with feathers on it in the front room. To finish it off, Kath let them keep the sideboard and drop-leaf table.

Just after they'd moved in, Myra pushed open the front door as she came in from work and heard Gran calling to her; there was something wrong with Billy the budgie. She reached into the cage to lift the bird out, but he was stuck to his perch. His feathers were crunchy to the touch, his eyes darted frantically around the room, and his legs made small tugging motions. Myra understood immediately what had happened: hairspray. He had been entombed since she left the house nine hours earlier. Myra gently prised his legs free, carried him into the kitchen and wiped the brittle covering off with a warm, damp cloth. Gran told her not to worry, at least he was alive. From then on Myra covered the cage with a large cloth before doing her hair.

I discussed with Professor Malcolm MacCulloch the change in Myra's behaviour after she started work. I was struck by how she seemed to calm down, and stopped fighting. 'Yes. But by that time much of her personality had been shaped. She had been taught to deal with violence from others, and to hand it out. These were not lessons she would forget.'

Myra liked Lawrence Scott's. In many ways it was the same as the streets on which she had felt at home as a child. Her life was made up of familiar faces and routines. The difference was that she had money, and did not need to scrap. But after a while she wanted to escape; it wasn't like school, where you could get away with bunking off. She began to feel trapped. Her friend and colleague Margie said that what they needed was a really good holiday. Myra loved the idea, and told her that she'd heard Butlin's at Ayr, in Scotland, was really good.

They got second jobs to help pay for it. After work they caught the bus to the Robertson's jam factory. The first thing Myra noticed as they drew closer was the sharp, thin smell of boiled sugar. Lorries from Kent roared in through the gate packed high with pallets of freshly picked strawberries. The factory needed to work flat out while the fruit was in season, and Myra found herself lining up with what seemed like hundreds of other women in front of a long trough. A supervisor stood at the front of the room and yelled instructions at them: wash your hands, put your apron on, tie up your headscarf. Myra did as she was told, and followed the others into the jam-making hall. Long wooden benches lined a conveyor down the middle of the room. The belt rattled into life, and a line of numbered boxes moved along it. Myra followed the example of the old hands, grabbed one and started plucking the stalks from the tops of the fruit. It was difficult to do quickly without damaging the strawberries, but she soon got the hang of it. In fact, she was pleased to note that she was one of the faster ones. When she finished a box, she wrote her number on the ticket and loaded it back onto the belt.

Supervisors walked up and down the rows making sure that the fruit was being prepared quickly enough, and to the right standard. Their work was checked too as the strawberries made their way into the large, shining steel vats to be boiled with sugar. To her left, Myra heard a sneeze. A supervisor yelled at the woman, told her to get to the washroom, re-scrub, and come back fast. The worker on the receiving end of the order looked shocked, but obediently scrambled for the sink. Every lost minute cost the women money.

At eight o'clock there was a tea break. Myra needed it: her back ached, her fingers were red and raw and she could feel the beginnings of a blister on the tip of her thumb. But as she stood up to take the short walk to the tea urn she noticed that some of the experienced workers stayed sitting at the bench. The trays kept on rolling towards them. One caught her eye and told her that when she was working she was earning. There was plenty of time for rest at home.

The following night Myra stayed on her bench during the break. She made more in piece work at Robertson's over a fortnight than she got in a month at Lawrence Scott's. She opened a post office account with the first week's takings, but was glad when she'd saved enough for the holiday. The work was far too tedious for her to stick at it. Strawberry jam never tasted quite the same again.

Ayr was not the warmest holiday destination, but it was an escape from Gorton. The camp hosts, or 'red coats', provided wall-to-wall entertainment, and when they stopped there was the warm embrace of boys she would never meet again. The freedom from expectation was welcome, as was the absence of prying neighbours, like Mrs Green, who complained to Nellie about the number of boys Myra kissed by her back door in Almond Street.

Most of the 'lads' Myra knew at home had left school and started work. They were having a few wild years before 'settling down' with a family, or being forced to do so by circumstance. She knew that her future probably lay in a relationship with one of them but, having just escaped Bob and Nellie's controlling influence, she did not welcome the prospect. Then she met Johnny; he was different. For the first time, thoughts of escape stirred in her mind.

Next to Gorton Monastery stands a rough patch of land known as Mission Croft. In the 1950s, once a year, the monks allowed travelling Romanies to run a small fair there. They set up camp on Loco Croft, next to the railway line. The painted caravans drew the admiration of children and the suspicions of their parents. Myra made a detour to walk past the slumbering encampment on her way to work. Its world seemed one of unimaginable freedom. In 1957, for a few glorious weeks, it opened up to her.

A beautiful Romany girl called Doreen fell for

Jimmy Rafferty, the grandson of Hettie opposite. Although he had a reputation for being wild, Doreen agreed to marry him and moved in. Gypsies, like Johnny, started coming in and out of the houses. With them came a sense of danger and excitement. Johnny had a slim face framed by unfashionably long curly hair, and he wore a white frilly shirt open at the neck. He came to stay at the Raffertys' because he needed to 'lie low' for a few days. Myra hung around, made cups of tea and spent hours listening to his stories. Johnny told Hettie Rafferty he'd like to hang his hat next to the blonde girl's. When the old woman told her this Myra was both excited and embarrassed. No one she knew spoke like that. Last thing at night, in her bedroom, she wrote Johnny love songs and imagined living in a caravan with him, far away from Gorton. She knew it was an impossible dream but she found it far more enjoyable than facing up to her future.

A few nights after Johnny moved in there was a screeching of tyres. Myra peeped through the curtains and saw two police cars, officers tumbling out of them, in front of the Raffertys. A sergeant hammered at the front door. By the time Jimmy pulled the bolt back Johnny had dropped from a windowsill into the ginnel at the back of the house. The following day Hettie came round to Gran's. Myra asked where he'd gone. Hettie said she didn't know, and didn't care. As far as she was concerned it was 'good riddance to bad rubbish'. Myra was outraged: Johnny wasn't rubbish, he was 'gorgeous'. Hettie said she'd soon learn not to judge a book by its cover.

Myra never saw Johnny again. That summer she started going out with Ronnie Sinclair. They'd known each other since they were twelve; she'd 'belted him one' after he pulled the ribbons in her hair during the Saturday matinee at the Plaza. He asked her to marry him, and they went halves on a second-hand engagement ring. But it felt like a game to her. She could not imagine living with someone who seemed like a boy.

A year after starting at Lawrence Scott's her boss, Bill Cockburn, announced that there were going to be 'cutbacks' on a last in, first out basis. Myra was devastated by the harshness of it but hoped that 'the change' might lead to adventure. Nanna got her and a bunch of friends weekend jobs with the Belle Vue catering department. Myra, Irene, Margie and Pauline worked Saturday nights from five till ten on the mobile food trolleys. Myra preferred selling tea to fish and chips as the smell didn't hang about your hair the same way. Either way the time flew by because they were so busy. It was a lot more fun than her new day job in a typing pool.

After a couple of weeks Eugene, the Belle Vue catering manager, said that Myra and Irene were 'wasted' on the food trolleys; would they like to have a go helping out in the German-themed 'beer cellar'? The girls, adhering to Nanna's instructions, tarted themselves up for work the following week. It would be good for tips, and it was important that the policemen who came in for a pint after their shift did not feel obliged to ask questions. The middle-aged barmaid – she looked just like Nanna, thought Myra: mutton dressed as lamb – gave them clear instructions on how to fiddle measures. They must only push the glass up three-quarters of the way, never right to the top. It soon mounted up. The barmaid also reached under the counter and pulled out a couple of packs of cigarettes, tossed them over, and told the girls to keep their mouths shut. Myra knew that by accepting the cigarettes she was entering a world of petty theft, but she didn't care. Every 'punter' who looked like a mug, or drunk, was short-changed by the price of 'a drink'. The girls told one another that it wasn't really criminal. The booze would have cost far more in a pub. The only time the thievery stopped was when the person the other side of the counter was a policeman.

Myra's third job was at Hinchcliffe's. She liked the other girls in the typing pool, Mary and Anita, but their boss was a bully. They sat facing his glass-fronted office, in a line, with their heads down, pummelling their heavy machines from nine till five. If they looked up, or started chatting, he would storm out and shout at them. His greatest pleasure lay in finding a mistake in their work. He would sit with his head bent over a large wooden desk and pore over every line, his balding head moving from side to side as he read. They would work away, pretending to ignore him, and wait for the inevitable, triumphant, 'Aha!' He would come out of the door smirking, waving the offending document before him, to humiliate whoever was responsible.

They spent their lunch hours scouring the back pages of the *Manchester Evening News* looking for new jobs. It did not take long before they found something. Wanted: Dictaphone typists. The jobs were at Burlington's Warehouses, a big catalogue company in the city centre. It had to be better than this! Anita was the first to go; she'd only given seven days' notice. The following week Mary and Myra were filled with excitement at the idea of their new adventure together. But on Friday afternoon the phone on Myra's desk rang. It was Anita, in a flap: Burlington's was even worse than Hinchcliffe's. She told Myra that patrols of 'blue caps' marched up and down the lines of typists, terrorizing them. If a girl looked up without good reason or went to the toilet for more than five minutes, her pay was docked. Anita had resigned.

The girls huddled together and discussed what to do. Mary said she was going to take her time. Ken, her fiancé, made good money and she didn't want to get it wrong again. Myra was in a panic: she couldn't afford to be off work. They lapsed into silence, then Mary remembered another advert in the *Evening News*, for a typist at Millwards. She'd worked there for a while; the pay was fair and the boss, Tommy Craig, was a really nice man. Myra sat at her desk, glowered at her boss's downturned head and picked up the phone. Had they filled the job yet? No, was she interested? Did she want to come over now? Myra stood up and, without asking permission, left to catch the bus for an interview.

It did not look promising: a cluster of old buildings tucked round a cobbled yard; two men in blue boiler suits loading barrels onto the back of a flatbed truck. But she liked the atmosphere as she walked into the office. The three men working there seemed relaxed, and there were no raised voices. Tommy sat her down in a side room with a typewriter and a handwritten letter to copy. She sailed through the test, chatted to him for a few minutes, and then he offered her the job. They were about to pack up for the evening, but why didn't she come and meet everyone?

The two men, Myra recalled in a letter to me, slowed the pace of their work as she came in but took care not to stare. She sensed that they didn't want to make her feel uncomfortable. The older one, who was sitting at a desk, stood up and held out his hand. This was Bert; she'd be 'taking quite a lot of dictation from him'. Then Tommy turned to a tall young man standing by a filing cabinet, and said, 'Myra, this is Ian. Ian, this is Myra.'

Book Two
The Moor

'He wanted to carry out the perfect murder, and
I was going to help him.'

Chapter One

'What's in it for me?' asked Malcolm MacCulloch.

'I beg your pardon?' I responded as I perched nervously on the edge of an expensive sofa.

'What's in it for me? It's the one question that precedes every decision.'

The forensic psychiatrist picked up and turned over each new piece of information, examining it for signs of human weakness.

'Why were you given the autobiography?'

'Because my source wanted the truth to come out.'

'Rubbish! Either they're deriving pleasure from influencing events or they're salving a guilty conscience. An altruistic motivation is almost always, at heart, selfish.'

Even though I was an experienced journalist, I found MacCulloch's view of the world reductive. He caught the expression on my face, and his eyebrows rose.

'Don't play naive. It's a truth you apply to get stories. You're good at it.' There was a mocking edge to his voice.

I stayed quiet.

'What you need to do,' he continued in a more placatory tone, 'is work out what the other people around her want and give it to them. You never know what you might find. Never, ever assume that there's nothing else out there.'

A month later I rang MacCulloch to report on progress.

'A church roof,' I said.

'Go on.'

'A friend of hers was wondering whether I might be able to make a contribution towards a new church roof.'

'And what's in it for you?'

'A later draft of the autobiography. It covers the relationship with Ian Brady, the murders and her attempted escape from prison.'

'Does it go further than the letters she wrote to you?'

'I'm told it's six times as long and far more detailed.'

'Good boy.'

I travelled to collect the 'new' draft of Myra Hindley's autobiography the following week. My source, who asked to remain anonymous, handed over a tattered carrier bag containing four faded cardboard folders. I climbed into my car and pulled out several hundred sheets of closely typed foolscap. They appeared to have been dropped at some stage as the pages were slightly crumpled and out of sequence.

It took me a month to read, and catalogue, the new discovery. The document was written in the late 1980s, after Myra Hindley had finally confessed to her role in the killings. It was invaluable as it helped to explain the formation of her relationship with Ian Brady, the circumstances surrounding the killings, and how the bond between them endured arrest and imprisonment. But there were large gaps in the story, only filled in by the letters she wrote to me more than ten years later. Taken together, the two accounts added significantly to knowledge of the case.

The evening following her interview at Millwards, Myra told me in a letter, Ronnie Sinclair was working a night shift. Myra didn't care; she went out with five girlfriends and couldn't stop going on about Ian. She told them he reminded her of Elvis, or Jimmy Dean. The girls were thrilled. They didn't say anything about her being engaged. Perhaps Ian was 'the one'. They only had to look about them to understand the importance of choosing the right husband.

As Myra walked back to Gran's she peered into the cracks of light between net curtains. She glimpsed fragments of people's lives: women knitting, men slumbering, the mess left behind by kids, an old couple sipping tea. Pieced together, they formed a picture of the existence Myra could expect if she married Ronnie. As she crawled under the covers to go to sleep she knew it would not be enough for her.

Patricia Cairns told me that Myra Hindley's instant, powerful attraction to Ian Brady meant there was never any doubt they would form a relationship. 'Once her mind was made up that was it, she would make it happen. She turned her beam on him. It's part of her character.'

'But she couldn't force him to fall in love,' I said.

'Who would have thought that a prison inmate could have achieved the things she did, had the friends she had?' Patricia asked. 'There was a real force of character there. She got me to move south, to live with David Astor, just so that she could see me twice a week in prison! I didn't really have any say in the matter. She wanted it and it happened. I've never come across anything like it.'

Myra described starting work at Millwards in her letters to me. The first morning, she took great care with her appearance. It was important to look good, but not as if she was trying too hard. Her skirt was tight but not too short; her blouse was fitted but not tarty. When she climbed the back steps to the office she told herself to be friendly but not gushing. Tommy Craig greeted Myra and showed her to her desk. She glanced over at Ian. His head was bent over a ledger; a Capstan Full Strength hung out of the corner of his mouth. She said good morning to him. He did not look up, just twitched his cigarette in acknowledgement and carried on filling in numbers.

Ian's coldness surprised her. She was used to a simple, direct response from men. There was not the slightest sign that he was attracted to her. She continued to glance at him between bursts of typing, noting details: waistcoat and tie; dark hair carefully cut, oiled and combed; shoes buffed mirror black. When he did speak it was in a formal, almost old-fashioned manner. She'd have laughed if he hadn't appeared so serious about it. Her hand tore across the shorthand pad as he rattled out words and figures in a softening Glaswegian accent. When Ian had finished he said, 'Thank you, Miss Hindley,' and went back to the ledgers at his desk.

Myra hoped that given time he would warm to her, and she set about gathering intelligence. She sat at her desk, pretending to work, and studied his conversations with Tommy and Bert. To her dismay, the main topic of discussion seemed to be horses. During the morning break the men spread a copy of the *Racing Post* out on a desk and pored over it, discussing weights, riders and ground conditions. At lunchtime Ian nipped out to put his bets on. If it was a big race – the Gold Cup, the King George VI, or Ascot – Tommy let them listen to the commentary in the bookie's. Otherwise, Ian got the results by ringing up the Tote.

During one of these calls Myra learned that Ian's

aloof, controlled exterior was a mask. She could tell from the set of his shoulders that he had lost, and expected disappointment. What followed was an explosion: he hurled the phone down and screamed a string of obscenities. Tommy did not show any surprise at his performance. It seemed that this was part of the office routine. He told Ian to calm down; if he couldn't lose he shouldn't bet. The force of Ian's anger was accentuated by the contrast with his sophisticated appearance. As he raged his accent slipped back towards the Gorbals. But his temper was nothing new to Myra; she had lived with fury all her life.

Tommy and Bert could talk about horses all day, but there was a definite change in atmosphere when Ian came over the intellectual. A glazed look fell over their eyes when he lectured them on his latest discovery – Nietzsche, de Sade, Dostoevsky. Myra realized that Ian wasn't interested in conversation; he was letting his colleagues know that, while he may be employed as a book-keeper, he was above all this. It was a temporary resting place before he went on to better things.

Ian was the first person Myra had met who studied 'proper' books, rather than thrillers or cowboy stories, in order to 'better' himself. The boys she knew had only ever opened a book because a schoolmaster told them to, and had usually accompanied their efforts with ostentatious displays of boredom. Ian's passion for literature was something she understood; she still spent hours reading, seeking refuge in a world created by someone else. But Myra knew from the way he talked that it was different for Ian. He didn't just escape into books, he used them to build a world of his own, a place in which he could live all the time.

Most of the men Myra knew got through life to the beat of an unchanging rhythm: work, bookie's, work, pub, bed and, at the weekends, football. Ian always seemed to be looking for a new tune. Myra smiled to herself when he told Tommy that he'd 'taken up the piano'. Then he replaced Boddington's bitter with red wine – a decision quite incomprehensible to Tommy and Bert. Ian's apparent sophistication, and distance, made Myra want him all the more. In spare moments between typing she recorded her feelings in a small blue diary she kept locked in her desk drawer. The police discovered it in the days following her arrest. It is a record of obsession.

2 August: 'Not sure he likes me.'
11 August: 'Been to Friendship pub, but not with
        Ian.'

Ian's experimental sartorial touches made him even more attractive: the red and white spotted hand-kerchief in a tweed jacket pocket; the long leather coat that reached almost to the ground. And all the time a coolness towards Myra. She did not know if he was immune to her or playing some sort of game. She poured her frustration into the diary.

13 August: 'Wonder what misery will be like tomorrow?'

24 August: 'I am in a bad mood because he hasn't spoken to me today.'

30 August: 'Ian and Bert have had a row. Tommy sided with Bert and said Ian loses his temper too soon.'

1 November: 'Months now since Ian and I spoke.'

6 November: 'Ian still not speaking. I called him a big-headed pig.'

I walked down the side of Ryder Brow school to where Millwards' offices once stood. They had been replaced with squat blocks of redbrick flats covered in satellite dishes. The bookie's was still there. I walked inside: formica floor, telly on above the door, sharp-eyed clerk behind a glass screen. He recognized straight away that I hadn't come to gamble. I decided on a direct approach and told him what I was doing. He was different from most of the people I had met in Gorton, relaxed about the past. Perhaps it came from the nature of his job.

'Brady? Oh yeah, I remember him,' he said. 'Awkward sod, never spoke to anyone.'

'Anything in particular make him stand out?'

'Only his betting name.'

'Which was?'

'Gorgonzola.'

'What, like the cheese?' I asked in astonishment.

'That's right.'

I wondered whether he had deliberately chosen an Italian dairy product as his alias or mistaken its name for that of the Gorgon – the snake-haired mythical creature whose glance could turn a man to stone. Perhaps he thought it was funny – Goon humour. The bookie gave me the answer.

'He dropped the "zola" bit after a while, like. Then it was just Gorgon.' He let out a small, dry chuckle.

Myra got hold of Ian's address when he put a bet on the Tote: 18 Westmoreland Street, Longsight. That evening she 'borrowed' Auntie Anne's baby son, Michael, and wheeled him east in his pram, or 'trolley'. There were some posher houses in Longsight – Victorian villas with stucco plasterwork, or mock Tudor façades – but they had seen better days and were now inhabited by working-class families. The spaces in between had been filled in with back-to-back redbrick terraces. The kids playing in the streets looked exactly like those in Gorton. Myra pushed Michael's trolley past the towering windows of the Daisy sewing machine works, down towards the black and white beamed houses on Westmoreland Street. She tried to look casual, in case she bumped into Ian, but her eyes swept over the faces on the Stockport Road hoping to find him. If she got him alone, away from work, he might just ask her out.

Over the next few weeks she came back almost every evening; Auntie Anne was delighted with how helpful she was being. Myra pushed the trolley up and down, past the shops on Hathersage Road, the Victoria Turkish baths, and the end of Eston Street, but there was no sign of Ian. As she passed the pub on the corner of Westmoreland Street she peered in through the windows. He wasn't inside.

On the long walk back to Gorton Myra came up with a plan. She called round to the Hills', and persuaded May to come for a drink in the pub on Ian's street. He was bound to go in there, it would be fun; they might even be able to persuade him to go to Chick Hibbert's, or the Ashton Palais. Myra and May took their time on the way into the pub – he might see them, and decide to follow. They spent hours lingering over their drinks. The locals welcomed the sudden, mysterious appearance of a couple of attractive girls, but Ian never did come in. They kept it up for a couple of weeks before May got bored, and Myra realized she'd have to come up with something else.

After a great deal of thought she resolved to lure him by showing that she too was interested in big ideas, that she too wanted to live in a place other than this. She went to Gorton library and prowled up and down the shelves. No good choosing something he knew more about than her. She had to appear an expert. She got to the poetry section, and there was just the thing: *The Collected Works of William Wordsworth*. Myra remembered it from school. She pulled it off the shelf and marched to the front desk.

She sat up in bed that evening, looking for the right poem. 'Daffodils' – far too obvious; 'Lucy' – too soppy and romantic; 'On the Extinction of the Venetian Republic' – too obscure. She finally settled on an excerpt from *The Prelude*. There was something about it that seemed right for Ian.

At lunchtime the next day Myra positioned herself in a patch of sunshine by the office door to the yard. Ian was sitting there playing chess with Dave, an invoice clerk. They seemed to take for ever between moves, staring in silence at the board. Eventually Ian glanced up, his eyes scanning the cover of the book, expecting to find some 'girly rubbish' he could mock. He was so surprised by what he saw that he seized the bait, and asked whether Wordsworth was 'any good'. Myra replied that his poems were 'marvellous', especially the long ones like *The Prelude*. Ian reached over, took the book from her and read a few lines. He riffled backwards and forwards through the pages to assess the worth of the material. As he handed the book back to her he said it looked interesting, he might get a copy from the library. Myra told me that she almost 'died from bliss' at his words.

The ice broken, they started talking. She did not push it though, waiting a few days before coming in with William Blake's *Songs of Innocence and*

Experience. Again he took it from her, and read. Ian lingered longer over Blake's clean rhythms and bold imagery. He asked her what sort of music she liked. Worried she might say the wrong thing she kept the answer vague: bit of pop, classical, big band, 'fairly catholic really'. Ian replied that he didn't like pop; he preferred music that was more intelligent, that had been properly crafted. He had a tape recorder to copy things from the library and off the telly. She could borrow some spools if she liked.

That Saturday, Myra recorded in her auto-biography, she put a deposit down on a Philips machine, just like Ian's. She signed an agreement to pay it off in weekly instalments, and carried it home to Gorton. She taped all sorts of things, mucking about with her friends. I found a police transcript of recordings at the National Records Archive. The conversations were unremarkable; young women bantering, razor-sharp Manchester humour. It was 1961, and the idea of being able to record voices was still novel.

Ian brought tapes into work for her to copy, stuff he said was 'good'. She could often tell where it had come from by the sound quality. There was jazz off the TV and classical music copied from library records. Occasionally, an older man or woman accidentally interrupted the recording, calling from another room or opening the door, and he barked at them to go away. The woman was Scottish, the man Irish. She

Myra, aged two, in a studio photograph paid for by her auntie Ann.

Myra (*right*), as a bridesmaid at her uncle Bill and auntie Kath's wedding.

Myra, in mismatching layers of winter clothes. By this time she had been sent to live with her gran.

Myra with her first dog, Duke.

Beasley Street, where Myra grew up with Gran.

Myra's father Bob (*centre*) drank every day and frequently got into brawls.

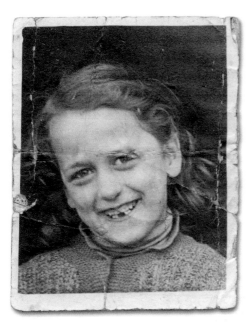

Myra, as she was losing her milk teeth. This is the age at which her father taught her to fight.

Myra and her class at Ryder Brow school. The head teacher, Mr Lloyd-Jones, stands to the left.

Myra, at the back, and friends on a day out from Gorton.

Ian Brady photographed by a member of a local camera club at Millwards Merchandising, where he was a clerk.

St Francis' monastery church, which Myra stopped attending after she met Ian. It was abandoned after her arrest and imprisonment.

The Steelie, where Bob and, later, Ian and Myra drank. (*Manchester Librairies*)

Belle Vue Pleasure Gardens, where Myra first met her secret lover, Norman.

Ian relaxing after work in Gorton.

Sunny Brow Park, where Myra and Ian read about the disappearance of John Kilbride.

Ian had his suits hand-made at Burton's.

Ian's beloved Triumph Tiger Cub.

Myra kept the watch Ian gave
her after the killing of Pauline
Reade for the rest of her life.

The documentation for Myra's Morris Mini pickup, used to abduct Keith Bennett,
was also among her papers when she died.

Myra bought a .22 target rifle from a Manchester gunsmith. Ian fantasized about using it for robberies.

asked Ian who they were. His mother and stepfather – he shared a house with them.

In Highpoint prison, Father Michael Teader visited Myra Hindley every week to hear her confession and take communion. They met in her 'room' on wing North 4, the segregation, or 'seg', unit for prisoners considered at risk from others. Afterwards they sat together, eating whatever treat he'd brought in, and chatted. She told him what it was that had drawn her to Ian Brady. 'She had never met anyone like him,' Father Michael said. 'He was completely different. Well read, intelligent, with a more sophisticated view of the world than any of the people she had encountered before. He seemed to offer her the chance of escape. It was what she'd looked for in the Catholic Church, and she thought she'd found it in him.'

Myra told Ronnie that their engagement was off. He was distraught, and rang her at work every day to beg for a reconciliation. At first this pleased Myra as it drew attention to her 'single' status. She smiled inwardly when Ian's eyes fell on the white line left by her engagement ring. But then he began to tease her about the calls. He sat across from Myra and laughed when she picked up the phone. She was worried that the disruption might jeopardize her job and decided that the best thing to do was to involve her boss. She told Tommy she couldn't take it any more, would he help? The next time Ronnie rang Tommy took the phone and warned him to stop pestering Myra or they'd have to call the police. He never called her at work again, and stopped mooning about on the corner of Beasley Street. Myra's description of Ronnie, in her letters to me and in her autobiography, was wistful. It was as if writing his name called up images of what might have been: marriage, kids, grandkids.

Where Lawrence Scott's had been large and organized, Millwards was small and informal. There was no 'social fund' for big occasions, and the staff organized parties themselves. They were therefore livelier, bordering on the riotous. Myra Hindley described the most important of these occasions in a letter to me.

As Christmas approached they began dividing up the jobs: sandwich making, baking a fruit cake, bringing in a record player, buying sausage rolls, wine and beer. At lunchtime on the day of the 'do' they piled the feast up on tables in the office and headed out to a pub where they'd booked a room. They talked loudly and drank quickly. Myra did not hang around Ian but kept an eye on what he was up to across the room. He seemed to be sinking pints very fast, even by the standards of the hard-drinking warehousemen, and was uncharacteristically garrulous. At closing time they bundled out of the door and made their way back to the office. The cold air had a sobering effect, and they drew together to keep warm, giggling whenever one of them stumbled.

Things began sedately enough. People had brought

in their favourite music and the old record player in the corner of the room was turned up to maximum volume. It belted out distorted hits as the men worked on their courage with beer, and some of the younger women started dancing about. Myra had a sandwich in one hand and a glass of wine in the other as she moved in time to Freddie and the Dreamers. She could feel Ian's eyes on her.

Things moved up a gear when Ron, one of the delivery drivers, crashed through the side door, swaying from side to side in an alarming manner and waving about a large, maroon-coloured bottle with a sailing ship on it. Naval Rum – 80 per cent proof! His thumbs pushed drunkenly at the cork and it flew out with a sharp pop, catching Bert on the shoulder. There was a loud cheer. The booze was almost certainly payment for allowing a couple of extra barrels to 'fall' off the back of his lorry, but nobody cared. Myra was about to swig some neat when her nose, still two inches away from the maroon liquid, filled with fumes. She frowned, trying to focus on the thick rivulets that clung to the side of the glass. Marge, the receptionist, told her to try it with a bit of Coke in. Myra found it went down a lot easier like that. She sat down and smiled as Tommy and a pretty young order clerk from downstairs started shuffling about. They only stayed upright by leaning on each other.

All of a sudden Ian loomed in front of her, rocking backwards and forwards on his heels, and asked if she wanted to dance. Myra wondered if she'd heard right. He didn't ask again, just reached down, put his hands on her forearms and leant back. She rose unsteadily to her feet, too drunk to savour the moment. They moved slowly about the room, occasionally bumping into other couples. Ian was a bad dancer as well as drunk, and he trampled all over her new shoes. There were a couple of glances in their direction, but no disapproval. They were young, single people having a bit of fun.

When the party finally ran out of steam Tommy asked Ian if he was coming. He had arranged to give him a lift; Myra was meant to be going with Jim and Doris. Ian replied that it was all right, Myra and he needed a bit of air and they were going to walk. They talked about the rum, how strong it was, as they wound down the path through Sunny Brow Park, crossed the small stream and climbed up the other side towards the Hyde Road. The winter sunlight, although weak, hurt her eyes. As they came out of the wrought-iron gate at the top he stopped and turned to her. He asked if she'd meet him that evening for 'a few drinks'. Myra did not hesitate to say yes, even though she was meant to be going out to a sporting club with the girls and they'd already paid for the tickets. She saw Ian onto the bus back to Longsight, then rang Margie, who she knew would be in, to say she couldn't make it, Ian had asked her for 'a date'. Margie, well acquainted with Myra's obsession, replied, 'At last.'

Myra told me in a letter that she pushed open the front door to find Maureen chatting to Gran and her cousin Glenys. She gave the girls some money and told them to go to the chemist's on the corner for a bottle of Yardley's scent and some mascara. They thought nothing of it. Her night out with the girls had been long planned, and it was natural to want to 'be her best'. Myra climbed the stairs to her room, lay on the bed and waited for the ceiling to stop spinning. She didn't notice Moby come into the room with the bottle of Yardley's, and her change. After a couple of hours she went downstairs for a cup of tea and a bacon sandwich. She didn't tell Gran where she was going.

It was dark when she pulled her coat on, and walked to the bus stop where they'd arranged to meet. One bus went by, then another; she thought he'd changed his mind, or had been leading her on. As a third bus appeared she saw a figure crossing the road towards her – Ronnie. She was about to make a run for it when the rear platform pulled level with the stop. Ian was standing there, motioning for her to get on. Myra took his outstretched hand and the bus roared away from Gorton into the night.

The evening passed in a blur; they were both blind drunk. There was none of the edginess and bad temper that usually characterized his behaviour. He spent much of the time doing impressions from *The Goon Show*. When they got back to Gorton Ian walked her home and asked if he could come in. Myra replied no, her gran might still be up. She knew she lacked the will to resist his advances and wasn't going to have him thinking her cheap. If he won her too easily she might lose him. Ian responded by pulling Myra into his arms and crushing his lips against hers. Even through the booze she could feel the pain. It was as though he'd never kissed a girl before. Myra pushed him away and took charge: she held his head in her hands and gently put her lips on his. He relaxed, and seemed to get the hang of it. After a couple of minutes she said he'd better go, someone might see them, and stepped back towards the front door. He stood there, gently swaying in the breeze, and said, 'You don't know how long I've wanted to do this.'

I was struck, reading Myra Hindley's letters to me, by the restlessness that followed her first date with Ian Brady. There was a sense of desperation at the thought that his affection might fade. The exaggerated intensity of her emotions reminded me of her reaction to the death of Michael Higgins. There was no sign, forty years later, that Myra was aware of the unusual strength of her feelings. The days to the New Year of 1962, she wrote, seemed to stretch for ever into the distance.

Ian remained formal at work, careful not to attract the notice of Bert and Tommy, but it was clear from his eyes that he did not intend to discard her. During one lunch break he asked if she'd like to go out with him at the weekend. There was a picture on in town,

King of Kings, and he thought she might like it. Myra knew about the film; it was a life of Jesus. She thought it kind of him to suggest it as he was an atheist. This time she did reveal to Gran that she was 'seeing' someone from work.

Ian turned up late at the bus stop again, and didn't bother to apologize. She understood that he had done it deliberately, but did not really mind. It was good just to be with him. The cinema was packed. There hadn't been a big-budget, speaking portrayal of Jesus before. Film-makers, wary of upsetting the Church, had kept him as an off-screen character and relied on over-the-shoulder shots or close-ups of 'His' hands. Nicholas Ray's production was a grand epic with a sweeping score by Miklos Rozsa, who'd written the music for *Ben Hur*. It featured Jesus's miracles, and the Sermon on the Mount with hundreds of extras. Myra thought that the lead actor, Jeff Hunter, was 'gorgeous'. She didn't agree with the reviewers who'd said he looked too young. Jesus had been almost exactly the same age as him when he died. The director used grandeur to drive home an unashamedly Christian message. It was a celebration of faith, and Myra loved it. As Jeff Hunter hung on the cross and groaned, 'Father, why have you forsaken me?' tears began to pour down her face.

The cinema lights came up, and she felt Ian's arm slide away from round her shoulder. She described in a letter how he leant back, stared incredulously at her tear-stained face and asked why she was crying. Myra replied that it was a beautiful, moving film. The cinema was filled with the sound of blowing noses. Ian snorted, stood up and announced that he needed a drink.

They went to the Thatched House and stayed until closing time. He picked the film to pieces, argued that the sole function of religion was 'to keep working people in their place'. It was all just man-made lies, mumbo-jumbo; religious people were weak. But Myra still went to St Francis' every week with Kath and could not accept what he was saying. She tried to argue back, pointing out all the good things the Church did for the people of Gorton. But he was ready with a trap. Was God good? Yes, she replied. If so, said Ian, how come he had let Michael Higgins drown? What good was there in that? Myra did not have an answer; she had never thought about these things before. The church had been a place to escape to, that was all.

Father Michael Teader discussed the demolition of Myra's faith with her during their weekly meetings. He told me it was built on weak foundations.

'This was pre-Vatican Two.'

'You've lost me,' I replied.

'The mass was in Latin – she didn't understand it. Religious teaching was by rote – she had no arguments to defend it. People were just meant to accept what they were told. If the Church had changed its policy earlier than the Second Vatican Council of 1962 she might have been able to deal with him. As it was, she didn't have a chance.'

Myra's infatuation and the absence of a defendable religious or moral code were a dangerous combination. Ian Brady was pushing at an open door.

They stumbled down Bannock Street arm in arm. She had Ian now and wasn't going to lose him. His arguments about religion did not repel her; in a way they made sense. At least, she reflected, he thought about life rather than simply accepting it like every other person she knew. When they reached Myra's house, she looked over her shoulder to see if anyone was watching and opened the door. The lights were off – Gran was in bed. She took her coat off as Ian slid home the bolt to the front door. Without saying a word he pushed her backwards, towards the living room; she fell to the floor, grabbed his face in her hands and kissed him ferociously. He responded, then gave her a small series of bites down the neck. She groaned at the pain.

Myra Hindley's description of her first sexual encounter with Ian Brady is raw and detailed. It portrays a naive girl stumbling into the arms of a brutal man. While there is no doubt that chance played its part, I did not feel that it explained everything. How many women would agree to see someone again if their first sexual encounter was unpleasant? I asked Malcolm MacCulloch why he thought she had not been repelled.

'She was used to brutal behaviour,' he answered.

'But wouldn't she look for something different in a lover?' I asked.

'No. If you have been treated brutally in childhood and you have a certain sort of temperament, you're going to develop a tough personality. And tough people, as well as having the capacity for sadism, often have masochistic tendencies. Rather than recoil from brutal behaviour, they seek it out.'

Myra did not want Ian to meet Bob and Nellie, but there was no way of preventing it. It was hard enough to hide the smallest secret in Gorton, never mind a relationship. In the end she decided to take him round to Eaton Street. Her parents' reactions were instinctive, and powerful. Bob thought Ian was a 'good lad'. He recognized a strength in him, and they seemed to have the same view of a woman's place. Nellie disliked him on first sight. When he had gone she pulled her daughter to one side. In a letter to me, Myra recalled Nellie's words: 'No good can come of that Ian Brady, you know.' Her mother thought that Ian's attitude to life was sneering and cynical. She also mistrusted his 'airs and graces'.

Patricia Cairns visited Nellie many times. They discussed Ian Brady at length. 'One of the reasons her mother didn't like Brady was that she could see the similarities with Bob. He was a bully. But there was nothing she could do. The attraction was too powerful.'

Ian stoked Myra's dissatisfaction with life. The further she stood from Gorton the closer she was to him. His outbursts were erratic. He would be behaving quite normally, lovingly even, and then the smallest thing would set him off – like Gran running the water in the kitchen. Why, he demanded, was there just one cold tap in Bob, Nellie and Mo's house? Why could you walk straight off the street into the front room? Didn't she realize it was just luck that had enabled her and Gran to escape from somewhere even worse? They were all trapped. Myra could see what Ian meant: she had always wanted more from life than Gorton had to offer. His rants made her want it even more. This shared resentment came to give them a common purpose, and identity.

May Hill and Pat Jepson noticed the change in Myra, and tried to preserve their friendship. They suggested she bring Ian to the Ashton Palais, or Chick Hibbert's; she told them it wasn't his scene. They tried to get her out when he wasn't there; she told them she wanted to stay at home in case he came round later. Over time, they slipped away from her.

In her letters to me Myra described how Ian changed the way she approached literature, taught her how to use it as a source of inspiration. Where she relaxed into a story, he hunted, looking for ideas he could use. The author had no control over him as he wandered through the pages, pilfering what he wanted. From Harold Robbins' bestseller *The*

Carpetbaggers it was the notion that rape, incest and paedophilia were adventures. If the opportunity to perform one of these acts presented itself, a man should take it. The fact that the main character of *The Carpetbaggers*, buccaneering multi-millionaire aviation pioneer Jonas Cord, is drawn as a grotesque completely passed him by. Ian got Myra to work fragments of literature into sex games. Books became fuel to their fantasies.

I found Ian Brady's copy of *The Life and Ideas of the Marquis de Sade* sealed in a see-through plastic wallet at the National Archives in Kew. It had a lurid orange cover in the centre of which was an enlarged reproduction of a dictionary definition: 'sadism (sad/izm), after Count de Sade (1740–1814): abnormal pleasure in cruelty; sadist *n&adj.*'. The book was made public, along with the rest of the trial exhibits and documents, in December 2005. Their release prompted a scramble by newspaper reporters. Details forgotten over the years were hastily plucked out and recycled as 'exclusives'. One correspondent, from a 'respectable' newspaper, even smuggled a trial file out of the archive's reading area and concealed it in a locker in order to confound his rivals. When the fuss had died down I read the documents closely, over a week, in a room with locked-off video cameras. The books discovered by the police range from the perverse, Edwin J. Henri's *Kiss of the Whip*, to the literary, Henry Miller's *Tropic of Cancer*.

But Ian Brady did not just plunder fiction, he stole political ideas as well. They were sitting in the front room at Gran's when he dropped a quarter-inch tape spool onto the spindle, flicked the catch that held it in position and started the machine running. '*Das Deutsche Volk muss glücklich sein zu gewinnen!*' Hitler, he informed her – great, wasn't it? Myra had to admire the sheer passion in the voice, the force of conviction. The roar of the crowd was intoxicating. They sat there, transfixed, until the tape ran out and slapped round and round against the heads of the machine. Ian explained how Hitler had been right about outsiders. Myra did not question his ranting against 'the Jews' or 'blacks'. Instead, she looked around her for evidence to support his views: the Jamaicans in Moss Side who 'sponge off our taxes'; Mr Ziff the Jewish tailor, who ran over her kitten in his big shiny car when he came round for his money. I found a payment book among her papers: 'Ziff: Personal Tailors'. Inside the stained brown card, inscribed in black ink, 'R. Hindley', and what he owed. The amount was never cleared. I wondered why she'd kept it. I supposed it was another reminder of a vanished past, never to be retrieved.

Ian's sadism was not confined to the bedroom; it also manifested itself as bullying at work. Myra's office, which was off to the side, was cold in winter. Even with the door open the warmth from the open fire in the main office died before it reached her. Seeing her shivering in a thick cardigan, Tommy put his head through the door and told her to come through. Myra said she was worried that the noise of her typewriter might put the clerks off. Tommy told her not to be so silly – what did she think he'd bought the new 'silent model' for? But as she worked Myra could see Ian out of the corner of her eye. He kept sighing, shifting his weight from one buttock to the other and dropping his pen on the desk. Eventually, he burst out, 'Christ, Myra, that machine's getting on my nerves. Come to that, so are you.' Tommy and Bert sat there in stunned silence. Myra didn't say a word. She just picked the typewriter up and walked back to her office. As she went she could hear Tommy shouting at Ian. There was no way he could understand what was going on.

Ian introduced her to the ideas of his favourite philosopher, Friedrich Nietzsche. But in philosophy, as in literature and politics, his way was that of a magpie. If it glistened, he stole it. It was an approach that survived long after his imprisonment. In 2001 Ian Brady published a book, *The Gates of Janus: Serial Killing and its Analysis*. Its pages are filled with references to Ludwig Wittgenstein. For an assessment of its quality I sent a copy to Professor Ray Monk, a leading authority on the Austrian genius. He called me within a day to denounce Brady's references to the philosopher as 'self-aggrandising' and 'pseudo-intellectual'.

I asked Patricia Cairns why Myra did not question

such extreme, disjointed views and behaviour. 'What you have to understand about Myra,' she responded, 'is that when she falls in love with somebody, turns her beam on them, she becomes like them.' She paused. 'She must have been getting some pleasure from it as well.'

Ian and Myra retreated further and further from their surroundings, choosing not to play by the rules of a society they scorned. But they used humour as well as radical ideas to mark out the boundaries of their existence. She called him 'Neddy' after a character in *The Goon Show*, and he called her Hess, both the name of Hitler's deputy and that of a famous concert pianist, Dame Myra Hess, who played the great German composers. He failed to recognize, or ignored, Myra Hess's fierce opposition to the Nazis. During the war she gave recitals of Beethoven and Schubert to packed rooms in the National Gallery. The performances were a joint affirmation of Hess's and the audience's belief that Nazi ideology, not German culture, had led to war.

'I suppose they were building a world apart,' I remarked to Patricia Cairns.

She raised a finger, shook her head and responded, 'A world above.'

Chapter Two

Gorton's pubs, many of which have been demolished, are preserved on the computer at Manchester Central library. There are dozens of pictures of the Bessie, the Shakie, the Steelie and the Waggon. Most are long gone, cleared when large parts of the area were knocked down and its people moved to bright new futures on the 'peripheral' estates tacked to the edge of British cities in the 1960s. The Waggon and Horses, however, where Ian and Myra drank after work, is still there, the large mock Tudor façade out of place on the Hyde Road. Perhaps its builder was inspired by the pastoral refuge of Far Lane rolling down the hill behind.

Any such delusion has long since vanished inside. I was greeted by looks of suspicion when I pushed open the bar door; the expressions turned to disgust when I ordered a Diet Coke. Although it was early, many of the regulars looked like they were on their third or fourth pint. But the Waggon is a large space, with dark corners. I walked round the bar and found a table opposite the giant TV screen showing racing from Haydock Park. The men sitting here were busy with the form, or talking about football. It's the kind of place where, once settled down, you can spend a lot of time without attracting too much attention.

Myra told me in a letter that she and Ian got into the habit of coming here. It was close to his bus stop, and easy for her to cut through the streets and ginnels to Bannock Street. Ian liked talking about current passions and resentments, but resisted divulging the past. When his history did emerge it was in fragments; Myra had to rearrange the pieces to build up a picture of the man she was in love with.

He told her that he had been born in Glasgow's Rottenrow maternity hospital. His mam hadn't been able to look after him so he went to live with the Sloans. Mum, Dad, four kids – they were nice to him. Myra told him that was just like her having to go and live with Gran. The difference was that Myra's start in life, however rough, gave her some sense of identity; Ian's made him feel a complete outsider. The mother who abandoned him, Peggy, was a tearoom waitress; he never mentioned a father. Myra didn't push the point as he was so obviously skirting round it. She suspected that he was illegitimate. When Ian was little Peggy came to visit him most weekends, but later she married and moved south, to Manchester. This was when he started going off the rails, nicking things and hurting animals.

Ian killed his first cat, by throwing it off the top floor of a tenement building, at the age of ten. He told Myra that it screamed all the way down. He'd wanted to see the fear, and he'd enjoyed it. Later, he trapped a cat in a tomb, returning every day to see if it was still alive. But he said Myra needn't worry, he'd grown out of it, come to realize that it was far more satisfying to hurt people because it was on a higher plane. His first experiments involved extreme bullying. He persuaded a group of schoolmates to help tie a boy to a stake and pack newspaper round his feet. They thought Ian was joking when he said he was going to set fire to it. They still couldn't believe it when he got the matches out, and they stood there dumbly as the fire crept about the boy's feet. Only when the 'victim' started screaming did they react. Ian walked away, laughing, as they crawled around swatting at the flames with the arms of their second-hand jackets.

As their relationship developed, Ian revealed his fantasies to Myra. He was sexually inexperienced, but that didn't mean he lacked desire. It's just that what he wanted was hard to get. He started having violent thoughts as a teenage schoolboy. The other lads had these pathetic pornographic cards; Ian had far better pictures in his head. When he read de Sade for the first time it was like looking in the mirror. Myra was the first person he'd been able to tell, and try his fantasies out with.

Ian's words, Myra told me, excited her. His cold indifference to authority, his reasons for holding it in contempt, showed that you could live your life as you pleased. There *was* an alternative to the mundane repetition of your parents' existence.

Professor Malcolm MacCulloch told me that such fantasies are a common feature in the development of sexual sadists. 'Rapists and murderers often act out their fantasies before they commit them,' he said. 'They'll integrate them into other criminal acts – masturbating during a burglary, for example. When they're ready they'll move on to the next stage. The point is that these things develop over time. He had a script; what he needed was someone to help him act it out.'

MacCulloch first worked on Ian Brady's case while a trainee psychiatrist in the 1960s. When Brady developed symptoms of chronic mental illness at Gartree prison in Leicestershire in the mid-1980s the professor was asked to assess his condition by the Home Office. Over the past twenty years a succession of psychiatrists had recommended his transfer out of the prison system, but the Home Office had consistently refused to act. There was a worry that a move to hospital might make the government of the day look 'soft'.

MacCulloch interviewed Brady at length and concluded that he was suffering from a serious psychosis.
The professor's report advocated his immediate
transfer from Gartree. 'It's pretty clear he would have
died if he'd remained in prison. Some people might
say, "So what?" I take the view that it's better for all of
us to understand what makes a man do the things he
did.' The decision to send him to Ashworth Special
Hospital, on Merseyside, was taken by the Prime
Minister, Margaret Thatcher. Over the next few years
MacCulloch got to know Ian Brady better than any
other psychiatrist.

As I sat opposite the professor I wondered what had
made Brady open up to him rather than any other
doctor. It had to be more than the forensic
psychiatrist's ferocious talent for 'working' people –
Brady would have seen straight through that. Perhaps
it was his contagious enthusiasm for understanding
the extreme reaches of human behaviour. I could also
see that Brady might have been flattered to be the
focus of a sharp intellect.

Ian began stealing soon after he started secondary
school, at Shawlands Academy. But he was an in-
different thief and kept getting caught. His
law-abiding foster-parents were horrified; they could
not understand what caused his behaviour. But they
never rejected him. Although this made no difference
to Ian's fate, it was an act of kindness he never forgot.

Even after he had been imprisoned for decades he remained vulnerable to mention of the Sloans.

When he left school Ian worked as a butcher's assistant, but the pay was lousy and the urge to steal uncontrollable. In 1954, when he was seventeen, a Glasgow Sessions magistrate gave him a choice: go live with your mother in Manchester or go to gaol. He chose Manchester, and caught the train south. His natural mother, Peggy, met him at Victoria station.

She and her husband, an Irish fruit merchant called Pat Brady, lived in a small house in Moss Side. Ian moved into their second bedroom, took his step-father's surname and accepted the offer of a job as a fruit porter at Smithfield Market. Apart from drinking too much, and complaining continually about the number of Jamaican immigrants on the streets of Moss Side, he seemed to have 'straightened himself out'. But Ian had been stealing for too long to stop just because he had moved south. He got away with the robberies he carried out, Glasgow style, on businesses and private homes, but he was not so lucky at work. The Bradys were mortified when he was caught trying to smuggle a sack full of stolen lead seals through the gates of Smithfield Market.

On remand, Ian did a spell in the dingy Victorian warren of Strangeways prison. No other gaol in the country dominates the surrounding city in quite the same way. Its tall red spire looms over the prisoners as a reminder of their failings, and over the inhabitants of Manchester as a deterrent. It is a place that speaks of retribution rather than rehabilitation. On the first day of October 1955, just a year after arriving in Manchester, he was taken from Strangeways to the city's magistrates' court for trial. Ian's lawyer did not have a lot to work with, and his client was surly and unprepossessing. As he stood in the dock awaiting the verdict, Ian told Myra, he tossed a coin in his head. If it landed heads – not guilty – he'd go straight; if it landed tails – guilty – he'd remain a criminal. The magistrate looked up. 'Ian Brady, I find you guilty as charged.'

Because he was under eighteen Ian was sent to Borstal for 'training' rather than prison. Myra told me that he was a diligent student, but not of the subjects the magistrate who sentenced him had in mind. The only difference between the people in Borstal and those in prison was their age. Ian met accomplished thieves who had worked with professional gangs. They told him how to do bigger jobs, how to avoid getting caught so often, and where to find 'fences' for the things he'd knocked off. For the first time he made friends, petty criminals Dougie Woods and Gilbert Deare. It was the happiest time of his life so far.

Ian was released on 14 November 1957 and returned to Moss Side. He tried labouring, but hated it. He got a job in a brewery, but was fired. He decided the only way out was to 'better' himself, went to Longsight library and took out a set of manuals on book-keeping. He astonished the Bradys by spending hours in his room swotting over ledgers until he felt sure he could excel at interview.

He bought the *Manchester Evening News* in search of a job 'with prospects', and a set of clothes to look the part. The first few companies didn't want to know: what good was a clerk who'd done time for theft? But in February 1958, just three months after getting out of Borstal, he got an interview at Millwards Merchandising, a wholesale chemical company based at Ryder Brow in Gorton. Ian was in luck: the boss, Tommy, was a Scot. He took a liking to the smartly dressed young man and decided that he deserved a 'second chance'. He gave him a job at £12 a week and told him he could begin work on the Monday.

The following month the Bradys moved to a larger house at 18 Westmoreland Street in Longsight. The shots in Manchester Central library show two lines of Victorian villas facing each other across a cobbled street. Children stand about staring at the camera; they are clearly not used to posing for pictures. There is a sign at the end of the road: DESIGNATED PLAY STREET. It is a portrait from a distant, more innocent time.

Ian almost always returned to Westmoreland Street after work, before heading back into Gorton. His mother still cooked and washed for him, and his dark-room was there. When he was sure of his ground with Myra, he suggested taking some pornographic

pictures; not ordinary stuff, but the kind of thing de
Sade might have approved of. He bit her before he
fucked her, he bit her as he fucked her, and he bit her
again afterwards. Her body was covered in small oval
eruptions of burst blood vessels. The whisky dulled
the pain but did not block it completely. Only when he
was sure that the marks would show up in a black and
white picture did he pick up his camera. He snapped
away with the twin-lens reflex, twelve shots a roll, until
he had what he wanted. He taped the film up, tucked
it into his jacket pocket and staggered outside to catch
the bus back to Longsight.

Ian often failed to appear, and was slow to tell Myra
where he'd been. It came out later, much of it at trial:
the Rembrandt pub in the city centre, Canal Street,
round the back of Central station. The sorts of places
'respectable' types – lawyers, teachers, policemen –
went for sex with each other, and with rent-boys. To
them it was a shared secret; to him it was just another
experience that fuelled his contempt for the
'hypocrisy' of ordinary life. Patricia Cairns says
that Myra Hindley knew about these sexual
adventures. 'Myra accepted that. If it was what he
wanted, he could do it. After all, it was just sex. He
needed her on a far deeper level.'

Malcolm MacCulloch peered at one of the photographs showing Myra Hindley, fully clothed, crouched
down on a picnic blanket, staring up at the camera –
a pose at once submissive and suggestive. 'This

relationship is very strong,' he commented. 'She is happy in a sexually sadistic relationship; he has found someone who can help to realize his fantasies. It is a very unfortunate concatenation of circumstances.'

Myra Hindley and Ian Brady soon began to turn fantasies about violence into reality. In its court reports the *Manchester Evening News* regularly featured cases of animal cruelty and always printed the address of the person who'd been convicted; sometimes there was a photo too. Myra and Ian read these stories with a shared sense of outrage. Now that he had decided to hurt people, Ian had come to feel a powerful affinity with animals. This, and a shared contempt for those they considered beneath them, lay at the heart of his and Myra's relationship. They decided to punish the perpetrators. It became a ritual: they would choose a victim out of the paper, go round to their home, and give them 'what they deserved'. Sometimes it was a brick through the window. If the opportunity presented itself and they were able to follow them somewhere quiet, Ian gave them a beating. One night they stalked a man in his local all evening just so that Ian could 'get him'. The joint endeavour of the enterprise, and its secrecy, made them feel as one.

I am sure that Myra Hindley included this story in her letters to me in order to demonstrate that she *did* love animals, that not everything she and Ian did was bad. But read in conjunction with her autobiography and other private papers, it simply reinforces the impression of a flawed character falling into a fatal alliance.

Ian, fed up with catching the bus back to Longsight, saw an advert for the Triumph Tiger Cub motorcycle – 'Fabulous Little Four Stroke'. It showed a smart, slim man in a tweed jacket, leather helmet and gauntlets chatting confidently to a pretty blonde girl in a chunky-knit sweater with her hands in her pockets. The flawless landscape was rural, autumnal. It was just £150. He put down a deposit on the model with a tall windscreen. It opened up their world. At weekends, and in the evenings, they travelled on the bike out into the hills of Cheshire and the Peak District. There is a shot of Myra sitting side-saddle in a twin-set in front of a cottage. Brady taught her how to use his twin-lens reflex, and there are endless images of him on the bike, grinning, looking dapper. One day, climbing the long, winding hill out of Greenfield, they came round a bend and there it was – Saddleworth Moor. Its magnificence captured their imagination. They returned week after week until they knew every stream, hill and gully. From the granite of Greystones to the grit stone at Hollin Brown Knoll, they made the moor their own. At its heart lay an enclosed bowl of heather and grass on the banks of Shiny Brook. They put wine in the stream to chill while they explored and, after a picnic, had sex in the cotton grass.

It was on the moor, Myra Hindley told me, that Ian

Brady finally revealed his great secret: he was a bastard. She'd long guessed it, and tried to console him: her gran was illegitimate, as was her gran before her. But they both knew that while generations of Hindley women had overcome their difficulties with the help of their families, Ian's mother had cast him adrift.

The moor was a place of solace and fascination to Ian. He named the rocks that dotted it. An outcrop from where he could survey the Shiny Brook valley became 'Eagle's Head' after Hitler's Eagle's Nest. Greystones was his Stonehenge. He set up the camera to take a shot there. They sat on a great slab of granite wearing leather motorcycle helmets, and he put his hands round her neck as if strangling her. He released the shutter by squeezing a vacuum bulb, as she grinned at him.

'Landscapes seem to have had a special meaning for him,' Malcolm MacCulloch told me.

'They have an effect on lots of people,' I replied.

'No, no. From an early age. He suffered some sort of attack, had a vision in Scotland when he was a teenager. They had a pantheistic, almost religious significance.'

The professor said that on a trip out of Glasgow with his adoptive family Ian had fallen into a trance at the sight of mountains. It had taken the Sloans several minutes to bring him round. A decade later, Ian became so attached to the rocks, boulders, valleys and streams of Saddleworth Moor, Myra told me, that he imagined they were talking to him. This sense of belonging made him feel secure in his separation from 'normal' life.

Ian told Myra that he did not intend to spend the rest of his days as a stock-clerk at Millwards. He'd learned lessons in Borstal and planned to apply them; he had contacts; he knew how to get rid of stuff. They rode to Bradford on his bike to try to track down Gilbert Deare, with whom he'd been locked up, to see if he wanted to help on 'a job'. Myra knocked on the door, pretending to be an old girlfriend, but he wasn't there. Ian told her they'd have to go it alone. She pointed out that he'd never done a big robbery before – they were bound to get caught! She was right to be concerned. Years later the police revealed to her that Ian and Gilbert Deare had once attempted a hold-up with knives. It had gone wrong, and they'd fled empty-handed, narrowly avoiding capture. But Ian was adamant. He told Myra that one way to avoid getting caught was to 'hit' the people who carried money to and from banks and businesses – the messengers. They were alone and unarmed. He got her to stand around on street corners, tracking movements, working out the best time to attack. The softest target seemed to be an electricity showroom on the Hyde Road. He fantasized about hurting the messengers, but she thought he would never go through with it. Then his mind seemed to wander, to go in search of bigger things.

A key moment in the development of Ian Brady's fantasies was his discovery of the book *Compulsion* by Meyer Levin. He devoured the text, then handed it to Myra and demanded she do the same. I found a copy for sale on the internet. When it arrived, a few days later, I tore open the brown paper packaging. The cover featured two smartly dressed young men, who bore more than a passing resemblance to Ian Brady, scowling out of a blood-red cover. The blurb at the bottom of the page boasted, 'Bestselling novel of the most cold-blooded crime of the Century.' Set in the centre of the back page were the words, '*You know why we did it? Because we damn well felt like doing it!*'

When she'd finished the book Myra told Ian it seemed like 'a rubbish thriller'. Why had he wanted her to read it? Having studied my copy, I had no doubt about Ian Brady's motives, and I found it hard to believe that Myra had any either. *Compulsion* is not a 'rubbish thriller'. It is a non-fiction novel written by a liberal, politically motivated former newspaper reporter. Levin's book deals with the murder of a Chicago schoolboy, Robert Franks, by two wealthy, good-looking young men, Nathan F. Leopold and Richard A. Loeb. Their only motive was to commit 'the perfect murder'. The killers picked their victim up in a hired car, beat him to death with a chisel, burned his face, hands and genitals with hydrochloric acid, and hid him in a drainage pipe before trying to secure a ransom. Levin's purpose in writing the book was to examine how the protagonists' background and psychological make-up contributed to their actions. In many ways, his work prepared the ground for Truman Capote's *In Cold Blood* and Norman Mailer's *The Executioner's Song*.

Ian told Myra that he couldn't believe the mistakes Leopold and Loeb had made. They bungled the pick-up and were seen by people who knew them; they beat Franks to death in the car so there was blood everywhere; then they hid him in a drainage pipe but left a foot sticking out. Finally – silly buggers – they rang the victim's father to try to extract a ransom. The way to commit the perfect murder was to plan it properly. You had to make sure that the body was never discovered. Ian laid it all out for her. She would help him pick up a child, wearing a disguise; they would then drive to the moor where he would rape, kill and bury it. Everything would be carefully prepared: the grave, the body disposal plan, the clean-up afterwards. Nothing would be left to chance. There was no way they would be caught. He was going to commit the perfect murder, and she was going to help him.

This is the point at which most people, however infatuated, would have reached the limit of their endurance. Her agreement to participate in sado-masochism and fantasies about robberies can, at a stretch, be explained away by the force of her infatuation; child murder cannot. But rather than flee the relationship with Ian, or try to talk him out of 'the perfect murder', she allowed things to continue. I wondered whether he would have been able to proceed without this tacit approval.

Myra was a useless driver; she failed her driving test three times. Ben Boyce, a grocer who had 'a soft spot' for her, occasionally lent her his Ford Prefect van to practise in after work. It was a big, black old thing and Myra never had it long enough to master the controls, never mind navigate the traffic with any skill. But in July 1963 Ben bought a new van and offered to let her drive the old one all the time, in return for help with deliveries.

Ian and Myra drove round east Manchester in the van and parked up watching children. They did not attract any attention; they just looked like a 'courting couple' getting away from the prying eyes of their parents, or neighbours. Ian liked to pick out an imaginary victim and describe what he'd do with 'it'. But these trips were about more than feeding sexual fantasy: he was working out the details of a successful abduction, and how to avoid the errors that Leopold and Loeb had made.

When he could get away with it, Ian took photos. I found an envelope crammed with negatives of boys playing football behind the railings of Ryder Brow school. There was something odd about how the pictures had been shot, so I went back to see what he had done. As I lined the pictures up with the railings

I realized that they were all taken quite low down. At first I thought he must have knelt. But I could see no reason for doing this – it messed up the shot. Then I worked it out: he'd fired the shutter from the passenger seat as Myra tracked her old school's perimeter in the Ford Prefect. The distance between shots was determined by the speed with which he was able to wind the crank of the camera. 'These photographs are part of the rehearsal,' Malcolm MacCulloch said as he laid the images out side by side on the polished wood of his dining-room table. 'He is planning what to do, and at the same time transferring the script in his head to her. But she is not fighting it. She is a willing participant. People have features to their personality which are brought out by circumstances. I think that Brady's knowledge, attitude, personality and what he wanted to do had this effect of bringing out the cruel, determined streak in Myra Hindley.'

The idea of 'the perfect murder' became part of their sex life. They talked through the abduction, what they would say to a child to persuade it to get into the van. As time went on what had seemed a fantastic idea became a possibility, but Myra still needed a final push. In a series of letters, she told me how Ian Brady finally persuaded her to help him turn fantasy into reality.

One day she woke up on the settee, at around one p.m., with a shocking hangover. Gran was standing over her, going on about the state she was in. Her clothes were unbuttoned and twisted awkwardly around her body. Myra couldn't remember what had happened the night before. She was a regular heavy drinker but usually knew when to stop. Embarrassed, she struggled into fresh clothes, had a wash and drank a cup of tea, but she still felt awful. Through the front window she saw her neighbour John Booth's bike leaning against the kerb opposite. Myra staggered outside and asked his mother if she could borrow it. A few minutes later she was careering down the road on the bike, the wind in her hair, blowing away the hangover. On and on she went, for mile after mile, factories and terraces going by in a blur. But her reflexes still weren't quite right. At Crown Point, in Denton, she lost concentration and slammed into the back of a bus at a red light. The traffic queued down the road as she picked herself up off the floor and sought refuge on the kerb. Why was she feeling so groggy?

Ian supplied the answer a few hours later: he'd drugged her with Gran's sleeping tablets. It took a while for the meaning of the words to penetrate her hangover. What the hell had he done that for? Ian was quite calm: he was going to commit the perfect murder, and she had to help him.

Myra kept her head down at work the following morning. She was barely able to type. She loved Ian, and the world they had built together, but the drugging worried her. She could live with sadism, enjoy it even, but, as she stated in a letter to me, she did not want to end up as his victim. When five o'clock came round she accepted his offer of a lift to the top of her road on the bike. Then she climbed off and walked the last few yards home, without glancing over her shoulder.

Myra knew he would not come round that evening, so she went to visit May Hill. It was ages since they'd seen each other, but it did not take long to fall back into the conversation of old friends. May confided in Myra that her boyfriend had given her the push for refusing sex; Myra admitted that she was fed up with Ian. They decided to drown their sorrows at the bar of the Steelie. The girls drank heavily, and as they walked home alcohol set the truth in motion. May said that no one liked Ian, and Myra was getting a shocking reputation by sleeping with him. May's words, Myra told me, played on her fears, and she decided to write a letter to be given to the police in the event of her disappearance. Sitting at the Hills' kitchen table, she scrawled out instructions on where they would find her body: close to the lay-by on Saddleworth Moor, probably by the rocks. She shielded her words from May and made her promise not to deliver the letter unless 'something happened'. They rolled back the Hills' sofa and tucked the envelope beneath the carpet. If not an insurance policy, it at least ensured that Ian would not get away with killing her.

The following Saturday Ian came round again. As

Myra put a fresh pot of tea down on the coffee table she saw him fishing in his pocket. He pulled out a small folder, drew the table up to the couch, and began spreading out photographs – shots of her, naked, close up, in a series of pornographic poses. Newspaper had been spread on the floor to hide the rug. Where you could see her face, Myra told me, she had a 'stupid drunken expression' on her face. She had no memory of posing for them. He told her that he'd taken them while she was out cold; she would do what he wanted. The teapot stood steaming between them in the ensuing silence. After a short while Ian scooped up the pictures, slipped them back into his pocket and walked out of the door. When he had gone Myra walked briskly round to the Hills', hammered on the door and asked May to get the envelope for her.

Myra's decision to retrieve the letter did not fit with the case she was building in her letters to me that she was bullied into taking part in the murders. If she had truly been terrified, surely she would have left the letter there, or gone straight to the police? Rather, it suggested that she realized he would not kill her, and she made a conscious decision to go along with his plan for the perfect murder. I asked Professor MacCulloch for his opinion. 'I find the idea that she was frightened into taking part in the murders unconvincing,' he said. 'I accept that there's a balance here but, on balance, the attraction of the relationship, and what's going on, is more powerful than being abused. She doesn't have a normal reaction to that sort of behaviour. Besides, she must have realized that he needed her to pick up a child.'

Myra did describe other attempts at 'escape' in her letters to me. She applied for a job with the NAAFI in Germany, went for an interview in London and was accepted. But when she got back to Manchester Ian was waiting for her at Piccadilly station. Myra told me that he took her home, threatened her family, and anally raped her. But still she stayed with him.

In her autobiography Myra described how, far from fleeing Ian, she allowed him to further 'educate' her about his background and motivation. He told her she should see where he came from. Ever since the day of his banishment by a Scottish magistrate he had made regular trips back 'home'. They loaded up the van with food and headed north. Because Myra did not have a driver's licence they stuck to the back roads; there were far fewer police there than on the motorways. In Glasgow, Ian directed her towards the Gorbals. The tenement he had grown up in was all but derelict. Most families, like the Sloans, had been moved out. Ian walked about in his long coat, a lightmeter round his neck and camera in his hands, and recorded the places where he'd grown up. Myra followed him as he walked into one of the blocks and ran up the steps, two at a time, like a boy coming in from school. He leant backwards out of the staircase window and called up, in a mock child's voice,

pretending to be 'Sloany' the misfit again. Myra
collapsed laughing. On the way back to the van they
glanced through the door of a pub. The first thing
Myra noticed was the sawdust on the floor, and the
spittoons, but she retreated under the force of
the drinkers' suspicious expressions. Ian told her that
they did not like women in pubs. He also warned her
to keep her mouth shut as her accent would not go
down well.

From the Gorbals, they followed a bus out to
Pollock. The Sloans had moved here in the hope of a
better life when Ian was still a boy. They parked the
van at the top of the road and sat watching the small
house he had grown up in. It was identical to all the
others. After a few minutes Ian grew restless, told her
he was worried about being observed. He jumped out
of the car and strode towards a low block of flats
opposite. They climbed the stairwell to the third floor
and continued to watch the Sloans' house from there.
Myra tried to imagine Ian playing down there with
childhood friends.

They were disturbed by a young boy coming up the
stairs. He gave them a wide berth and knocked on the
door of the flat opposite their look-out. A girl
answered; Myra guessed she was about twenty. When
the door had closed, Myra could feel her eye on them,
through the spyhole. Five minutes later the door
cracked open. What the fucking hell did they want?
Myra was taken aback by the girl's venom. Ian turned,

said they weren't bothering her. The girl spat back that they 'fucking were'. Ian's jaw clenched tight, and his cheekbones seemed to stand out. Myra thought he was going to slap her, but he simply turned and walked down the stairs. In her autobiography, Myra recalled his words as they walked back to the van: 'I'd never hurt one of my own.'

They sat outside the Sloans' for hours. Ian sent Myra out for fish and chips; he stayed hidden in case anyone recognized him. Just as she returned, Ian's stepsister, May, emerged from the front door of the house. Ian pulled Myra's head down so that it obscured his face until May had passed. She did not notice him, bought her chips and walked briskly home, pulling the door to behind her.

Myra asked Ian why he didn't just go in. He did not reply, just sat there staring straight ahead. They spent that night sleeping in the van, outside the Sloans' front door, wrapped in their coats. In the morning, stiff with cold, they drove to the public wash-house at Glasgow Central station for a bath. As she lay soaking in the hot water Myra decided to put a couple of blankets in the back of the van for future excursions.

The trip to Scotland helped Myra to understand Ian's hunger to 'rise above' the 'confines' of the working class. Committing the perfect murder was a way of asserting his superiority. But she was still not quite ready to help him. Nevertheless, he insisted that she go out looking for a victim. Myra described in a letter to me how she drove round and round Gorton. She looked at kids and imagined telling them she'd lost something, taking them up to the moor and handing them over to die. Ian knew that every time she went out there was a chance he would get to fulfil his ambition. Everything else was in place. His frustration grew every time a victim failed to materialize. When Myra returned empty-handed yet again he wanted to know what the hell had happened this time. Her excuse was lame: there were too many people about. He grabbed her round the neck and slapped her repeatedly, told her that he'd been watching on his bike and she'd bottled it. He released her and slammed out of the door.

Myra, as her letters to me reveal, was not the only one affected by her sexually sadistic relationship with Ian Brady. One morning Myra stood over Gran in her work clothes, shaking her by the shoulder. She was fast asleep. A fresh cup of tea stood steaming on the bedside table. No matter how hard Myra shook, Ellen did not move. She ran round to Eaton Street to get Nellie, then down the road to Dr Chadwick's. The doctor prodded Ellen and listened to her chest before announcing that there was nothing wrong. Did she use sleeping tablets? Myra held the packet out to him, and blanched. Dr Chadwick nodded understandingly; the old dear had got in a muddle and taken one too many, that was all. But an image from the previous evening had come into Myra's mind: Ian making a cup of tea and taking it up to Gran. He'd doped her too.

Myra rang in sick and stayed at home to look after Gran. That evening she heard the Tiger Cub come down the street and pull up. She struggled to control her temper as she waited for Ian to come inside. He was quite calm, and did not bother to deny what he'd done. He told her that he'd had no choice, as she kept backing out. He knew it was difficult, but she'd enjoyed the fantasy so she'd enjoy the reality. They both would. Besides, all she had to do was hand them over. The rest could stay up here, he added, tapping the side of his head.

Myra recorded in a letter to me that she knew he was right. Every time she climbed behind the wheel of the black van she was a step closer to 'doing it'. Her account of this period is filled with foreboding. There is the sense of an actor rehearsing his part, over and over, in the certain knowledge that he will eventually take to the stage.

Chapter Three

On a warm summer's evening I walked down Taylor Street, turned right opposite the Steelworks and, a minute later, left into Froxmer Street – the site of the first abduction. The low sun shone through a willow and danced on the wall of Gorton Foundry. I turned and looked back in the direction Myra Hindley would have come. There was Peacock Street Primary. It seemed extraordinary that they set out to abduct someone so close to home. Perhaps it added to the excitement, the feeling that they had a secret no one else was party to.

The account of the first abduction, in Myra Hindley's letters to me, is extraordinary in its detail. It was just after eight on Friday, 12 July 1963. Myra's stomach fluttered as she signalled left by Beyer Peacock. She had watched the pretty girl in a party dress turn into Froxmer Street and knew she was alone. She glanced in her rearview mirror. Ian flashed the Tiger Cub's headlights on and off, on and off, then roared past the van to the end of Froxmer Street. The bike disappeared out of sight, but Myra listened for the engine note and heard it die as he cut the ignition. She pulled the van to the side, leant over, rolled down the window and asked the girl where she was going. Pauline Reade, whom Myra had known since she was little, turned and smiled in recognition. A dance at Openshaw. She'd fixed up to go with Pat Cummings, but she'd had to cancel. Yes, thanks, a lift would be great.

Myra could see Ian parked up on his bike in an alley next to the Vulcan pub at the end of Froxmer Street. As the van rolled past him Myra asked Pauline if she'd mind a small detour to look for a glove she'd lost near Greenfield; it had been a present from her boyfriend. She'd drop Pauline back at the dance after. No problem, said Pauline.

Myra Hindley's senses were so sharpened that every one of this evening's experiences etched itself into her memory. Each word, sound and smell read as though it had been lived and committed to paper the same day. 'The clarity of her recollections is very striking, and important,' Malcolm MacCulloch told me. 'It means that the omissions are likely to be obvious, and significant.'

Myra glanced across as she steered the heavy old van down the A635. Pauline had on white gloves, a pastel blue coat over a pink dress and white high-heeled shoes. She was wearing only a little make-up and her hair had been newly curled. Her perfume was light and fragrant. It reminded Myra of her own – June, by Saville. She stuck carefully to the speed limit as they drove through the outskirts of Manchester, Stalybridge and Greenfield. The Tiger Cub's headlight bobbed up and down in her wing mirror. To pass the time, Myra told Pauline how Ben's new van had broken down and she had agreed to help him tow it when they got back to Gorton. It was 'only fair', as he'd let her borrow this one. Pauline asked Myra where her boyfriend was. Oh, he'd had to go off on an emergency, she replied. He'd join them later if he could.

The light was failing when they turned the corner to the moor, and they sat in silence for a few moments. Then Pauline asked if Myra was all right – she was gripping the steering wheel ever so tight. Myra flexed her fingers, flashed a smile and explained that she was still getting used to driving the big old van.

Ian had counted all the buttons on their clothing before they went out. His shirt, jacket and trousers; her blouse, skirt and coat. Every number had been written down on a piece of paper to be checked off when they got home. He'd also listed all the things they would need to do afterwards: burn shoes, cut up clothing, wash spade. Myra knew exactly where to park when they got to the moor and what to say so that their stories fitted together. Unlike their inspiration, Leopold and Loeb, they had left nothing to chance.

They reached the lay-by; the Tiger Cub stood at its edge, concealed between a couple of large rocks. Myra feigned surprise as she greeted Ian. He 'suggested' that she park round the corner while he and Pauline started looking for the lost glove. The light was disappearing fast now. Myra glanced in the rearview mirror as she pulled onto the road and saw Ian leading Pauline onto Hollin Brown Knoll. She was having trouble walking in her white high-heeled shoes. He had taken her arm to lend her support.

It was almost dark when Myra pulled the Ford into the smaller lay-by, two wheels on the verge, two on the tarmac. She sat staring at the moor and noticed a couple of ditches that had been dug for new gas pipes. Other than a soft wind drumming against the slab-sided van, it was quiet. She was almost certain that Ian was raping Pauline.

After twenty minutes there was a scrabbling sound. Ian slid back down the hill to the van. He banged on the window and gestured for her to get out. Myra walked at his side, careful not to twist her ankle. Even though it was dark Ian knew exactly where he was going, and he guided her round the newly dug ditches. The first things to emerge from the darkness were Pauline's white gloves and shoes, caught in the moonlight as the cloud broke in the black night sky. Myra asked whether he'd raped her. Of course he had, said Ian matter-of-factly. He told Myra to wait while he went and got the spade.

Myra stared down at the body. Pauline's clothing had been pulled up and blood was seeping from a deep wound in her neck. She was surprised: Ian had said he was going to strangle the victim. She heard him coming back. He grumbled about not having been able to find the spade easily in the dark, jumped off a rock and landed next to her. The peat juddered with the impact of his weight. He told her to get back in the van. As she walked off Myra noticed, with dismay, that his clothes were covered in blood. This part of the moor was completely exposed in daylight. At night-time car headlights cut through the darkness, their drivers' eyes locked on the road in front. Myra knew that Ian would enjoy the fact that 'normal' life was hurrying by with no idea of the horror he was perpetrating.

When Ian got back to the van he carefully wrapped the spade in a plastic sack and the knife in cloths before stowing them. He told Myra to head back to the other lay-by. She bungled the three-point turn and had to repeatedly back up and down between the verges before the van was finally facing the right way. Ian swore at every missed gear and stamp on the brake. When they reached the bike they pulled a couple of planks out of the back of the van to make a ramp and pushed the Tiger Cub inside. It was a tricky manoeuvre but they had practised it in daylight. As she climbed behind the wheel Myra asked Ian the time. Ten thirty, he replied.

They sat in silence as the van rattled back down the hill to Manchester. On the edge of the city, Ian said, 'If you'd shown any signs of backing out you'd have ended up in the same hole as her.'

'I know,' Myra replied.

As they passed the foundry they saw Joan Reade with her son Paul, looking for Pauline. Myra stared straight ahead and pretended not to notice their obvious distress.

Gran had banked up the fire to keep the front room warm. Ian carried the knife and spade in through the back door and locked them in a cupboard. Then he reminded Myra about Ben's van. Myra swore; she was exhausted and did not feel up to pretending that everything was normal. But Ian insisted; they mustn't draw attention to themselves by changing their behaviour. He buttoned up his overcoat, to hide the blood on his shirt, and pushed her out of the door.

At Ben's house Myra saw, through a crack in the curtains, that he was fast asleep in front of the fire. She knocked. It was a couple of minutes before he came to the front door, yawning. Rather than put the job off till the morning, as Myra had hoped, he pulled on his shoes. She apologized for being late, said that they'd stopped in Whaley Bridge and hadn't been able to get the van going again afterwards. Ben said not to worry, the old banger was always doing that, it could happen any time. Ian chatted away to the grocer as they drove, and helped him hitch a rope to his broken-down van so that Myra could tow it back to Gorton. Ben tapped the roof of her Ford and climbed behind the wheel of his vehicle. Myra started the engine and let out the clutch. The first time she used too few revs and stalled; the second, she pulled away so fast the rope almost snapped. Ben got out and walked up to her open window. Would she like him to drive? Ian jabbed Myra in the ribs; they hadn't cleaned the back out yet. No, no, it would be fine. She was just a bit tired.

When they got home Myra filled a bucket with hot, soapy water in the kitchen and carried it out to Ian. He washed every inch of the van and wiped the surfaces down with strips of sacking stolen from work. They moved quietly so that the neighbours wouldn't hear, and spoke to each other in a low whisper. Myra hissed at him, demanding to know why he was washing the tyres. He replied that he didn't want to leave behind a single fingerprint. Leopold and Loeb's car had been full of 'forensic'; the only way to be sure was to wash everything down. Myra shone a torch over the surfaces as he worked. He was methodical, turning small circles with the cloth, obliterating every trace of Pauline and the moor.

Back inside, Ian laid out his list and spread a large plastic sheet on the floor in front of the fire. Myra came out of the kitchen, pulling on a pair of washing-up gloves. She told me in a letter that he snapped at her, 'What do you need those for? Don't be so fucking squeamish. It's only earth.'

She replied, 'I'm not having grave-dirt under my fingernails!' He slapped her, sat down and started cutting his clothes into strips. They hissed lightly as he laid them on the coal. Myra half-filled the sink with soap powder and scrubbed the spade clean, even though there was no blood on it, and he'd wiped most of the dirt off on the rough tussock-grass. Myra asked Ian what they should do about her clothes. The plan had been for her to stay in the van, but she had walked across the moor and stood next to the body. He said she hadn't touched anything so she'd be fine if she sponged off any flecks of peat and wiped her shoes.

Ian pressed on the handle of the knife, trying to snap it off. But it was too well made and the steel rivets clung stubbornly to the wood. In the end he gave up and threw the whole thing in the fire. He told her that the heat would burn off any blood; they'd have to get rid of the blade in the morning. Myra vigorously scrubbed the bottom of the cupboard where the knife and spade had been. It was 4.30 in the morning by the time they had finished. Myra crept upstairs, swallowed a couple of Gran's Nembutal and pulled on clean underwear and a dressing gown. She and Ian fell asleep next to each other in front of the fire.

Myra woke with a start at 6.45, rousing Ian, who swore. He noticed his black coat lying over the arm of a chair, caught in the light fingering its way through the lace curtains. The collar was coated in blood. Worried that Gran might wake up, he carried it straight to the sink and sponged off as much of it as he could. Then Myra put the kettle on while Ian retrieved the burnt knife from the fireplace and wrapped it in pages pulled from the *Manchester Evening News*. After breakfast they headed into town in search of a dry cleaner's. He told her to book the coat in under the name of the US president, Kennedy, while he sat round the corner with the bike engine running. When she'd done that she climbed on the back of the bike and they headed out along the Stockport Road. They were going to dump the knife far away from home and Saddleworth Moor.

After twenty minutes, while they were still in Manchester, Ian pulled up by a newsagent's. He called over his shoulder, as he kicked out the sidestand, that he was just going to get some fags. Myra waited for him on the pillion. A short while later Ian emerged holding a packet of Capstan Full Strength, and handed Myra a Crunchie bar. She slipped it into her pocket for later. Ian did not climb straight back onto the bike, as she expected, but stood there looking down at her with a lop-sided smile on his face. He asked, why didn't she eat it now? Was she put off by the fact that he'd bought it with the four half-crowns in Pauline's pocket?

Myra growled at him through gritted teeth. He'd drummed the law into her: you could still get hanged for treason, killing a policeman, and murder in the furtherance of theft. She ordered him to go back up to the moor and replace the money. Ian looked at her as though she were mad. Who was going to find out? It was the perfect murder. Myra snapped at him. He was going to do it, and she was going to watch. It didn't matter how angry he got, she wasn't going to swing from the gallows for his pride. He pulled a Capstan out, lit it, pushed his foot down hard on the starter, kicked the engine into life and roared off down the Stockport Road.

Ian picked a quiet lane and rode slowly up it until they came to a suitable place. There was a river on the other side and some children were skipping stones on the water. They leant the bike up and wandered casually past the kids looking for somewhere quiet. After a few minutes they were on their own. Ian glanced downstream, checked no one was watching, and threw a few stones to test the depth of the water. Satisfied, he pulled the package out from under his jacket, unfurled the newspaper and tossed the knife into the stream. The blackened blade sank quickly out of sight. He lobbed a couple of large rocks after it, in the hope that they might rest on the burnt steel, pinning it to the bottom of the stream. Myra sat on her haunches and watched the sunlight catch on the water. He snapped her out of it, told her it was time to go. They walked back to the bike, pausing briefly by a wall so that he could set fire to the newspaper he'd wrapped the knife in.

* * *

Myra denied to me that Pauline was targeted as a victim, even though she'd known her all her life: 'all the victims were in the wrong place at the wrong time – it could have been anybody that was "chosen".' The random selection of targets was part of Ian's plan as it gave the police fewer leads to follow; Leopold and Loeb were caught because there were too many connections to their victim. In that sense, the choice of someone so close to home was a mistake. It was an error, I reflected, that would have driven most people to distraction, yet Myra was able to keep functioning.

Malcolm MacCulloch took a sip from a glass of water, and picked up his notes.

'Her reaction is abnormal. This is one of the most horrendous things that can happen to anybody. A person of a more nervous disposition, or with less fortitude, would disintegrate. They would become distressed, anxious, develop post-traumatic stress disorder. There is no evidence of any of this.'

'How does that further our understanding?' I asked.

'There are lots of people with tough personalities who do great and brave things – save nations, get the VC. Under other circumstances they might be labelled abhorrent psychopaths. It's really a question of who you meet.'

Myra stood on Hollin Brown Knoll and watched Ian scatter the half-crowns. He didn't drop them on the grave, but around it. When he was satisfied with their position he crouched down and pushed them into crevices in the peat. The coins would not lead anyone to Pauline's body, but if the police did somehow discover her they would also find the money. Myra looked on approvingly. Then she noticed something on Ian's hand, and asked him what it was. A plastic glove, he replied; he'd wiped the coins clean before scattering them. Had she forgotten? This was the perfect murder. No one was going to catch them.

When Myra and Ian got back to Gorton the living room was packed, and noisy: Gran, Mam, Maureen and cousin Glenys were sitting there chattering about Pauline's disappearance. Amos Reade had been on the phone to the police several times during the night, but they had only come in the morning. 'Young girls often go missing, sir,' they told him. Now they were questioning poor Amos and talking about dredging the canal and reservoirs. What did Myra think? asked Nellie. Ian smiled. He had warned her to act normally, told her this was bound to happen. Oh, she hardly knew the girl, Myra replied. Pauline was Maureen's friend really, wasn't she? Maureen agreed, then recalled, wistfully, that David had gone out with her for a while. Myra turned up her nose at the mention of Maureen's new boyfriend, David Smith. He was a thug with a long list of convictions for violence.

That night, after a meal with his mother, Ian came round. On the doorstep he pulled a bottle of Drambuie from under his leather coat, to 'celebrate'.

Myra, already half cut on wine, smiled and stood back to let him in. They talked late into the night, and went over the killing again and again. Ian, Myra told me in a letter, was ecstatic. He'd finally done it, after all these years – the perfect murder. He reached over, pulled Myra to him, and stroked her hair. Warmth flooded through her and she lay there, breathing deeply, staring into the flames. They soon fell asleep, and Myra did not suffer any nightmares.

The following week, for her twenty-first birthday, Ben gave her the van. He could no longer afford to keep three vehicles on the road. The tax and insurance had only two weeks left, and it needed an MOT. Ian bought a tin of white gloss and they spent a weekend painting the interior, front and back – it was certain to get rid of any 'forensic' that might be left. When they'd finished Ian said he'd like to get the outside resprayed as well. The electricity board lettering still showed through, made it too memorable.

Ian's twenty-first birthday present to her, eleven days after Pauline died, was a gold-plated Ingersoll wristwatch. I found it among her possessions in its original crocodile-skin-effect brown cardboard box. The receipt was neatly folded underneath a red plastic plinth. A rusting staple held it to the twelve-month guarantee.

Those days and weeks after the murder of Pauline Reade were Myra Hindley's last opportunity to run. The version of events she presented to me – that Ian

Brady forced her into the killings – might just have worked. She'd probably have done a few years for being an accessory. Her decision to stay with Ian, sleep with him, wear the watch he gave her, meant that there was no turning back.

Chapter Four

Gran snapped at her: she'd been caught. Myra's heart gave a lurch, but she tried to keep her face expressionless. A policeman had been round earlier about the tax on her van. Gran had told her to get it sorted but it was always Ian this, Ian that. Myra hid her relief.

The *Manchester Evening News* and *Gorton and Openshaw Reporter* were still full of Pauline Reade's disappearance. The police dragged the canal and the reservoirs. There were house-to-house enquiries; Maureen's boyfriend, David Smith, was interviewed twice. Ian questioned Mo closely about what they'd asked. Did they have any theories? Did they suspect anyone?

Myra and Ian returned to the moor many times. Seeing Pauline's grave, Myra wrote in her auto-biography, made Ian calm, reminded him that he really had committed the perfect murder. There is a photograph of him, wearing a dark suit and glasses, standing on the rocks of Hollin Brown Knoll; another of her grinning in a long woollen coat, a transistor radio at her feet. She noted that the song playing on the radio was 'My Guy' by Mary Wells. They were in front of Pauline's grave. Myra's clear recollection of posing by the grave, and the gleeful expression on her face, did not seem to me to be the actions of someone who was living in fear; rather, they suggested that she was complicit in savouring the murder. 'That is the sort of thing that happens with sadists,' Professor MacCulloch told me. The photographs were spread out on his dining-room table. 'They review what they've done. Either they remember it in fantasy, and that reinforces them, or they have souvenirs – body parts, hair, pictures – through which they're able to relive what happened.'

Ian printed the pictures of Pauline's grave in his darkroom at Westmoreland Street. The negatives were large 6cm × 6cm professional quality medium-format images. He took great care to make sure that they were processed and washed correctly. Rather than make enlargements he produced 'contact prints'. By the red glow of a safe-light he pressed the negative straight onto photographic paper, then exposed it for twenty seconds to the white light of the enlarger. It was a fast way of working, and it meant that the resulting pictures were the right size to stick straight into his new tartan-covered picture album.

Myra avoided passing by the Reades' house in case she bumped into Pauline's mum, Joan. They had often walked to work together when she was at Lawrence Scott's. She did once encounter Pauline's dad, Amos. He looked drawn, was staring into nothingness, and did not see her. His daughter's disappearance was the main topic of conversation at work. There was a wild rumour that Pauline had run off to Australia with a man from the fair because she was pregnant and couldn't face telling her strict Catholic mother. Complete rubbish, Myra said. Pauline was far too reliable a girl for that; she'd known her all her life. Myra told me in a letter that she coped by walling herself in and operating on a different plane from everyone around her. It was the same strategy she'd used to cope with the violence at home when she was a child. Only this time she was not alone. The shared secret of the perfect murder made her feel even closer to Ian.

Gran waited up with Myra for the police night patrol to come round about the tax disc. Ian had told her to act normally and gone back to Longsight to keep out of the way. Somehow, Gran's nervousness made it easier for Myra to detach herself; when the knock of leather on wood finally came she was quite prepared. The sergeant said that he wouldn't have booked her as she'd never been in trouble with the law before, but now it had to go ahead. The probationary constable at his side, who had written the ticket, shifted uncomfortably. Myra complained that the van did have a disc in the window – Ben had lent her one. That was the other problem, the sergeant explained: because there was a third party, and deception, involved they'd really have to charge her. Gran, listening to everything from the kitchen, was horrified. She went round all the neighbours telling them it was 'just a traffic offence'.

Myra decided the best thing to do was to come clean with Tommy Craig. She didn't want her boss to hear about it from someone else and think that she might have something to hide. He told her not to worry. It was just a 'misdemeanour' and she'd probably get no more than a caution. A week later the papers arrived summoning her and Ben to appear at Manchester Magistrates' Court.

She heard the thunk-thunk of the Norton's engine coming down Bannock Street long before she saw it. It was a sound, Myra noted, quite different from the phut-phut of Ian's little Tiger Cub. Rising over the top of the engine note was another noise: the chatter of a shortwave radio. Myra and Gran watched from behind the net curtain as the policeman dismounted and strode up to the front door, unbuckling his helmet. Gran hovered, demanding to know what she'd done this time. Nothing, replied Myra, irritably, it was probably just about the van. She stood in the darkness behind the front door and waited for the knock.

When the door swung open, light flooded in and

there stood 'the tallest, best-looking man' Myra had ever seen. The officer, who introduced himself as PC Norman Sutton, had heard about her 'spot of bother' and wondered whether she intended to keep the van. A friend of his had a refrigerator business and needed something just like it. Gran scuttled across the road to the neighbours to let them know that Myra wasn't 'in trouble' again. Myra asked PC Sutton if he'd like a cup of tea. It was clear from his behaviour that he liked her. She told him he could have the van, but Norman insisted on giving her £25 for it. He said, with a sly smile, that he couldn't hand over the cash on duty; how about meeting up one evening for a drink so that they could settle the deal? Myra agreed. Gran came back and stood fidgeting in the doorway. The noise of that radio was a bit unsettling; was there any chance the constable might be able to turn it down? Norman took the hint, stood up and said he'd see Myra next Wednesday. Gran did not say anything. Meeting a different man from Ian Brady might do Myra 'a bit of good'.

Ian and Myra were having a picnic in a field when she told him about the van. The sound that came out of him astonished her: it started as a low hoot and dissolved into hysterical laughter. He lay on his back in the grass, the beer bottle in his right hand shaking with the power of his convulsions. They'd used a van to commit the perfect murder, and she'd sold it to a policeman! Myra had to admit it was funny.

After the murder of Pauline Reade, Ian's 'absences' became more frequent, and more lengthy. He spent hours out on his bike in the evenings, cruising round Manchester. His thirst for killing slaked, he needed new 'experiences'. Myra sat in and waited for the sound of the Tiger Cub turning into Bannock Street, the engine cutting before it rolled to a standstill outside number 7. Even when he wasn't physically there she was with him.

In order to pass the long evenings, Myra enrolled for night-school classes back at Ryder Brow: English on a Wednesday, Maths on a Friday. Miss Webb, the English teacher, appeared amused to see such a diligent truant walking back through the school gates. Once she'd set the class a task she slipped into the desk next to Myra. She said she was surprised to see her there; English had been her best subject. Myra could probably teach it better than she did! Wouldn't it be better to catch up on the subjects she'd bunked off from? Myra replied that she liked English and wanted to get even better at it. The teacher nodded, stood up and resumed the lesson.

After class, Miss Webb told Myra what had become of the other girls in her year – this one was a nurse at the Manchester Royal Infirmary, that one a secretary. There was one surprise among them, a police officer. Myra's ears pricked up. That sounded interesting, she was meeting a constable for a drink later on. Well, said Miss Webb, if Myra ever wanted to join the police force she should let her know. A lady friend was an inspector at Mill Street station. She'd be happy to recommend her.

Norman was waiting outside, standing next to his 650cc bike. If anything, he looked even better out of uniform – grown up and fashionable. They walked in the opposite direction to West Gorton in search of a 'discreet' pub where no one would recognize Myra. As they sat down with a rum and Coke for her and a pint for him, Norman said he'd known her right away. What did he mean? Myra asked. The policeman replied that he'd been a regular at Belle Vue when she was a barmaid. Myra fished in her memory, trying to remember him. It had all been a blur, the faces just 'punters', not people. Norman added that May, the manageress, was his mam. Myra gasped in astonishment. Her old boss and the pleasure gardens belonged to a different time.

Norman gave Myra the money for the van and took her home on his bike. The house was dark: Gran was in bed and Ian was out, prowling about. Myra had no idea whether he was going to appear that night. She agreed to let Norman come in, but said that if Ian showed up he'd have to pretend he'd just popped round with the cash for the van, and leave. Myra put the small TV light on and went into the kitchen to make a cup of tea. Norman sat down and stroked her dog, Lassie. He asked if she was serious about Ian. Myra replied that she was. The only problem was that

Ian had said he would never get married, or have kids. Myra set the tea things down on the small table, stirred the pot and poured. Norman eased the dog off the settee and pulled her to him. They kissed; it was long, slow and gentle. Myra wanted him; he was a new 'experience'. If Ian could have them, why couldn't she? They arranged to meet again after her next night-school class.

In the early 1960s the police were not as remote as they are today. People were in and out of the station; the front desk even provided change for people to feed the gas and electricity meters, which both discouraged the 'fixing' of coin slots and meant that officers had day-to-day contact with the community they policed. Myra felt relaxed, she told me in a letter, about going to Mill Street station for an interview. She'd talked over the prospect of training as a police-woman with Norman, who'd agreed it was a good idea. It might give them a future together. The inspector gave her a grilling on her past, but it was easy to deal with: she just blocked out the memory of Pauline's death. It was a convincing performance, and she was passed fit for training. The business with the van wouldn't be a problem, they said – none of us was perfect! Myra was handed the paperwork to complete a formal application to join the force and she trotted down the station steps and into the cool autumn air clutching the forms.

When she got back to Bannock Street Ian was

waiting for her. At first, he was shocked at what she'd done. But as he thought about it his enthusiasm grew, and he encouraged her to join the police. Just like selling the van to Norman, the idea heightened the excitement of having committed the perfect murder. Ian demanded to know if she was sleeping with 'the policeman'. Myra refused to answer. He said, casually, that he might just kill him. That night Ian and Myra made love, and he bit her hard on the shoulder from behind.

Ian was now disappearing for as many nights as he was around. Myra saw more and more of Norman. They went dancing at the Levenshulme Palais, for rides on his bike, and for drinks in pubs. Then they made love. It was quite different from the sex she had with Ian. But Myra knew the relationship was temporary – Ian only allowed it to carry on because it amused him. She still belonged to him.

Myra Hindley only ever told the story of her relationship with Norman in her letters to me. I believe that she included it in order to try to show that she was looking for a means of escape, that she would have been 'normal' if she'd never met Ian. But as I read it I suspected that the policeman got caught in a game between them: he became a means of heightening their sense of danger and excitement.

I tracked down Norman Sutton to a nursing home on the outskirts of Blackpool. His name was 'kept out of the papers' by his sympathetic colleagues after the arrest of the Moors murderers. The *Sun* newspaper sniffed him out years later and put the story on the front page. It revealed that he was divorced and living in Bolton. Norman had refused to comment to the paper but was captured on the end of a long lens peering round a doorway. He looked frightened. Myra Hindley read the piece in her cell, and cut it out; it was there when she died. In a letter to me she wrote, 'I hoped he hadn't suffered from the press exposé . . . I do still treasure him in my heart.'

As we walked down the antiseptic corridor to Norman's room the nursing home sister told me that he had ME. 'He's not in a good way, but he'll see you.'

Norman Sutton was lying on the bed in blue and white striped cotton pyjamas, hacking into a screwed-up handkerchief. The small space was dimly lit with a bedside light. He gave me a baleful, suspicious look as I came in. At first, he denied having a relationship with Myra Hindley. Then I told him what she had written.

'Oh Jesus!' he said.

As he shifted in the bed I could see that his frame, now racked by illness, had been that of a strong man.

'I just want to check the story.'

'All right. It's true. Brady was a complete maniac. He came round when I was there, having a cup of tea. The bastard started screaming at me. He wanted to kill me.'

'But you were a policeman.'

'I was married when I met Myra, and couldn't do anything. It ruined me when it came out. I ended up leaving the force. I've got nothing, nothing.'

Before I left, Norman asked whether I could spare some cash for cigarettes.

One Friday evening Ian and Myra packed up and headed north, to Scotland, for a break. It was to become part of their routine between murders. Away from Manchester, they relaxed. Ian led Myra across the hills around Loch Lomond, and they took a trip across the lake on a paddle steamer. Everything was recorded with Ian's camera: him leaning against the rail of the ship; her with a transistor radio round her neck. They listened to *The Goon Show* sitting by the lake shore. Their conversations were shot through with black humour. Ian was particularly pleased with a picture of Myra sitting on a monument painted with the words 'Maggie Well burnt as a witch in 1776'. She stared, inscrutable, straight into the lens. Ian printed the pictures and stuck them into the tartan album alongside the ones of Pauline Reade's grave.

As requested, I had regular conversations with Greater Manchester Police detectives to inform them about what I had found in the new material, and what Professor Malcolm MacCulloch thought of it. As a result, they decided to do more work on Ian Brady's photographs.

DC Gail Jazmik handed me a reproduction of the tartan album. We were sitting in a corner of the headquarters' canteen. 'All the meeting rooms are booked,' Jazmik had explained. She wanted to know whether any of the pictures I had been given might lead to the grave of Keith Bennett. 'Do you have any photographs that aren't in this album?'

A group of secretaries at the next table were shouting about how drunk they'd got the night before. I screened them out and studied the heavy black pages. There were four to six monochrome pictures per side. At first sight, the album could have belonged to anyone. The moorland scenes were interspersed with snapshots of dogs, friends and family; Nellie and Bob Hindley glued in alongside shots of Ian's mother and the Sloans in Glasgow. There was also a shot of a kilted soldier playing the bagpipes. The only hint of mystery lay in the strange way in which the images were arranged. Technically superb pictures were interspersed with the kind of thing a good photographer would discard as soon as it emerged from the developer: Bob Hindley's blurred back shuffling through a doorway; Ian, overexposed, holding a tiny baby. The absence of an emotional narrative was also striking; this was no complete world the photographer was trying to present. Where there was humour or warmth it showed up the colder, unsmiling pictures for what they were.

'There are a few pictures that don't seem to be here,' I said.

I handed DC Jazmik a stack of compact discs with thumbnail images on the back. She held them close to her glasses and stared intently, scribbling notes when she came across any she didn't recognize.

'I can see three we haven't got. Would you mind doing us some prints?'

'No problem.'

I ran off three landscapes for her. There was nothing that appeared to point to a grave, but at least the police could be sure that they had all the evidence available if there were further developments.

Myra finally passed her driving test on 7 November 1963, at her fourth attempt. The following Sunday she and Ian were sitting watching *Sunday Night at the London Palladium* when Ian turned to her and said he wanted to 'do another one'.

Myra wasn't really paying attention and asked, 'Another what?'

'Another murder. What did you think I meant?'

She could not believe what she was hearing. He'd wanted to commit the perfect murder, and had achieved it. Why did he want to do another? Ian replied that he just did.

Myra met Norman after her night-school class, made love to him, and told him it was over. He asked her why, said he didn't understand what she saw in Ian. She told him that it was impossible to put into words. The ending of this relationship freed Myra to concentrate once again on helping to realize Ian's desires.

Chapter Five

'What I'm looking for are patterns, repetition,' Malcolm MacCulloch said. 'He was systematic in the way he operated. By understanding this we can untangle his crimes. It may even, one day, contribute to the case being closed.'

'You mean, something may have been missed?'

'Exactly. But then that's hardly surprising as this material has not been available before.'

Myra recorded in her autobiography that the only way Millwards' warehouse foreman, George Clitherow, could hold Ian's attention was to talk about guns. He was an expert. Small-bore, large-bore, Webley, Smith and Wesson – George seemed to know it all. What's more, he was president of Cheadle gun club. Ian was careful, though, not to make his interest in weapons too obvious. If George picked up on it and invited him along to shoot, he'd have to refuse. There was no way he could get a firearms certificate with his criminal record. Myra, however, was a different matter. Ian told her to 'work on' George and get an invitation to Cheadle. When the offer came, Myra did her best to look surprised. After work, Ian rode her into town to apply for a firearms certificate. The police at Bootle Street station were not bothered by the traffic offences on her record. Not exactly Al Capone, is it, love?

The following weekend, Myra found herself flat on her stomach, eye clamped to a sight, loosing off .22 rounds at a target. Not bad, said George. She wasn't much of a shot but he seemed to like her enthusiasm. Myra sensed that he was surprised at her interest, and by the fact that Ian allowed her to spend the weekend like this. He asked her whether she'd like to come for a drink after.

Myra took great care to be sociable. She had instructions to get to know people, to find out where they got their guns from. Firearms were expensive; there was bound to be a black market. She finally secured an 'off-ticket' pistol from a mate of George's for £5. She also bought a target rifle, legally, from a gunsmith's in town for £10.14s. It came with a certificate stamped 'to be used on approved ranges only'.

Myra and Ian rode across the moor to a lay-by at the head of Hoe Grain stream. They needed privacy to shoot the gun. Ian, Myra told me, was like a small child as they made their way deep onto the moor, skipping over the rough landscape with excitement. They had to cross and re-cross the rapid water, swollen with winter rainfall, as they made their way to the confluence with Shiny Brook, and turned right. The rifle, in a canvas bag, was slung over Ian's shoulder with a leather cartridge belt Myra had stolen from the gun club. After twenty minutes they arrived at a stone sheep pen, in the middle of a large, secluded clearing. Ian turned and held out his right hand, shaking it impatiently. Myra started to hand him empty tins – she'd been collecting them all week – and he lined them up on the wet, grey rock. Ian grinned at her, got the gun out of its case, and walked twenty paces back in the direction they'd come. Myra went with him: he'd never fired a gun before. She'd had to show him how to clean, load and handle it.

The loud crack of the weapon was followed by silence. The bullet buried itself deep in the peat; a second ricocheted off rock; then he found his target. They stayed there for two hours while Ian blasted away at the tins. He only stopped when all the bullets had gone. It was relaxing; Myra took pleasure in his childish satisfaction. When they had finished they gathered up the bullet-riddled tins and spent cartridge cases.

I found endless pictures of Myra and Ian posing with the guns. The shots of her are carefully posed, pin-sharp; those of him are often blurred. She did not have his knack for bracing the camera against her body, to keep it steady at slow shutter speeds. Myra's face is expressionless in the pictures with guns, picking out some imaginary target with a hunter's eye. Ian is grinning in some, scowling in others. The most alarming shows him wearing a leather helmet and his long black coat, pointing the rifle barrel straight at the lens.

Myra was angry, but hiding it well. The man at Warren's Autos, next to Piccadilly station, had told her she couldn't hire a car with the pink slip of paper that said she'd passed her test; she needed a full licence. Ian would be furious. They had worked out all the details of the next killing and planned it for the following afternoon. Myra's licence arrived a few days later. She went straight back to Warren's Autos to reserve a car for the weekend. The man behind the counter said he was sorry but they only hired with a week's notice. Myra bit her lip and reserved a car for the following Saturday, 23 November. Ian was beside himself with impatience, but he agreed that she'd done the right thing, sticking with the plan, staying calm.

On the morning of the 23rd, Ian gave Myra a present, Gene Pitney's 'Twenty-four Hours from Tulsa'. They listened to it as she got ready to leave for Warren's Autos. The American's trembling falsetto echoed round the kitchen; the words were about not coming home any more. It was a grim play on the fate of their next victim. Myra groaned inwardly when she saw the Ford Anglia washed and ready on the forecourt. The bright white lettering of the number plate, 9275 ND, matched the rest of the car. It would show every speck of peat. Ian exploded when she picked him up, at eleven a.m., on the corner of Westmoreland Street. He raged that the thickest plod would be able to see exactly where they'd been. Myra fought back: what was she supposed to do, wait another week? How would he have taken that? Ian eventually calmed down and accepted she was right.

In order to create an alibi they drove south to Staffordshire and took photographs of themselves against a jagged line of rocks, Ian slim and formal in his old-fashioned clothes, Myra looking staid – a secretary on her day off. When they were done they headed north to Huddersfield, stopping off for a coffee and a Danish. Myra couldn't finish hers. Ian grabbed the sugary pastry, wolfed it down and told her it was time to go shopping. The hardware shop had everything she wanted: a roll of thin cord, a small kitchen knife with a serrated edge, and a spade. She was wearing a black wig she'd bought in Lewis's on Piccadilly Gardens, and a headscarf to hold it in place. She tried to act as normally as possible when she paid, to blend into the background. Ian was waiting for her round the corner in the Anglia. He got out as she walked up to the car and swiftly opened the boot, which was lined with black plastic. She carefully laid her new purchases alongside the freshly cleaned rifle and a torch.

Myra pulled away slowly and drove round the small town looking at all the cinemas. Ian chanted to himself in the passenger seat: hadn't seen it, no good, hadn't seen it, no good. Then they found what they were looking for, and Ian laughed. *From Russia with Love*. They'd gone to that last week. If they needed an alibi for the evening they were in there watching it.

Ashton-under-Lyne is a small town on the edge of Manchester. It has a strong sense of community, and feels gentler than the city. In its centre, surrounded by robust municipal buildings, stands the market. Bright canvas canopies protect shoppers from the rain sweeping in off the surrounding moor. When Myra and Ian arrived it was dark, but the stalls were still lit up. There were lots of kids hanging about, scrounging and mucking about. Ian was irritated when Myra told him that she needed the toilet. She told him it would affect her concentration if she couldn't go. He growled something about behaving inconspicuously. A group of women was gossiping in the toilet block; they did not look at Myra as she came in. She caught her reflection in a mirror and noticed that the wig needed re-clipping. Turning her face from the women, she backed into a cubicle to sort it out. As she washed her hands she checked it, gave a small nod of satisfaction, then walked out into the night to meet Ian.

He'd 'seen one', buying left-over food. Could she remember the script? Myra nodded and walked alongside him as they made their way down the back of a line of stalls. John Kilbride was sitting on a wall eating a bag of broken biscuits. Ian and Myra walked past him, arm in arm, scanning the area for witnesses. When they were satisfied the coast was clear, she turned and delivered her opening line.

'You're out late for such a young boy, aren't you?'

Ian picked up the cue. 'We've got kids, and we'd be worried if they were out like you, with it getting dark.'

Myra smiled reassuringly and offered the young boy a lift home. He agreed, stuffed what was left of the bag of biscuits into his jacket pocket, jumped down off the wall and walked with them to the white car. Myra asked him his name. He said he was called John Kilbride, but people called him Jack. He told them that he lived nearby, on Smallshaw Lane.

Ian hung back a few paces as they walked to the car. When they reached it he dived into the back seat, feigning innocent enthusiasm, and told John to get in the front. Myra slid behind the steering wheel, leaned across and locked the passenger door. She asked John if he'd like an adult treat, a bottle of sherry. The boy responded with enthusiasm. It was all so easy. As they pulled away, Myra looked in the mirror and saw Ian checking over his shoulder. She told the boy that they'd have to go home to get it for him. They lived in Greenfield, was that all right? John nodded. He did not suspect anything.

In a letter to me, Myra recalled Ian's words as they came into the village on the edge of the moor: 'Now that we're almost home, why don't we drive up to where we picnicked this afternoon and get that pair of gloves you left? I've just remembered them.' He told John that they were a present for their wedding anniversary and had a sentimental value. The boy was untroubled, staring out of the window, enjoying the ride. Ian had already chosen where he was going to be raped and buried.

When they got to the lay-by Ian asked John to help him, got the torch out of the boot, and walked off down a shallow incline onto the moor. A half moon lit their way. After a couple of minutes Myra drove off down towards Greenfield. She got the rifle out of the boot and laid it on the floor, next to a bag of bullets. She sat there fidgeting and glancing at her watch every couple of minutes. Ian had said she'd be less conspicuous there. If anyone 'suspicious' came up the hill she was to follow and, if necessary, shoot them.

At eight o'clock she headed back to the lay-by, flashed her lights twice and pulled in. Almost immediately there was an answering flash from the moor. As she opened the boot she noticed that, as well as the spade, Ian was holding a shoe. He told her that it must have come off while he was raping the boy; he'd only noticed it while filling in the grave. Myra asked if he'd hurt John. Ian replied, no more than he had to. The point was to rape, kill and bury – it was the ultimate thing. He wasn't interested in hurting. Myra replied that he hurt her during sex. That was different, said

Ian, he wasn't doing the 'ultimate thing' to her. Then he changed the subject, complaining that the knife she'd bought was too blunt. He'd had to strangle the boy with string.

Back in Gorton, they fell to cleaning up. Everything had been planned so carefully that, even though it was only the second time they'd done it, it felt almost routine. Ian cut up his clothes and shoes and burned them alongside John's in the fireplace. He threw the small knife on top and wiped down the spade before putting it in the cupboard with the gun. The one 'improvement' lay in how they cleaned the car. Ian had covered almost every surface in plastic sheeting. Rolling this up and wiping down the surfaces was far faster than washing down every inch of carpet and upholstery. He and Myra threw buckets of hot, soapy water over the wheels and white paintwork. 'He was unusually forensically aware,' Geoff Knupfer, the former head of Greater Manchester CID, told me. 'Remember, this was the 1960s, and most people did not know about these things. The level of planning was quite extraordinary.'

When they had finished, Myra drank off a bottle of wine in one; Ian followed suit. The third bottle went down more slowly, and was followed by whisky chasers. Myra was still drunk when she dropped the Anglia back at Warren's Autos at nine the following morning. *Another* hangover, Gran shouted at her as she came in. Myra had to stop drinking so much; she was only twenty-one but looked old and haggard! Her mam and the Hills were right, that Ian Brady was no good. Myra told Gran to stop lecturing her. The old lady fell silent, handed her a cup of tea and some aspirin and encouraged her to go to bed.

It is clear from Myra's letters to me, and the different drafts of her autobiography, that the relationship with her family had lost all meaning. She went through the motions, did the least that was expected of her, but there was no longer any real emotional connection. Gran, Nellie and Maureen knew that there was something wrong, and that Ian was 'the cause'. But they had been unable to exercise any control over her as a child. Now that she was an adult they had no chance.

Myra and Ian read about John Kilbride's disappearance the following afternoon, as they sat on a bench in Sunny Brow Park, in the *Gorton and Openshaw Reporter*. The police were doing house-to-house enquiries, and they had sniffer dogs out. She gazed out over the lake, remembered playing there as a kid. Ian read from the paper: John Kilbride lived at 262 Smallshaw Lane; he went to St Damian's Church School; his father was from Ireland – they were all Catholics, breeding like animals. Myra ignored the jibe, but he continued: that was two fewer Catholics in the world today. Myra couldn't take any more. Her head was throbbing from the hangover, and she told him to shut up.

The talk about John Kilbride's disappearance was incessant. Myra, glad that it was busy at work, kept her head down and muttered noncommittally whenever anyone mentioned it. Gradually, as had happened after Pauline's disappearance, the story faded from the front pages then stopped appearing altogether. There was simply nothing new to write.

In a letter to me, Myra related how, soon after the killing of John Kilbride, she and Ian were sitting on the sofa in front of *Sunday Night at the London Palladium*. Bruce Forsyth's camp voice filled the room: 'I'm in charge!' Ian leant across to her and asked, 'What do you think I get out of doing what we've done?' Myra replied immediately that it was about being in charge, having the power of life and death. Ian smiled, said good, she knew where he was coming from. It was the same for her, wasn't it? I felt sure that Myra told me this story in order to explain Ian's motivation and how driven he alone was. But I found it unconvincing. She must also have been caught up in the feeling of power, and superiority, to continue helping him.

A few days later Ian told her to wrap up warm, they were going for a ride on the Tiger Cub. When he turned onto the Ashton Old Road she banged him frantically on the arm. The bike wobbled a little, but he ignored her. They sat on Smallshaw Lane, opposite the Kilbrides' house, for what seemed like an eternity. A small girl came to the gate and peered up and down the road. She didn't give them a second glance.

A couple of weeks later they went back to the moor. Ian took a picture of Myra squatting down, peering at the ground, holding her new dog Puppet wrapped inside her coat. She was on the grave of John Kilbride. They talked about killing, agreed that it put them 'in charge' and freed them from 'the confines of the working class'.

Professor MacCulloch put his notes down. 'They used very similar methods in both murders. They rehearsed each killing and took pictures on, or by, the graves afterwards. This could be a system.'

On New Year's Eve, 1963, Ian and Myra rode back up to the moor on the Tiger Cub. In her autobiography Myra recalled that he parked up in the lay-by next to John Kilbride's grave, held his whisky bottle to the full moon and said, 'To John!'

Chapter Six

'Duncan, these negs are absolutely filthy.'

Tim, the manager of Redcliffe Photographic Laboratories in Bristol, had to clean each of the images by hand. His cotton-gloved fingers were stained nicotine brown. He stared at them and grimaced.

'I've already had to throw one pair away!'

He pulled his gloves off and handed me a set of prints.

'I was on my own here last night. These really disturbed me.'

He was pointing to the shots of boys in football kit at Ryder Brow.

Ian Brady developed the pictures of John Kilbride's grave in his makeshift darkroom. He laid a towel over the crack below the door, to stop light leaking in, and tacked a heavy piece of material over the window.

Then he turned out the light. He was careful not to crease the film as he transferred it from its roll to a developing spool. It was a relief to be able to slide it into a tank, fasten the lid and turn the light back on. Then the comforting smell of chemicals: ten minutes for the developer; thirty seconds stop bath; four minutes fixer; twenty-minute rinse, just to be sure. He pulled down the material blocking out the light and a low evening sun angled into the room. Large square negatives dripped onto the floor. The one of Myra and Puppet was well exposed and sharp.

Outside his window, between Westmoreland Street and the Daisy Works, ran a path. Several nights a week Keith Bennett, his brother Alan and his sister Maggie walked along it on the way to their grand-mother's house. They spent the night there while their mother Winnie went out. Sometimes they walked close by Myra's van, parked up, waiting for Ian. She'd bought an Austin, kept it for a couple of months, and traded it in for a brand-new Mini pick-up.

Myra told me in a letter that on the evening of 18 June 1964 she drew up into her usual place, glanced around for any witnesses, and calmly pulled on the black wig. She felt at one with Ian; they stood on one side of a chasm that divided them from the rest of the world. They had stowed mementos of their killings in a suitcase at a left-luggage office. That morning he'd given her Roy Orbison's 'It's Over'.

Ian walked swiftly up to the Mini, climbed into the

back and they drove off. Keith had just turned off Stockport Road, where his mother left him on her way to 'the bingo', and was walking towards his grandmother's house. Myra said that the instant she saw him she knew that Ian was going to tap on the glass for her to stop. She pulled over, wound down the window and asked if he'd mind giving them a hand with some boxes. It was so easy, Myra thought. They trusted her just because she was a woman.

Now that Ian had found he preferred children, he wanted time with them. He led Keith more than a mile from the road to the confluence of Shiny Brook and Hoe Grain streams. It was their 'special place' where they came to shoot, picnic and have sex.

I followed Professor John Hunter down Hoe Grain. The moor at Shiny Brook is a constantly shifting world. Each change of light and tilt of the wind makes it feel different. The only constant is the fast babbling of water. The noise rises and falls with the rain, but never stops.

'It's a long way from the road, John.'

'Yes. But the better you know the terrain the easier it is to move across it. Even if you are leading someone who has never been here before.'

Myra followed Ian and Keith. She thought that the boy looked like a lamb going to the slaughter. Ian knew exactly where he was going; he had chosen the spot carefully and hidden a spade there. As they got close he motioned to Myra to climb the plateau that rises above Hoe Grain and Shiny Brook. She sat down there with her back to the stream and listened to the echo of the wind in the grass and the fast-running water. Off to her right she could see the tall, Stonehenge-like shape of Greystones.

After half an hour a high whistle pierced the sounds of the moor. She looked down and saw Ian waving for her to join him. They made their way back up Hoe Grain towards the car. On the way they buried the spade in the shale of the steep left-hand bank.

It was late when they got back to Gorton. They had to be at work the next day, so there wasn't much time to clean the car out. Ian wiped it down and burned their shale-scarred shoes. His had specks of blood on them. The last thing he threw on the fire was the thin cord he'd used to strangle Keith.

Myra dropped him back at Westmoreland Street, the twin-lens reflex hanging inside his coat. He'd taken a photograph and wanted to develop the film. The negative he pulled off the developing spool showed Keith lying in the peat. But Ian was disappointed, he later told Myra: the picture was out of focus. He showed it to her, and said he was going to burn it.

'There are pictures of her in this area,' John Hunter said.

'Yes,' I replied, 'they all show her on Shiny Brook. The two most easily identifiable are by the waterfall. There's one of her at the top and one at the bottom. The question is, are they significant?'

Hunter looked down at the fast-flowing stream. 'We don't know if they're markers, so I have decided to concentrate my search on gullies where Brady would have had complete cover to do what he wanted.'

It is only because Keith Bennett has never been found that his murder stands out from the others. Indeed, the most striking thing about the way Myra described it to me in her letters was the brevity of the account, and the language used. It was as if the routine was so well worn by now that its finer points no longer needed explanation. She was locked into the relationship with Ian Brady, mechanically going through the motions. It was just another murder.

Chapter Seven

While Nellie Hindley's dislike of Ian Brady was based on intuition, the loathing of her other daughter's fiancé, David Smith, was grounded in hard fact. Although only seventeen he already had a long criminal record: one stabbing, at the age of eleven, and three further counts of actual bodily harm. When David and Maureen got married at All Saints register office on 15 August 1964, she refused to attend. Ian and Myra stayed away too. He thought it best not to attract attention by being seen to approve of Smith. But Myra, as she related in a letter to me, wanted to avoid a rift. She arranged a day trip to the Lakes and a celebratory meal at a 'nice' hotel, with wine. Things they had never experienced before.

Myra drove, and Maureen sat next to her; Ian and David squatted in the back with bottles of wine. She looked in the mirror and could tell that they were getting very drunk. They were telling each other about the things they hated, crimes they had done time for. By the time the Mini pulled up outside the hotel the two men could hardly stand. She began to fear that admitting Smith to their world had been a mistake.

Myra and Maureen had grown closer with the passing of the years and the fading of their parents' divisive influence. On the way back to Manchester they talked about the future. Mo wanted to know why Myra didn't marry Ian; she replied that she didn't need a ring on her finger or a piece of paper to feel secure. Myra knew that Ian's love for her would never die. Maureen said she didn't feel that way at all. She was sure that now she and David were married he would 'settle down' and stop looking at other women. Myra tried not to show her feelings. She doubted that David Smith would be able to stay out of prison, never mind settle down.

Myra, Ian, David and Maureen saw more and more of one another. The routine never seemed to change: they all got blind drunk before 'the girls' retired to bed and 'the boys' slumped in armchairs, rambling away into the small hours. David confided that he beat Maureen; Ian told David that he hit Myra too, it was nothing to be ashamed of. He gave him a copy of de Sade's *Justine* to read. But there was a difference between the sisters' situations. Where Myra was a willing participant in a sexually sadistic relationship, Maureen was a victim. She was not hardened to violence and had no idea how to cope. Myra's mistrust of David Smith turned to dislike. She recorded in her autobiography how his violent behaviour led her to seek revenge.

One evening there was a hammering at the door. Myra pulled it open to see David standing there, dripping with rain. She demanded to know what he was after. He said that Maureen had run out on him, and was in hiding; Myra must know where she was. David's words gave Myra an idea, and she softened her tone. Moby had gone to Blackpool, she was on her way to see her, did he want to come? David swallowed, tried not to look too surprised, and nodded his head.

The Mini's small windscreen wipers lashed back and forth as the rain kept on coming, streaking down the glass and making it almost impossible to drive. Myra stayed silent: to do anything else would have aroused David's suspicion. When she thought he'd drifted off to sleep she kicked her heel hard against the base of the footwell. What was that knocking? she asked loudly, as though alarmed. David jerked to attention. Myra pulled down the left-hand indicator stalk and turned onto the hard shoulder. She told him to get out and listen by the front wheel while she revved the engine. David, still thinking about Maureen, did not see the trap. The instant he stepped onto the hard shoulder Myra floored the accelerator and roared off. She glanced over her shoulder and saw him, dumbstruck and soaking, staring after her.

In September 1964 a letter fell through the door at

Bannock Street: a notice of compulsory purchase by the council. The Corporation of Manchester was demolishing many of Gorton's oldest streets and moving their occupants to large new overspill estates on the fringe of the city. It was the latest fashion in 'town planning'. Myra and Gran were allocated a brand-new, pre-fabricated concrete house on the Hattersley estate. Gran was nervous. She was leaving almost all her friends behind. Her anxiety was eased only slightly by the news that the Hills – John, Maggie, May, Winnie and two married daughters with children – had all been allocated houses just across the road. Nellie helped Myra to get the house ready, installing a new cooker and curtains, before she and Gran moved in. Myra kept telling Gran that it would be like a home from home: she'd be able to bring Mam from Gorton to see her in the car. But Ellen knew things would never be the same, and fell into long silences. These were all but impenetrable when Ian was around.

Then Myra suggested that he move in; it would be 'a help with the bills'. It took a couple of trips to move all of Ian's stuff. Besides all of his photographic equipment there were the suits he'd had hand-made at Burton's to transport. He wasn't going to have them crushed, even if they were made from the latest crease-proof polyester. Life at Wardlebrook Avenue settled into an uneasy rhythm. Ian and Gran made an effort to be civil to each other but there was no warmth there. She saw the change he had wrought in Myra, and did not like it.

Forty years on, Hattersley is a desolate place. Manchester's social problems, removed from the centre of the city, have been accentuated by isolation. I went there the day after the community centre was burnt down. Many of the shops were boarded up, and the one newsagent open had a special offer on three-litre bottles of White Lightning cider. The small plastic signs on the lamp-posts, KILL YOUR SPEED NOT A CHILD, seemed like a tasteless joke. As I walked past the gap where number 16 stood until the council pulled it down, a shaven-headed, bare-chested man tumbled out of number 15 spitting four-letter words.

But Myra told me in a letter that she loved this place when it was new. For the first time in her life she had an 'upstairs bathroom'. The best thing was that you could see the countryside from Wardlebrook Avenue, imagine yourself in it. The hills above Hattersley are fringed with heather – the beginning of the moorland. Myra and Ian were out in the van all the time, exploring with their dogs Puppet and Lassie. It was a friendly road, and they worked hard to 'fit in'. Some people disapproved of them for 'living in sin', others were won over and allowed their children to go on 'excursions' with the young couple.

'They used to go out of their way to be friendly,' Carol Waterhouse, who was ten when Myra and Ian moved in next door, told me. 'I first met Myra when she came round to borrow an onion. That tells you how poor we were.' Ian and Myra offered their neighbours generous hospitality. 'My brother David and I used to wash the car out for money and sweets. They seemed so sophisticated. They drank wine. Well, for a working-class person like my mam to be invited in and offered wine was quite something. It just didn't happen.'

Most of the children from Hattersley who accompanied Ian and Myra on 'outings' to the moor remained anonymous. But Patti Hodges was later dragged into the glare of public scrutiny for one simple, horrific reason: she was taken to picnic by the grave of John Kilbride, at Hollin Brown Knoll. And Patti, as Myra Hindley revealed in her autobiography, was not alone. Carol and David Waterhouse were taken to the Shiny Brook area, where Keith Bennett died. When I spoke to Carol it turned out that the police had not been back with her since it was confirmed, in the mid-1980s, that Keith was a victim of the Moors murderers. I asked whether she would be willing to return with Professor John Hunter and his assistant, the former head of the West Midlands Police murder squad, Barrie Simpson.

Carol was nervous, but Barrie put her at ease, giving her time and allowing her to lead the way from the lay-by at the edge of the A635 onto the moor. As she picked her way over the rough tussock grass, Carol said, 'I'm looking for broad, yellow stones you can walk up the middle of the stream on.' She led Barrie, John and me down Hoe Grain to the confluence with Shiny Brook and turned right, towards the Wessenden Head reservoir. Nothing quite matched the picture in her memory. There were yellow stones, but it would have been impossible to navigate them, whatever the water level. She turned and headed back up Shiny Brook.

'How did they behave towards you?' asked Barrie.

'They were adults, but not like parents. That's what made them so attractive. She was quiet, he was chatty. He kept his sunglasses on all the time. We had a great day. This is it!'

We were heading upstream, towards the waterfall where Myra posed for two pictures.

'You can walk up the centre of the stream on the rocks. David and I stood in the middle and Ian took photographs. We all had a picnic together on the bank.'

'Can you remember exactly where?' asked Barrie.

'No, I'm afraid not. It's so long ago . . .'

Myra told me in a letter that Patti Hodges spent most of Christmas Eve 1964 with her and Ian in the lay-by at Hollin Brown Knoll. They got home in the small hours, shivering from the cold, and dropped Patti home. While Myra was banking up the fire in the front room, Ian made an announcement: he wanted to 'do another one'. They'd get the victim from a fairground he'd seen advertised on a booze run to the new Tesco at Newton Heath. He added that this time he wanted to bring 'it' back to the house so that he could take photographs. He could sell them.

The recklessness of the idea, and the speed with which Ian wanted to proceed with the murder, alarmed Myra. She felt that he was getting careless. She tried to dissuade him, but he would not be moved. At breakfast on Boxing Day, Ian gave Myra a copy of 'Girl Don't Come' by Sandie Shaw. It was the one part of their ritual he chose not to abandon. The song was about tears filling eyes, hurting inside, wanting to die.

They went over the final details of the killing in snatched conversations, making sure that Gran didn't overhear. He said they'd do the same as before: get 'it', a girl, to help carry some boxes back to the car, then make off without attracting any attention. Myra was surprised that he wanted a girl.

Myra drove Gran round to spend the day with relatives. Ian stayed at home to rig his camera lights in the upstairs bedroom. He hid his reel-to-reel tape recorder, microphone attached, under the sheet of the divan bed. When Myra got back they headed for the new Tesco and bought just too much shopping to carry comfortably.

In Myra's letters to me, the story of the fourth murder ended abruptly at this point, with the words, 'Thank God I'm out of space. That murder is the one which haunts me most. I'll try and write again over the weekend. Best wishes, Myra.' But she never did write about the killing of Lesley Ann Downey, or explain it to me in one of our regular telephone conversations. It was the case that led to her conviction and directly implicated her in an act of unspeakable cruelty. She did, however, talk about it to the police when she gave them a confession in early 1987.

The Stones' 'Little Red Rooster' was playing as they staggered between the rides at the fairground with their boxes of food and drink. Myra dropped her shopping next to a girl who appeared to be on her own. The girl bent down to help, told her that she was called Lesley Ann, and said she was ten. She called Myra Mam and Ian Dad. They had no trouble getting her into the car.

At Wardlebrook Avenue, Ian took the girl upstairs while Myra locked the dogs in the kitchen. She heard a scream and ran upstairs. He was trying to pull her coat off.

'Please, Dad, no!'

'Shut up!' Myra didn't realize Ian had already set the tape recorder running. She was worried people would hear, shut the window and switched on Radio Luxembourg to cover the noise.

After raping Lesley Ann, Ian strangled her, wrapped her in a bed sheet and put her in the back of the Mini. Myra glanced out of the window to check the weather. It was snowing, so she rang the AA. They told her only to travel if it was absolutely essential. Ian swore, furious at having to change the plan. They'd have to get Gran to stay the night at the relatives' house.

The following day they drove to the moor. Ian ran onto Hollin Brown Knoll with Lesley Ann slung over his shoulder. As Myra watched him she thought of the hours they had spent practising this routine – her hanging limp, like a corpse, while he learned how to move over the rough ground. He came back for the spade and buried the child in a shallow grave, sweeping a dusting of snow over the top to disguise it.

The photographs Ian took of the girl were far too strong to sell, never mind put in the album. Myra told me in a letter that she begged him to burn them. He refused, put the pictures in a suitcase, along with the tape recording, and stowed them under the bed. A few days later they went back to the moor and Ian took shots of Myra standing by the grave. Innocuous 'snaps' that would not stand out from the others in the tartan album.

'I'm struck by the consistent themes,' Malcolm MacCulloch said. 'Here is another murder that was carried out in a systematic, sadistic manner. Once again the burial location appears to have been selected beforehand, and recorded afterwards.'

'What does he get from the pictures?' I asked.

'He is reminded of the fact that he has committed the perfect murder, and that the bodies remain undiscovered. They are his possessions.'

* * *

Ian put a lock on the spare bedroom door after the murder of Lesley Ann. He used it to store his 'personal' things – mementos of the murders. Occasionally he'd get something out and show it to Myra. Ian tried to make the evidence less incriminating by hiding key parts of it outside the house. As well as the left-luggage office, he had taken to using a disused filing cabinet at Millwards. The coded body disposal plans hidden there would mean nothing without the names and photographs of the victims.

Four months after the murder of Lesley Ann Downey, David and Maureen's baby, Angela Dawn, was rushed to hospital and died. David and Maureen, their marriage already under strain, slipped into despair. Myra thought it might be better if they moved from Gorton to Hattersley, and helped to sort out a flat in Underwood Court, two minutes' walk away. Ian was delighted. He and David spent hours together in the upstairs bedroom, drinking and talking. Maureen told Myra that she was baffled by the books David was bringing home: *The Carpetbaggers*, *Kiss of the Whip*. He sat for hours in the front room copying out long extracts about child rape and sadism.

One night, Ian suggested that they all drive up to the moor together – it was a full moon, it would be beautiful. He told Myra to park in the lay-by where they had 'toasted' John Kilbride, then turned to David and suggested going for a walk as there was a fantastic moonlit view of the reservoir. David clambered out of the car and followed him a short distance onto the moor where they paused, in silence, to drink in the atmosphere. They were standing on the grave of John Kilbride.

Chapter Eight

Myra Hindley's old Olivetti typewriter broke while she was writing to me. I said I'd try to get it mended, and we arranged for a handover to take place at David Astor's house in St John's Wood. I sat with a coffee, chatting to his wife Bridget, while we waited for an unnamed courier to arrive.

After a short while Pat Hepburn, David Astor's secretary, put her head round the door. 'She's here. Could you go outside?'

I stood on the pavement and waited. On the other side of the road a short, dark-haired woman was bent over, rummaging in a car boot. She pulled out a black bin-liner, strode across, thrust it at me and turned without saying a word. I stood staring after her, wondering who she was – prison warder, lover, friend?

When I got back to my office I split the bin-liner open. The smell of Myra Hindley's prison cell escaped into the room – roll-ups and detergent. The Olivetti turned out to be broken beyond repair. I supplied a new machine, on long-term loan, and had it delivered.

Myra called me the following weekend.

'There's a problem, Duncan.'

'What, Myra?'

'They won't let me have the typewriter until it's been tested for safety by an electrician.'

'Oh no!' I groaned.

'Don't worry, I'll find a way round it,' she replied. 'And, Duncan?'

'Yes?'

'About this loan. You can have the machine back when I get out.'

I heard her laughter bouncing off the walls of the prison corridor.

The following week a tape arrived. I loaded it into my cassette machine and pressed play. She was speaking in a whisper, and had Radio 4 on in the background so that no one would discover her recording how Edward Evans came to die. Every now and then the story was punctuated by the sound of her dragging on a roll-up.

There was a knock at the front door, Myra began. It was David Smith, standing there clutching a letter from the council, looking sorry for himself. David told Myra it was an eviction notice; he and Mo had to be out by next Saturday. He'd used her sister's name to try to evoke sympathy. He wanted cash. Myra told him it was no good: she was broke, so was Ian. There was nothing they could do. But then Ian appeared at her shoulder and told David to come in. The men climbed the stairs to the spare bedroom. Myra dropped onto the settee and listened to the radio, fidgeting. She didn't trust Smith.

When Ian came downstairs, Myra recalled, he announced, 'We're going to roll a queer!' She had never heard the expression before, though it hardly needed explanation. She was deeply worried at Ian's recklessness. It had been safe when there was just the two of them. Myra understood that while she was in love with Ian, David Smith was in awe of him, and she did not feel that their bond was strong enough.

On 5 October 1965, David and Ian came down from the upstairs bedroom with two suitcases. Ian told Myra that he wanted her to take them to Central station. Didn't want anything incriminating in the house, did they? Myra demanded to know what was in them. Ian glared at her; she was showing him up in front of David Smith. He told her not to be so stupid. In the past Myra had trusted Ian to manage the evidence: keep what he wanted, destroy the rest. But now that Smith was involved she felt things were getting out of control. Ian was making mistakes, like Leopold and Loeb had done. Myra wanted to believe that there was a way of preserving what they had.

When they got home, Ian took Myra's mother-of-pearl prayer book out of the bottom drawer of the dresser. It was her confirmation present from Bert and

Kath. He slowly turned the book over. It had a latch
and lock to keep it shut – a symbol of virginity. Ian
smiled, pulled the left-luggage ticket from his pocket
and tucked it down the spine before replacing the
book on the shelf. Myra told Ian that she was worried
about Smith: he knew too much, they couldn't trust
him. In that case, asked Ian, should he kill him? It
would be easy. Myra said no, it would upset Maureen
too much.

The following morning they were sitting down to
breakfast when Ian held a flat, rectangular brown bag
out to her. 'Here you go, girl.' She looked at him. 'It's
All Over Now Baby Blue' by Joan Baez. The song
bothered Myra; it wasn't just the words about the dead
left behind, but the reference to the vagabond rapping
at the door, in the clothes she once wore. Ian was
teasing her about the involvement of David Smith.

Myra worried as they drove into town. She did not
want their world to end. Her mind was jerked back to
the present when a dog ran out into the road, its owners
looking on helplessly. The car ahead of them hit it.
Myra braked, opened the door and jumped out. Ian ran
after her. She found the animal whimpering in an alleyway and gently felt it all over for injury. The breathless
owners finally caught up with them. She offered to take
the dog to the vet – it was no trouble. Ian looked down.
The couple said no, he'd be fine, thanks anyway.

Myra parked the car outside Central station. Ian
got out, slammed the door and walked off to find a

victim. Myra noticed the assurance in his stride. Again, he knew exactly where he was going. Myra lost herself in thought about Smith. Maybe Ian should kill him once this was over. It would be for the best.

She was startled by a sharp rapping on the car window next to her head. A policeman stood there, motioning for her to wind it down. He told her she was parked on double yellow lines, she'd have to move. Myra apologized, and explained that she was waiting for her boyfriend. The officer replied that he was going to walk round the Theatre Royal block. If she was still here when he got back he'd have to book her.

A couple of minutes later Ian appeared with a slim, dark-haired teenager. He introduced Myra as his sister. The boy said he was called Eddie, Eddie Evans. He told them he was an apprentice and had just been to see Manchester United play Helsinki. Eddie had meant to go with his mate, Jeff, but he'd had to stay in to mind his sick mother.

At home, Ian opened a bottle of wine while Myra let the dogs out. They had planned this, to create a relaxing atmosphere. Eddie settled into his chair, and Ian motioned at Myra to go and get her brother-in-law. David answered the buzzer immediately and told Myra to come up. Maureen was in bed. David quickly pulled on his shoes and jacket. As he walked out of the door he picked up his heavy dog-walking stick. On the tape, Myra recorded that she asked David why he was taking it. He replied that he always did so at night. She replied, 'You're in the frame, you are.'

Myra told David to wait outside; she would signal for him to knock on the door by flashing a light. He did not have to wait long. Ian opened the door, greeted David, and asked him if he'd come for the miniature wine bottles. The men stepped inside; Myra went off to feed the dogs. Her hand was turning the can opener when there was a loud crashing and the sound of a chair flying across the living room. Myra looked through the serving hatch and saw Ian grappling with Edward Evans. She ran into the hall to find David standing by the front door. She shouted at him that they were fighting – he should go and help! Gran's voice quavered down the stairs, demanding to know what was going on. Nothing, replied Myra, she'd just knocked something over. Myra stood and guarded the bottom of the stairs as the scuffling subsided. It was replaced by the rhythmic thunk of Ian's axe going home.

When the house finally fell silent, Myra went into the front room. She had never seen such a mess: the walls were covered with blood. Ian stood there with the axe in his hand, hopping on one leg – he'd sprained his ankle. Edward Evans was too heavy for David to carry to the car on his own. They wrapped the body up in plastic sheeting and put it in the spare bedroom. David said he would come back the following evening with his dead daughter's pram to shift it. It took them hours to clean up all the blood. They did not finish until three in the morning.

Just a few hours later Myra got up to make Gran a cup of tea. When she came down Ian was sitting on the couch, with his sprained ankle up, writing a letter to Tommy Craig to say that he would not be in that day. He looked up sharply at the sound of a knock on the back door. Myra opened it to a bread delivery man wearing a white jacket with Sunblest on the pocket.

'You've got the wrong house, we have Mother's Pride,' she said.

'I'm a police officer. Is the man of the house in?'

Myra realized immediately that David had shopped them. Superintendent Bob Talbot walked into the room to find Ian sitting, with his foot up, in the front room. Uniformed officers swarmed through the house. Talbot demanded the key to the back bedroom.

'I've no idea where it is,' said Myra.

'Give him the key,' said Ian.

Had Ian Brady been content with committing the perfect murder he would probably have got away with it. But, perhaps inevitably, turning fantasy into reality gave him a thirst for more, and Myra's complicity made it possible for him to keep on killing. But repetition bred boredom, and the only way to reinvigorate himself was to take ever greater risks. Ian and Myra may have been cleverer than Leopold and Loeb, but in the end it was the same thing that brought them down: hubris. Their defiance of the gods was far from over.

Book Three
Prison

'Dear Mam . . . keep all the photos for us, <u>for reasons</u>, the one of dogs, scenery etc . . .'

Chapter One

The last thing I lifted out of the car boot and carried down to my office was a clutch of bulging supermarket carrier bags. I moved carefully as the plastic was so old it had begun to break down; it felt tissue thin. I laid the bags on my desk and looked round. Every available surface was covered with Myra Hindley's personal effects. In order to get at what mattered I was going to have to sort through a lot of detritus.

'She was a hoarder,' Father Michael Teader told me. 'She lived in prison but longed to be outside. Every scrap of paper or small gift was a connection with the real world.'

I pulled the lid off a faded Quality Street tin. It was filled to the rim with old 45s – Joan Armatrading, Tim Hardin, Joan Baez. At the bottom of a Tesco bag, rattling around among dozens of old cassette tapes, was an old pair of large-framed eighties-style reading glasses. In another carrier were fifteen-year-old Christmas cards from people she had never met, but whose words had moved her in some way. Many were religious and contained quotations from the Bible, or poems full of hope. There was a card from 1990 with a picture of a cartoon cat hanging upside down. The inscription read, 'Hang on! You're almost there! This year is the beginning of a new decade – it will be a time for you.' Something about the way the card was signed, with smiley faces, made me think that it had come from a lover.

Balanced on top of my photocopier were box upon box of legal documents – a record of every twist and turn in an increasingly desperate campaign for freedom. Tucked inside a sheaf of papers to her solicitor was a letter, written in an uneven hand, begging for information about the whereabouts of Keith Bennett. It was written by the missing ten-year-old's stepfather, Jimmy Johnson. 'All the bodies of the victims have been found except our son, Keith . . . please help us, Myra.'

I reached inside an old Woolworth's bag and pulled out a thick wad of paper covered in small, neat handwriting. The pages had darkened with age but the words were clearly legible. I was astonished at the contents. In my hands were the letters Myra Hindley had written to her mother over a period of thirty-six years in gaol. The change in paper size marked the passing of the decades: black-lined, folded A5 sheets in the 1960s and 1970s; blue-lined, flat A6 sheets in the

1980s and 1990s. The prison paper seemed to get cheaper with the passing of the years, but the heading on the letters never changed: M. Hindley, 964055.

I started reading, and did little other work for the next three weeks. I discovered that the letters from Myra to Nellie have the value of a diary. The contours of a story appear fixed when captured from a single point in time; set that same story alongside a day-by-day record and the way it has been shaped emerges. Each shift in loyalty, change in circumstance is laid bare.

'Almost every one of these letters contains an instruction for it to be destroyed,' said Malcolm MacCulloch. He was skimming through the four bound volumes I had made for him. The professor ran his finger down the page, using the index to skip straight to key events. 'How did you get hold of them?'

'Nellie ignored Myra's instructions,' I replied. 'They have been passed on in case they are of any use in resolving the case.'

MacCulloch paused, then said, 'So at the time Myra Hindley wrote her autobiography, and the letters to you, she had no idea that her own, contemporaneous account still existed?'

'No.'

'Excellent, excellent.'

Records locked in a vault beneath Greater Manchester Police headquarters explain why officers did not arrest

Myra straight away. They had a body, a prime suspect and a witness. It was difficult to know what to make of the rest of Smith's story – robberies, guns, bodies on the moor. Given his history of violence they were certainly not going to take it at face value. He might even have killed Evans himself.

Myra Hindley's arrest, interrogation and prosecution are also recorded in her autobiography. When the police cuffed Ian to take him to the station, she demanded to go too. The reality of the situation hadn't sunk in. The officer in charge, Superintendent Bob Talbot, agreed; he had 'a few questions' for her anyway. Then Myra remembered Ellen. She said she was going to have to get one of the neighbours to look after her, and asked if she could tell them she'd 'run someone over'. The bewildered policeman agreed, so Myra scooped Gran up and took her round to the Hills'. Neither Maggie nor May believed the story about an accident: her Mini was parked, undamaged, on Wardlebrook Avenue. And there were far too many police around for that.

In the back of the panda car, on the way to the station, Myra remembered Ian's words: 'Say nothing.' Puppet rocked back and forth on her lap as she stared out of the window. The strategy held up until she was in an interview room, facing Constable Philomena Campion. I found a verbatim record of this conversation, and all the police interviews, at the National Records Archive.

'This morning the body of a man was found at your house. Who is that person?'

'I don't know, and I am not saying anything. Ask Ian. My story is the same as Ian's.'

'What is the story of last night?'

Myra told the policewoman that they had bought some wine and been for a picnic at Glossop. The officer let her go on, then gently steered her back to events at Wardlebrook Avenue.

'All I'm saying is I didn't do it and Ian didn't do it. We are involved in something we did not do. We never left each other, we never do. What happened last night was an accident and it should never have happened.'

Philomena Campion softened her approach to try to get Myra to open up. 'It is in your interests to tell the truth of what did happen,' she said.

The police were suspicious of Myra's sullen defensiveness. But it was possible that her behaviour was born out of loyalty to Ian, rather than guilt. In order to weaken her resolve they left her 'to stew' for a few hours.

Meanwhile, the forensic team worked its way slowly through the house at Wardlebrook Avenue, taking samples: carpet, cigarette butts, dog hair. One officer was given the job of lacing up and playing every one of the tapes they found with the two Philips machines: a recording of *The Goon Show*, a speech by Winston Churchill, a man, woman and child talking.

Superintendent Talbot flicked slowly through the pages of a tartan-covered photograph album. Days out. Family snaps, endless shots of dogs – it looked innocent enough, almost too innocent. The house was full of photographic equipment: an enlarger, safe-lamps, rows of chemicals, stacks of trays, 149 negatives, 170 prints. There might just be a connection to the killing here, he thought. He clapped the album shut, and tucked it under his arm.

In the afternoon, eight hours after the discovery of Edward Evans, a Home Office pathologist climbed the narrow stairs to the spare bedroom at Wardlebrook Avenue. Charles St Hill found the body trussed up in plastic sheeting, just as Ian had left it. The doctor gingerly lifted up the three books on the victim's head: *Tales of Horror, Among Women Only (La Dolce Vita – Love and Sensation in Post-war Italy)* and a children's book, *The Road Ahead*. He cut the string holding the polythene wrapping in place, and carefully removed it. Superintendent Bob Talbot and Chief Superintendent Arthur Benfield watched in silence. The unease they'd felt at the sight of the books only increased when the doctor pointed out a ligature round the victim's neck. It looked as though it had been put there *after* the fatal blows to the skull. The scene bore the hallmarks of ritual, not a spontaneous killing after a fight.

Ian sat there, calm and in control, when Arthur Benfield came in. The policeman had never seen any-one arrested on suspicion of murder behave that way.

Ian was captivated by dramatic landscapes.

Ian in a photograph
that Myra said
marked the grave of
Pauline Reade.

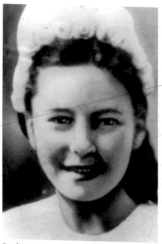

Pauline Reade. Disappeared 12 July 1963, aged sixteen; body recovered 1 July 1987.

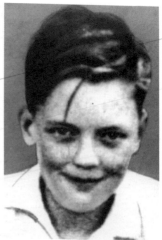

John Kilbride. Disappeared 23 November 1963, aged twelve; body recovered 21 October 1965.

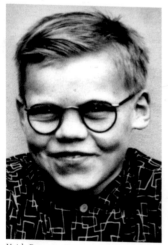

Keith Bennett. Disappeared 16 June 1964, aged twelve; still missing.

Lesley Ann Downey. Disappeared 26 December 1964, aged ten; body recovered 16 October 1965. (*Rex Features*)

Edward Evans. Disappeared 6 October 1965, aged seventeen; body recovered 7 October 1965. (*Rex Features*)

Ian Brady. Arrested 7 October 1965. (*Empics*)

Myra Hindley. Arrested 11 October 1965.

A furious relative is restrained as the Moors murderers arrive at court.

Police search the moor, using rods to probe the ground, after Myra and Ian's arrest.

Scores of ordinary people queue to see the accused.

A special dock was constructed at Chester Assizes to protect the defendants from attack.

Ann West (*right*), mother of Lesley Ann Downey, at Lesley's funeral (*above*).

Myra, photographed using the camera of her lover Trisha Cairns, shortly before her failed escape attempt from Holloway prison. Myra and Trisha planned to work as missionaries in South America.

Below left Myra poses in front of a copy of *Papillon* – the story of a prisoner's amazing escape.

Below right Myra in 'graduation pose' after receiving an Open University degree in the humanities.

Myra and Trisha made impressions of Holloway's keys in Camay soap and plaster of Paris. The teapot, PG Tips box and clock were used to hide the escape kit. (*TNA UK*)

Police photographs of Myra's first-floor cell, and the wing along which she and Trisha planned to escape. (*TNA UK*)

Above Alan Bennett (*left*) and Professor John Hunter (*second right*), searching for Keith's body.

Above right Alan Bennett and the former head of West Midlands murder squad, Barrie Simpson, pause for a cigarette.

Above Peter Topping's team abandoned the search for Keith Bennett two months after the discovery of Pauline Reade.

The Bennett brothers: left to right, Alan, Ian and Keith, shortly before Keith's murder.

The transcript of the interview shows that he was determined to find out why.

'Inside the wallet are several pieces of paper on which are written certain words and abbreviations. Would you care to tell me what they mean?'

'Yes,' replied Ian. 'That was the plan for the disposal of Eddie. We planned that after it had happened. We sat up doing it.'

'What does "Det" mean?' asked Benfield.

'Details,' Ian replied.

'Stn?'

'Stationery.'

'Hat?'

'Hatchet.'

On and on Ian went, so confident that he might have been in charge of the interview. He laid everything on Smith, trying to protect Myra.

The hours dragged by as Myra waited to see Ian; she needed to get instructions, it had all been so rushed. Just before nine p.m. the policewoman assigned to her, Philomena Campion, came back with Dr Ellis, the police surgeon. She told Myra the doctor had come to take some 'samples': nail clippings, saliva, blood, hair and pubic hair. Pubic hair? Myra was outraged, but the police constable stood firm and she had to relent.

When the doctor left they let Nellie and Bert in; the hope was that they might 'bring her to her senses'. The police gave the family a few minutes, then had another go at breaking Myra's resolve. Arthur Benfield, with Philomena Campion at his side, used a firm, fatherly approach.

'Do you wish to say anything to me about what happened last night?' he asked.

'No, not until you let me see Ian first.'

'He's been charged and will be up in court in the morning.'

Myra refused to respond. They decided to let her go. There was no evidence that she had helped to kill Evans.

Myra told me, on tape, that Bert took her back to Reddish for the night. He and Kath questioned her closely about what had happened and were not satisfied by the answers. They tried to persuade her to 'come clean', to look after her own interests, but she wouldn't listen. The following morning she left the bungalow to return to the police station with something approaching a sense of relief.

Myra was desperate to see Ian, and she hovered in the court doorway hoping to catch his eye as he was led in. He appeared from the cells below, with a policeman on each arm. When their eyes met he turned to the officer at his side and asked whether he and Myra could share solicitors – he'd thought she was going to be charged too. The policeman recorded the slip and passed it on to his boss.

Ian was charged, and remanded to Risley. Myra was pulled straight back in for questioning by Arthur

Benfield. She was furious that she hadn't been able to see Ian, get the story straight. They'd planned all the other murders so carefully. If only it hadn't been for David Smith.

'Ian and I didn't do it, and I didn't do it,' she blurted out, then sat there, square-jawed, staring at the superintendent and ignoring Constable Campion.

'Well, who did?' he asked.

'I am saying nothing else until I have seen Ian's solicitor.'

Frustrated, and mystified, the police again decided to let her go. Myra agreed to come back on Monday, after she'd seen Robert Fitzpatrick, Ian's solicitor.

On the Saturday morning, Myra told me in a letter, she and her mother carried a large bag of washing to the launderette opposite Millwards. While Nellie stuffed clothes into a machine, Myra crossed the road to work. Tommy wasn't in yet, but the office fire was burning in the grate; Myra realized that the cleaner must have been in. She walked quickly through the main building to the store at the back. This was where the records to the orders were kept – Ian's domain. She riffled through the files until she found what she wanted – the body disposal plans.

Myra knew it was only a matter of time before she was arrested. They were bound to find the ticket to the left-luggage locker. Why the hell had he hidden it down the back of her confirmation prayer book? One by one she fed the papers into the fire, made sure that they crumpled in the heat and turned to ash. Mesmerized by the flickering light, she wondered if she would have to go to prison for long. When Tommy arrived Myra asked him to sack her. He refused, said he was sure that whatever had happened was nothing to do with her and the typing job would be kept open until everything had been 'sorted out'. What about Ian? Myra asked. That was a different matter, replied Tommy. He'd have to go.

On Monday, 11 October 1965, Myra got off the bus in Stalybridge, crossed the street to the police station and reported to the desk sergeant. She performed each action mechanically, her mind incapable of turning itself from Ian. His solicitor, Robert Fitzpatrick, was waiting for her. The interview was halting; she did not know what to say, did not have her instructions. She told the baffled lawyer that she agreed with whatever Ian had said. Afterwards they took her back to Hyde and hurled questions at her. She sat there in stony silence, refusing to answer. Superintendent Benfield told her they had all the evidence they needed. There was Evans's body, Smith's confession, and she and Ian hadn't been as clever with the clean-up as they thought. There was a blood-stained cigarette butt in front of the fireplace, blood splatter on her shoes. How was she going to explain that? Why didn't she help herself by telling the truth? At three o'clock, WPC Campion and Superintendent Benfield watched in exasperated silence as DS Carr read out the inevitable words: 'Myra Hindley, I am charging you with being an accessory after the fact in the murder of Edward Evans.'

Myra's first ever letter to me recorded the events which followed. They took her out of the room and led her down the grand stone steps at the centre of the police station, one WPC on each arm, a plainclothes detective walking ahead. He pushed open a pair of swing doors and led the group down another staircase. Stone turned to concrete, daylight to tungsten. Instead of offices they were now passing cells. The corridor was so narrow that the officers had to bunch together as they pushed Myra along. Then the detective stopped, turned to his left and kicked open a re-inforced wooden door. They led her to a chair in the middle of the room and pushed her down. Myra told me that she thought she was going to be interrogated, and clenched her teeth defiantly in expectation of a slap. Instead, there was a blinding flash of light – a police photographer had captured her image. On the way back up the stairs, Myra wrote, the WPC holding her left arm leant towards her. 'Come on, love. If you stick up for him you'll go down for ever. He's a man; he probably made you do it . . .'

Re-reading this letter, I reflected on why Myra chose to begin her story with the taking of her arrest photograph. It is clear that she recognized the power of the picture, and all that it symbolized. She needed to demolish this image in order to convince people that she was bullied into the killings by Ian Brady, and win her freedom. If only she'd known it was coming, she was saying, she'd have struck a different pose and the world might have seen her as she really was.

The red and white brickwork of what was once Hyde's municipal heart – a combined town hall, magistrates' court and police station – looms over the market place. It is a decaying symbol of Victorian rectitude. I told the caretaker what I was doing and he let me into the derelict area once inhabited by Cheshire Constabulary, deep beneath the building, where Myra Hindley and Ian Brady were held.

'Why is it like this?' I asked.

'The council don't know what to do with it. Been this way for years.'

A string of sixty-watt bulbs led the way down below ground through narrow, dusty corridors, pale orange in the tungsten light. The paint on cell doors had peeled and cracked; their name-plates were empty. I pushed one open. The walls were covered in grubby white tiles, and cobwebs breathed in and out at the barred windows. The cells had stood empty for years, a monument to Manchester's shame. From the abandoned monastery of St Francis to the clumsy omission of Myra Hindley's name from picture captions, it was the same. No one quite knew how to deal with the legacy of the Moors murders. It was painful to admit that they had happened, but impossible to consign them to history for the case was still alive: a mother still yearned to bury her missing son, and refused to fade away until she had done so.

Detective Chief Inspector Joe Mounsey, police records show, was troubled by Ian Brady's negatives. Why had he kept them all? The ones of Myra and him posing in front of the Mini were easy enough, but what about the empty stretches of moor? David Smith's words about there being 'other bodies' washed into his mind and would not recede. Lying on the desk was a notebook that PC Roy Dean had found at Wardlebrook Avenue. It was full of scrawls, doodles and names: 'John Birch, Frank Wilson, Alec Guineas, *John Kilbride . . .*' There was also a receipt for the hire of a white Ford Anglia on 23 November 1963, the day the twelve-year-old boy had disappeared from Ashton market. Mounsey called the photographic officer, Ray Gelder, and asked him to print up the negatives, see if he could find out where they had been taken.

In her autobiography, Myra recorded that she and Ian travelled in different cars to Risley. They may have been separated, but there was a sense of relief in knowing that they were going to the same place. Ian had given her a look at the remand hearing that told her to keep quiet – they only had the one body. The connection between them felt unbreakable; if anything, what was happening strengthened it.

The officer on reception demanded to know her religion. Myra took a while to reply: none. The officer sighed and wrote 'C of E' in the ledger. Did she have any birthmarks? No. What was that behind her right ear then? Myra apologized, she'd forgotten it was there. Did she have any false teeth? Myra asked if the officer was joking – she was only twenty-three! They had to ask, came the weary reply. People often took them out to hide fag stumps in their gums.

They put Myra in a room on the hospital wing, away from the other prisoners. The next morning she woke early, instantly aware of where she was, and stared at the prison uniform draped across the back of the chair: two grey skirts, two brown blouses, thick lisle stockings with a seam, baggy knickers, a suspender belt and a bra. She was desperate to go to the toilet but couldn't face the humiliation of the chamberpot under the bed.

Myra got dressed and fiddled with the stockings, trying to get the seams straight, while she waited for breakfast. Eventually, the cell door cracked open and an officer handed her a small brown envelope. It was very thin, and had no stamp on it. Myra turned her back on the guard, slipped her nail under the flap, and tore it open. It was Ian's 'reception' letter – every prisoner was allowed one on their first day. She read it over and over, smudging the black ink with her tears. He wrote that she'd be out in no time, but he was going to get life. It was not something he could face – three months in Strangeways had been enough – and she'd have to be brave *like Emmy*. The last two words chilled her heart. The actress Emmy Sonnemann was married to Hitler's deputy, Hermann Goering. On 15 October 1946, rather than be hanged – the Allies had refused him permission to be shot – the head of the Luftwaffe crushed a cyanide capsule between his teeth. Emmy was released from Straubing prison in March 1946 and lived on until 1973. 'My influence will pall,' Ian wrote, 'and you can begin a new life.' But Myra knew that she could never let him go. He ended the letter 'I love you.' It was the first time he had openly expressed the sentiment.

Myra asked the governor for an 'inter-prison' visit before their next court appearance, in three days' time. She whiled the hours away acquiring the skills that women at Risley taught one another: how to use cigarettes as currency, forge a cheque and carry out an abortion.

Myra described that first 'visit' with Ian in her auto-biography. She walked into the room, and he smiled at the sight of her in prison clothes. He was wearing a smart three-piece suit. She just sat there, drinking in the sight of him. They were separated by a sheet of glass, and a guard stood at each of their shoulders. Didn't she know, he asked, that there was no need to wear prison clothes as she hadn't been convicted? Myra replied that she did, but she wanted to preserve her smart clothes for court; they'd only get messed up doing the prison cleaning. They made small talk and tried to appear relaxed so that the guards would get bored and start thinking about what they were having for tea or what was on the telly. Ian told her she'd go mad if all she did was talk to the other women. She had to keep her mind outside; she should order books from the prison library. Suddenly, he asked if she'd got the luggage ticket. The guards looked as though they had drifted off. No, whispered Myra, she hadn't been able to get back in the house. Ian's face barely registered an expression – he did not want to attract the guards' attention. She told him that she had been able to get the stuff at Millwards though. He nodded to show his pleasure, and swiftly changed the subject.

Detectives hadn't found the ticket yet, but they had been told by David Smith that Ian and Myra hid evidence at a left-luggage office. British Transport Police went through Manchester's stations looking for a locker containing two cases – one brown, one blue. On Friday, 15 October, they tracked them down at Manchester Central. The contents confirmed Joe Mounsey's suspicions: the killing of Edward Evans was not a one-off.

The brown case contained nine pictures of Lesley Ann Downey, naked, with a scarf tied around her mouth. Her limbs had been arranged in a succession of pornographic poses; the negatives were in a halibut liver oil tin. There were also two tape spools. Police records show that the red leader on one was damaged;

Superintendent Bob Talbot watched as a technician replaced it with new, yellow, tape and laced it up. Ian's voice boomed out, 'This is Green track one.' Music filled the room. 'This is Green track two'– a recording of *The Goon Show*. 'This is Green track three' – a commentary by the BBC announcer Freddie Grisewood. 'This is Green track four':

CHILD: (*screaming*) Don't, Mum – ah!
WOMAN: Shut up!
CHILD: Please, God, help me. Ah. Please. Oh.
WOMAN: (*whispering*) Come on.
　　　　(*Footsteps.*)
WOMAN: (*whispering*) Shut up.

The recording was just thirteen minutes long, but the officers in the room never forgot it.

Professor Malcolm MacCulloch asked to hear the tape when he was treating Ian Brady and working with the police to find Pauline Reade and Keith Bennett in the mid-1980s. 'There's no element on that tape which betrayed any sympathy towards a little girl who was plainly in great fear,' he said. 'No sympathy whatsoever. It's brusque, aggressive, commanding, tough, impatient. It's very distressing to listen to.'

The tape galvanized the police into action. A team of officers worked its way down Wardlebrook Avenue questioning every man, woman and child. They all said the same thing: he was a bit aloof, she was friendly, great with kids. Then officers knocked on the door of number 12, and Elsie Hodges answered. Oh yes, her Patti was always out with Ian and Myra. Detectives interviewed the small, frightened girl. Her witness statement explains that the first 'outings' with Myra were to pick up Ian from Longsight. They waited for him in the van down a little side street just off the Stockport Road. Myra had told her she didn't like to go in because Mrs Brady kept her chatting for too long. After a couple of weeks Myra suggested a trip to the moors. Patti thought it was a great idea.

The police were already digging on the Moors, acting on Ian Brady's 'landscapes' and David Smith's claim that there were bodies buried in the peat. The *Manchester Evening News* splashed the story under the headline POLICE IN MYSTERY DIG ON MOORS. Myra heard the news on the canteen radio. But the police team was at Woodhead Pass, eight miles from Saddleworth.

When DC Clegg and WPC Slater drove Patti out of Manchester on the A635 she told them that she, Ian and Myra went to Saddleworth, not Woodhead. They climbed out of Greenfield, up the steep hill and round the left-hand bend that took them onto the moor. That was it! The little girl was quite sure. That lay-by was where they'd parked, by the road sign warning of a dangerous bend ahead. The landscape matched the pictures in the tartan album.

* * *

The taxi driver, Myra recorded in her autobiography, was silent all the way from Risley to Hyde. On the outskirts of town the prison officer sitting next to her turned and suggested she pull her scarf up over her hair. Myra was startled. Why on earth should she do that? There may well be photographers, said the officer; the case had been getting a lot of attention. Silently, Myra pulled the material up and over her head. As the driver swung sharply left through the back entrance of Hyde Magistrates' Court and the flash bulbs exploded, she ducked and stared at her feet.

Ian squeezed her hand as they sat in the dock. The remand hearing was short, the atmosphere low key. They both pleaded not guilty, and the magistrate ordered them to be held for another seven days. The proceedings hardly seemed to matter to Myra. She was looking forward to seeing Ian afterwards with Mr Fitzpatrick.

Robert Fitzpatrick was a partner in a local solicitor's practice, more used to divorce and conveyancing than murder. The lawyer met them after the hearing, in Hyde police station canteen; officers were moving about on the other side of the serving hatch. He told them that they couldn't possibly have joint legal visits; it was unusual enough to have the same solicitor! They had to, Myra said. Mr Fitzpatrick insisted: they would need different defences. Ian told him that they wanted the same defence. Reluctantly, the solicitor agreed. When the meeting was over he slid down the bench to allow them a few minutes alone together.

In her autobiography Myra recalled the words she spoke to Ian. 'I love you!' she said. 'I've always loved you and wanted to tell you so much that I did. You told me you loved me in your letter. I can actually say it to you now. I love you.' Ian, she wrote, replied, 'I love you too.'

Police records reveal that the search party arrived on Saddleworth Moor at 9.30 a.m. on 16 October 1965. An aerial photograph shows how Detective Chief Inspector Mounsey and Detective Inspector Mattin spread their men out: one party to the left of the A635, one to the right. The officers hacked at the peat all morning, slowly working their way further onto the moor. They tested the ground ahead of them by jabbing in long sticks, 'tamping rods', and smelling them for signs of corruption. The work was slow and frustrating. After lunch, Joe Mounsey decided that he and Norman Mattin should return to Manchester. Detective Sergeant Eckersley could always send for him if they found anything.

The day's searching was drawing to a close, just before four p.m., when Constable Bob Spiers wandered a little deeper onto the moor to relieve himself. As he stood there he spotted something sticking out of the ground – bone. Sergeant Eckersley ordered his men to dig out a small test pit before sending for Joe Mounsey. No, he told him when he arrived, it definitely wasn't a sheep.

Lesley Ann Downey's exhumation was carried out under the supervision of the pathologist, Professor Poulson. The body was buried so close to the surface that half of it had decomposed, and part of the forearm was missing. Wild animals, probably. The operation was recorded by photographic officer Ray Gelder. Every now and then he was called forward to take a picture. He worked with the rapid skill that comes from years of experience, but his mind kept wandering. There was something about the photographs Joe Mounsey had given him. He moved away from the burial party until it was framed by the landscape, with the hills in the background, and took a series of pictures. He was standing in the same place Ian had stood to take his 'landscapes'.

Myra walked into the interview room. Chief Superintendent Arthur Benfield sat behind a large table, the two cases open in front of him. His fatherly manner, police records show, had gone. 'What is this?' he asked, tossing the black wig on the table. Myra remained silent. 'And this?' A photograph of Lesley Ann Downey. And this, and this, and this, and this, and this? Benfield scattered the contents of the cases in front of Myra, who remained silent.

'Please, Mam, no!'

Myra's head jerked up. They were playing the tape. She listened in silence. Thirteen minutes later the machine stopped. Benfield fired questions at her but she just sat there shaking her head, saying nothing.

As I read through the police accounts of the interviews, and her own recollections, I was amazed at Myra Hindley's resilience. It's one thing to live a lie, quite another to maintain it under skilled and determined interrogation. 'It's the same toughness that made it possible for her to carry out the crimes in the first place,' Malcolm MacCulloch told me. 'It is very, very unusual.'

The paper rocked to and fro in the developing tray, under the glow of a red safe-light. Detective Constable Peter Mascheder watched intently as chemical reacted with silver halide. Myra Hindley, clutching Puppet in her arms, slowly appeared. The officer used tongs to drag the paper first into the stop bath, then the fixer. He had to force himself to leave it long enough. Two minutes later he held the dripping sheet in his hands. Ray Gelder had been right about the neg: she was staring at the ground instead of the dog. He plunged the sheet into the washer and went to find Joe Mounsey.

Ian sat with his head bowed as the tape played; DCI Haigh was taking notes, Chief Superintendent Benfield and Superintendent Talbot were watching.

Police records contain a transcript of the ensuing conversation.

'You know the tape,' said Superintendent Benfield. 'The voices appear to be those of yourself and Myra, and, I believe, that of Lesley Ann Downey, whose photograph you admit taking.'

Ian replied, 'She didn't give the name of Downey, it was something else.'

The officers were stunned by the coldness of his reaction. In order to try to jolt him, Benfield threw the dead girl's shoes and socks onto the table.

'Look at these photographs. Do you agree that the shoes and socks on the photographs are similar to these?'

It didn't work. Ian continued to deny all involvement. He'd 'only' taken the pictures, not killed the girl.

At eleven a.m. on Thursday, 21 October, Peter Mascheder faced north on Saddleworth Moor and held the photograph of Myra and Puppet in the air, trying to line it up with the hills behind. Joe Mounsey stared intently at him. Mascheder nodded – this was it. Even the rocks at Myra's feet were in the same place.

Detective Inspector John Chaddock of the West Riding Constabulary walked up to the two men. His witness statement records what followed. Mounsey told him to look at the stones and at the picture. His meaning was clear. Chaddock leant forward and put the tip of a probe between two of the stones; he pushed the rod into the peat, then withdrew it. The stench of decomposing flesh was unmistakable. The officers fell to the ground and scraped at the bare peat. Nine inches down they discovered a boy's black shoe and, beneath it, a foot. They had found the body of John Kilbride.

Superintendent Bob Talbot stood in the front room at Wardlebrook Avenue. The boots Myra had worn on the grave of John Kilbride lay bagged up by his feet. In his hands was a white prayer book – an odd discovery among the sexually sadistic material Ian had used to fuel his fantasies. He flipped the gold catch and read the inscription: 'To Myra, from Auntie Kath and Uncle Bert, 16th November, 1958.' It was a souvenir of her first Holy Communion. He feathered the pages and held the book up to the window so that the light spilled down the spine. There was something there. Talbot banged the book against the palm of his hand, dislodging a tightly rolled piece of paper. He unrolled it: British Railways Board left-luggage ticket No. 74843. The depositor had chosen not to fill out his name.

Ian and Myra's court appearances, she recorded in her autobiography, soon turned from administrative routine into public theatre. The roar of the crowd crashed against the walls of Hyde Magistrates' Court. Mostly, the competing cries of 'Hang them!' 'Bitch!'

and 'Bastard!' drowned one another out. But the occasional voice made its way through, bounced off the wood panels of the courtroom and echoed down the corridors of the police station. Everyone was on edge – everyone, that is, apart from Ian and Myra. They were completely unmoved as the magistrate remanded them for another week.

Their solicitor, Robert Fitzpatrick, tried to talk strategy with them in the police canteen afterwards, but he had difficulty concentrating. The people beyond the walls were his people and they might find it hard to understand why he continued to represent Ian and Myra. It was no great surprise when one of the uniformed officers on escort duty interrupted to say that they needed to go – it was getting far too dangerous.

Myra sat up and peered through the window of the Black Maria as it pulled out of the back gates. Fists hammered on the sides of the van. Ian smiled at her as she slumped back down, blowing her cheeks out. It was then that she realized something was up: the van had turned the wrong way for Risley. A wave of indignation built in her as the vehicle was driven to the outskirts of Ashton. A few minutes later it roared through the gates of the police station.

It had obviously been carefully planned. They were led to separate interview rooms as soon as they arrived. Waiting for Myra were Detective Inspector Mattin and Detective Chief Inspector Jack Tyrell. The police transcript of the interview shows that they wanted to know about the photographs.

'What were you looking at?' asked Tyrell.

'I was looking at the snow or the dog,' replied Myra.

'Who chose the place where you would kneel?'

'No one. We just took a photograph where we felt like it.'

Myra was sweating heavily. The officers thought it was nerves, but she had Ian's letters stuffed down the back of her skirt, underneath a heavy mohair coat. There was no way she was going to leave them in the cell.

They went on and on, showing her the photographs only she and Ian knew had been taken in front of Pauline Reade's grave. They also showed her the pictures taken around the grave of Lesley Ann Downey. But Myra wound the detectives up, deliberately misunderstanding the simplest of questions, playing stupid about where the shots had been taken or who had taken them. It was exasperating, but the policemen refused to rise to the bait.

'This photograph is taken very close to the grave of Lesley Ann Downey,' said Tyrell, 'and the spot you are looking at there is the grave of John Kilbride.'

'As far as I am concerned they are two normal photographs that I have had taken,' said Myra.

'It would appear,' Tyrell pressed on, 'that you and Brady took delight in taking photographs of graves.'

Myra broke off, told them she was thirsty. They

agreed to get her some tea. She drank three or four cups. For five and a half hours the detectives went over the same ground, but Myra did not give an inch. At 6.30, in exasperation, they left the room.

Twenty minutes later Detective Chief Inspector Joe Mounsey came in. He had been getting the same thing from Ian all afternoon, and he looked furious. He slammed down the picture of her kneeling on the grave, then slammed another of the boy's exhumed body on top, then another, and another. Myra told me, on tape, that she shouted, 'Take them away. I'm not looking at them.' Mounsey raged at her, pacing up and down, bellowing, 'Come to me little children and suffer.' It made no difference. He didn't break her.

The following day, Myra told me, the police changed tactics. Mam, Bert and Kath were allowed to see her. The police still hoped that they might get her to 'see sense'. Bert reminded her that she was quite normal until she met Ian; it was bound to be all right, if only she'd tell the truth! Myra refused. One by one her relatives broke down and sobbed, clinging onto her. Then the police escorted David Smith across the back of the room and out of a door. Her manner hardened. She'd had enough of this – she was going to stand by Ian! The police, watching from a distance, saw her reaction. They led her back downstairs to a cell.

Detectives suspected that she and Ian had also killed Keith Bennett and Pauline Reade. But there was no proof, so they abandoned the search for their bodies. They had all the evidence they needed to ensure that the Moors murderers would get life.

Robert Fitzpatrick was let in by the custody sergeant. He said he had some bad news for Myra. The police had asked a vet to knock out her dog, Puppet, in order to age him, but he'd failed to come round. What did he mean? asked Myra. Her dog was dead, replied the solicitor warily. Myra screamed that the police were murderers, they'd rot in hell for this. Her next letter home to Nellie was filled with bitter recriminations and an aching sense of loss. Myra remained firmly locked into the world she shared with Ian; Puppet was an important part of that world, so she mourned his death. The outrage at the killing of five children meant nothing, so she ignored it.

Chapter Two

Nellie kept all of her daughter's letters from prison. She carried them about from house to house until, in old age, she decided they were too much of a risk and had them stored away for safe-keeping. The change in tone over the years is striking, but the strength of Myra Hindley's voice never diminishes.

She did not write to her mother immediately. The first letter was dated 5 November 1965 – thirty days after the death of Edward Evans. Myra told Nellie that she wanted to look her best for the committal. 'If you could send to the station a decent pair of high heels, I'd feel a lot better than I do in these mules. I feel like a tramp in your clothes (only because they don't fit me properly).' There was not the slightest hint of remorse, or even mention of the crimes she stood accused of. There was furious criticism of the police for killing her dog: 'I feel as though my heart's been torn to pieces. I don't think anything else could hurt me more than this has. The only consolation is that some moron might have got hold of Puppet and hurt him.'

Myra told Nellie to retrieve Puppet's neck-tag and store it with the rest of her and Ian's possessions. 'This letter will probably be censored,' she concluded. 'If you should write at all, <u>do not mention anything regarding the cases</u>.'

Ian came into the visiting room. They exchanged letters every day. Myra still carried hers wherever she went. It wasn't just a question of security, they made her feel closer to Ian. She dropped the bundle onto the table, ran her eyes up and down his body, and sat down next to a woman prison officer. In her autobiography she recalled teasing him about his prison uniform, a kind of 'hairy jerkin suit'. She said he looked gorgeous. He replied that she didn't look so good herself in those lisle stockings and shoes – like Minnie Mouse! Humour had found room in their relationship again. They were able to relax, safe in the knowledge that they could see each other several times a week: at Risley, during meetings with their solicitor, and at court. They had insisted on their rights: all unconvicted, cohabiting prisoners were allowed to see each other. There was no reason, they argued, for them to be treated differently.

As usual, they shifted through apparently mundane topics of conversation in order to bore the guards.

They spoke about trips they'd taken, films they'd seen. The 'screws' didn't know what else had happened on those days. Ian told her that it might be an idea to get her mam to look after *all* the snaps. He did not know that the police had seized every picture and were going through them, looking for evidence of other missing bodies. Oh yes, said Myra. It would be a way of remembering the good old times, wouldn't it?

Myra wrote home: 'Dear Mam . . . keep all the photos for us, <u>for reasons</u>, the ones of dogs, scenery etc.'

Malcolm MacCulloch held the letter out to me, waving it. 'It looks like there *are* marker photographs for all the missing bodies,' he said.

'How can you be sure about that?'

MacCulloch shrugged. 'There was very little that was spontaneous or accidental about the way these crimes were carried out. If he retained reminders of one killing he is likely to have retained reminders of all of them. And remember, three of the victims had been recovered by this point – they were no longer perfect murders. He knew this and would have wanted mementos for the undiscovered bodies. That's why he wanted the photos!'

Myra did as Ian had suggested, and visited the prison library. The prison governor accompanied her. As Myra's eyes flicked up and down the shelves she noticed that many of the titles were religious, and complained. The governor responded that religion helped people to cope in here; it might not do her any harm to give it a go. Myra resisted the temptation to answer back, and walked between the sparsely stacked shelves. She found a copy of *Catch 22*, which had just come out, and Spike Milligan's *Puckoon*, which would remind her of Ian. She wrote an analysis of each book in her letters to him. From the beginning they made sure that they had things in common, something to talk about besides the murders.

In the front of the Black Maria there was a meshed window between the prisoners' and driver's compartments. Myra leant forward, hooked her fingers through the wire and looked ahead: Hyde Magistrates' Court came into view. Both she and Ian had newly trimmed hair, and Nellie had sorted out her clothes for her. It was pouring down, and the water drummed against the small, rectangular window, obscuring the view. But Myra could make people out, queuing three deep: press, photographers and ordinary women with rollers in their hair. She could not believe how many there were. She had avoided the papers, looked inwards, concentrated on Ian, and did not understand the true strength of public opinion.

I ordered the BBC news film on the case. It arrived in a couple of battered cans from the Windmill Road store in west London. Inside were twenty or so small, taped-up rolls of cellulose. I found an abandoned Steenbeck editing machine to view them on. But as I tried to load each clip it snapped. The edits had dried out over four decades. I went in search of help. 'This is going to take a while,' said Rex, the telecine operator, who was an old-school BBC craftsman. He painstakingly replaced every single edit before transferring the material to tape.

The pictures showed a surprising number of children clustered outside the court before the start of the committal. There was a sequence of Lesley Ann Downey's uncle attacking a Mini, sent out as a decoy by the police, imagining Myra Hindley to be inside. The camera was battered from side to side by still photographers fighting to capture the moment.

Myra and Ian were represented by junior counsel at the committal: Philip Curtis for her, David Lloyd-Jones for him. The defence opened proceedings by asking for the whole case to be heard in camera. The magistrates, two men and a woman, replied that they would hear the opening speeches in private before making a decision on the rest of the case. Myra and Ian smiled to each other as court ushers pushed disappointed members of the public and anxious journalists out of the door. But their happiness was short-lived: the prosecution won the day, and the 'hordes' were re-admitted.

David Smith, Myra recorded in her autobiography, was the first witness against them. Myra reached out and squeezed Ian's hand. They needed each other now. They would stand or fall together. A curious calm settled over her. She and Ian sat and stared, without once lowering their gaze, as the 'traitor' took the oath. Myra could feel Ian's anger as David gave his version of events. But to the rest of the world he looked aloof, doodling absent-mindedly on a pad, like a bored clerk at work. He never lost control in court. Myra took his lead, but struggled when Maureen stood up to say that her sister had gone off children once she met Ian. What about the hours Myra had spent caring for the Smiths' baby, Angela Dawn? The tears she'd shed when she died? In a letter home, Myra railed against her sister and David Smith. 'Did you read the lies Maureen told in court, about me hating babies and children? She wouldn't look at me in the dock, Mam. She couldn't. She kept her face turned away.' Myra went on, bitterly, that she knew the couple had sold their story to a newspaper. 'I noticed she was wearing a new coat and boots, and that Smith had a new watch on and a new overcoat and suit. I suppose he's had an advance on his dirt money.'

One by one, relatives of the dead children stood up to give evidence. Myra and Ian stared them down: Mrs Evans, bent double with grief; Mrs Kilbride, who cried as she talked about John. Then came Ann West, the mother of Lesley Ann Downey, who screamed across the court, 'How can you look at me after what you've done?' On and on she went, her voice filled with loathing, hurling insults at Myra, calling her a tramp. Myra recalled in her autobiography that she turned to Ian and said, 'I'm not a tramp!' 'No, I know you're not,' he replied.

Ian and Myra drew closer and closer together. She did not allow herself to feel any emotion in the face of the relatives' grief; he was completely unmoved by it. Committing the perfect murder, he'd told her, was an existential exercise. It was proof of their ability to reject an 'ordinary' life.

Myra maintained the fiction of innocence to Nellie and begged her not to believe all the things she read in the press. The reporters were being misled by the number of prosecution witnesses – eighty, can you imagine! Her lawyers would work on the defence once the committal was over. What Myra did not understand was that there was no possible defence against the tape of Lesley Ann Downey. By the time the child's words had stopped echoing round the courtroom she and Ian stood condemned in the eyes of the world. There was not a man or woman in the country who would acquit them.

On Thursday, the weather was so bad that the van couldn't make it back to Risley. Myra and Ian spent the night in the police cells, deep beneath the court. She was unable to sleep, and sat with a blanket pulled round her, shivering through the small hours on the board bed. In the morning the officer on duty refused to bring her make-up bag. Then she was given a cup of tea with salt in it. She kicked it over, and called the station commander, Chief Inspector Wills, to complain. Her only friend in the world was Ian. Myra wrote to Nellie, 'Nothing matters in the World as long as Ian is all right. If you'd drop [him] a short note and a box of Maltesers, I'd be glad. He says he doesn't want anything sending in, even from his mam, but I know he'll be glad you sent them.'

Years later, in her confession to the police and in her letters to me, Myra Hindley said she was 'under Ian Brady's spell' throughout the trial. This implies, if not resistance, at least a degree of passivity. I found this difficult to reconcile with the police record of her behaviour during her interrogation and committal. And a story in her unpublished autobiography shows she remained actively involved in the enjoyment of sadistic sexual fantasies even while on remand for child murder.

Just before Christmas their solicitor, Robert Fitzpatrick, came to Risley. He gave her a book of poems by Wordsworth. It brought back happy memories of meeting Ian and trips they had taken to the Lake District. Ian got a volume of Ovid. He seemed pleased, and tucked the slim book into his jacket pocket. While Mr Fitzpatrick's head was down, getting out his papers, Ian slipped Myra a notebook. It was filled with stories about harming children, written in a secret code. He also handed her a slip of paper on which he'd written the key. When she got back to her cell she began copying these 'messages' into an exercise book. She disguised them as verse and interspersed them with real poems. When decoded, one read, 'Why don't you throw acid on Brett?' Brett was the younger brother of Lesley Ann Downey; acid was what the killers in *Compulsion*, Leopold and Loeb, used to burn the body of their victim. The messages made her feel that they were still as one.

There were seven exercise books among her belongings. The pages had discoloured with age but the poems, written in blue biro, were clear. I recognized Housman, Tennyson and Wordsworth, but wasn't sure about 'A. C.' Clough and Charlotte Mew ('Moorland Night'). Inside one I found a fragment of one of Brady's letters, a violent invocation to love. It looked like fantasy, but it was difficult to be sure. I called Greater Manchester Police and told them what I had found.

DC Gail Jazmik and DS Fiona Robertshaw sat opposite me in a dingy BBC office on Whiteladies Road in Bristol. Lists pinned to a noticeboard showed that the last occupant had been a personnel officer. The notebooks were scattered on the desk in front of them. DS Robertshaw read in a flat Manchester accent, 'Moorland night, moorland night. Perhaps you will give back one day what you have taken.' The officers split the books into two piles and continued to read, only speaking to each other when they found something unusual or had finished a volume. As Fiona Robertshaw read, the lines on her forehead deepened. When she had finished she looked up.

'I want someone, an expert, to go through all of this to assess it,' she said.

'Right.'

'Would you let us borrow these to get them checked?'

'Of course.'

The police asked a cryptologist, supplied by GCHQ, to examine the notebooks for new evidence. The message came back: it was going to take him a while.

Ian and Myra were determined to spend their time inside well. They began by improving their knowledge of Shakespeare. She got *Richard III* from the library and gave him a copy of Richard Armour's *Twisted Tales from Shakespeare*, a comic history of the bard and his work – Goon-type humour. They wove quotations in and out of the coded letters. Myra sent Ian Richard's opening soliloquy. The first lines – 'Now is the winter of our discontent / Made glorious summer by this son of York' – were intended as a play on their situation. Myra felt that the latter part of the speech accurately described Ian's place in the world:

'Why, I, in this weak piping time of peace,
Have no delight to pass away the time,

Unless to spy my shadow in the sun,
And descant on mine own deformity.
And therefore, since I cannot prove a lover
To entertain these fair well-spoken days,
I am determined to prove a villain,
And hate the idle pleasures of these days.'

Ian enjoyed the letter, and responded with Edmund's words from *King Lear*:

'I grow, I prosper:
Now, gods, stand up for bastards.'

Myra dug out a memory to share in his resentment. Just before she went to secondary school, Bob and Nellie were arguing about whether she should go to 'The Franners' or Ryder Brow. Her father invited his old school friend, Father Roderick, round to work on his wife. Myra recalled that the monk sat there, over a steaming cup of tea, and lectured that because Nellie and Bob had got married in a register office rather than a church those two poor little girls were nothing but bastards. Bob may have sought Father Roderick's help, but he was not going to stand for that. He bundled the monk out of the front door and only stopped short of hitting him because he was 'a man of the cloth'. Myra ran round to Gran's to tell her that she was a bastard just like her, and her mother before her. They were all outsiders!

* * *

Towards Christmas, Myra sat on her bed to write home to Nellie. She had to be careful, her autobiography records, not to touch the red-hot radiator with her feet. She asked her mother to 'take care' of all the things left at Wardlebrook Avenue, to move them to Ian's mum's as quickly as possible. She said that 'Mr F.' was writing to the Attorney General to demand the return of anything that was not an exhibit. This included the tartan album, and almost every picture in it.

On Christmas Eve, Myra told Nellie, Ian's mother brought a meal in. They shared a roast chicken, turkey sandwiches and half a bottle of Sandeman's port wine. Ian ate heartily. It was the happiest time since their arrest – almost like being at home again.

In the run-up to the trial, Myra's family sought to rekindle her faith, hoping to break the bond with Ian. Auntie Kath, who had encouraged her to get confirmed, sent a 'holy' picture. On the back she wrote, 'Pray for me and I'll pray for you.' Myra told Nellie in a letter, 'I suppose she means well, but it means nothing to me.'

The Home Office paid for a psychiatrist, Dr de Ville Mather, to come and see Myra. Her lawyers said she should co-operate, and she did as she was told, but refused to give him any detail. The information he extracted would only be used by the prosecution. The doctor asked her what music she listened to, what books she read. Her taste was catholic, she replied, there was nothing he could learn from it. She viewed him with contempt. The defence then sent their own psychiatrist. She liked him, and things were going very well. Then he remarked that she was really very well read and articulate. Myra snapped, what, for a murderess? No, no, the doctor replied, it was intended as a compliment! Myra calmed down, and explained that she just didn't like being taken for a working-class idiot. The psychiatrist – Myra forgot which – suggested an EEG to pick up abnormalities in the brain. Myra declined.

Myra was still worried about how she'd look in court. She told Nellie in a letter that the governor of Risley had refused to let her get her roots done. 'I'll have to appear at the trial looking terrible with streaky, lifeless hair.' Her counsel complained to the authorities. Grudgingly, they relented.

Myra read in the *News of the World* about the changes to Chester Assizes for the trial: microphones, speakers, fitted carpets and security screens to protect her and Ian from assassination. It was reported that the Lord Chief Justice wanted to hear the case himself but was unable to leave London.

For the trial, Myra was given her grey striped suit and two blouses, one yellow, one blue. She washed them, ironed the suit, and polished her shoes. The black high-heels belonged to Nellie and were size 5; Myra took a 7, so they were agony when she pulled them on. She'd have to slip them off in the dock. The hairdresser came in to set and bleach her hair one last time. Myra was relieved to find that she did not give her a hard time, just chatted away as if she were working on her at a salon in Gorton.

The Sunday before the trial she wrote to Nellie. 'This is just a few lines before the "off" in case I don't have any time during the week to drop you a line. I had my hair done on Saturday. It looks so nice that I'm sorry that I'm all dressed up and nowhere to go (joke).'

Chapter Three

Ian and Myra clasped hands as they entered the darkness. The corridor, two prison officers to the front and two to the back, was a refuge from the courtroom. For five years they had been alone in their secret world. Now, Myra wrote in a letter to Nellie, lawyers were turning it over, in the company of 'scabrous' journalists, for strangers to judge. But they still had their love, and their secrets.

Mr Fitzpatrick was waiting for them in an oak-panelled meeting room. A stack of pictures lay on the table before him. Myra told Nellie that their solicitor had arranged a special viewing of all the photographs seized by the police so that they could pick out those pictures that were 'special' to them.

I asked Malcolm MacCulloch about the significance of this meeting. 'If I'm right about the existence of more markers, Brady would have derived enormous satisfaction from his superior knowledge.' He paused.

'And so, as his disciple, would she. The marker photographs tie her into the sadistic sexual enjoyment of the crimes more than any other piece of evidence. The tape recording of Lesley Ann Downey showed cruelty; this is the celebration of cruelty.'

Ian and Myra ignored most of the pictures, selecting just a few. Mr Fitzpatrick said he'd do his best to get these back after the trial, whatever happened. Myra's letters to Nellie reveal that she and Ian knew they were going down. The question was, for how long? Their lawyers' strategy was to sow doubt in the jury's minds about one or two of the charges. There was no hope of an acquittal.

The junior counsel who had represented them at the committal were replaced by senior QCs; Myra recorded in her autobiography that she was surprised to hear them called 'silks' as she'd never heard the term before. Ian's case was led by the highly experienced lawyer and Liberal MP Emlyn Hooson; Myra's brief was Godfrey Heilpern, who had achieved silk six years earlier at the age of just thirty-five. Opposing them, in a highly unusual move, was the Attorney General himself, Sir Frederick Elwyn Jones QC, MP. The judge, Mr Fenton-Atkinson, had overseen war crimes trials at Nuremberg. He spoke in a conversational voice, with natural authority. When he addressed the jury, the barristers in the pit below him stopped shuffling their papers in order to hear what he said. I found his notes on a large, buff sheet of cartridge paper at the National Records Archive. The words are carefully chosen, well ordered, and set down in an immaculate copperplate – the work of someone used to being in total control of their surroundings.

The judge, trial records show, was outraged when he discovered that David Smith, the principal prosecution witness, had done a deal with a newspaper. Not only did he stand to earn £1,000 in the event of a conviction, he and Maureen were being put up at a sumptuous hotel in Chester. Everywhere the couple went they were chaperoned by reporters. Mr Fenton-Atkinson challenged David Smith in court to reveal the name of the paper. 'Come on, you know the name. Tell it to us.' The judge leant forward, glaring at the mute and stubborn witness.

'I don't know if the newspaper would wish me to do that,' Smith replied, infuriating Mr Fenton-Atkinson still further.

'They may have some questions to answer about this. Who are they?'

The judge kept on pushing, but to no avail. David Smith had never had the chance to make so much money, and he wasn't going to squander it. Only his importance to the case saved him from being charged with contempt of court. Nevertheless, the judge demanded an immediate investigation by the Attorney General. 'It sounds to me like a gross interference with the course of justice,' he said.

It is illegal to take photographs in English courts,

but the temptation proved too much for one snapper who, somehow, smuggled a camera in. The photograph appeared in newspapers around the world. I found it in the *Toronto Star*; it is still forbidden to publish it in Britain. The picture shows Myra and Ian standing beside each other in the centre of an imposing, oak-panelled room, facing the judge. George I and William III stare down on the proceedings. Ranged in front of the dock are lines of defence and prosecution lawyers. At the back of the court, wedged in on tiered, horseshoe-shaped benches, are members of the public, press and relatives. The most striking thing about the defendants is their sense of strength and togetherness.

'This is where the picture was taken from.' The manager of Chester Court, Mark White, was standing in an ornate wooden gallery just yards from the judge's chair. I marvelled at the photographer's nerve. 'The thing is, it's not a press gallery. This is where guests of the court – dignitaries – would have sat.'

'You mean, a photographer got someone to take the picture for him?' I asked.

'Must have done,' he replied.

The defendants sat dressed as if for work at Millwards: Ian, sober in made-to-measure Burton's terylene, and Myra, prim in her grey wool suit. Every few days she changed her hair. At the beginning of the trial it had a lilac tint, by the end it was ash blonde. She wore make-up too – Ponds' Angel Face, shade

Golden Rose. She'd asked Nellie to get a bottle for her. They listened attentively to the evidence and wrote notes with rapid, composed efficiency. Every now and then one of them tore off a sheet and handed it forward to a lawyer. Ian emerged three times to give evidence, Myra twice.

Myra recorded in her autobiography that they sustained themselves through shared love and shared secrets, some serious, some silly. One day Myra smuggled a Quality Street Easter egg from Nellie out of Risley. She and Ian sat scoffing it in the back of the van on the way to Chester. They both felt sick by the time they reached the sandstone city walls. Myra ended up flushing most of it down the court toilets.

Ian's calm, undisguised arrogance did not endear him to the jury. Neither did his pedantry. The court transcript records that, ten days in, the Attorney General cross-examined him for the second time.

'You admit it was you that killed Evans?'

'I admit that I hit Evans with the axe.'

'Are you suggesting that you did not kill him?'

'No. Somebody else has.'

'Who?'

'The pathologist said it was accelerated by strangulation.'

'The questioning of the pathologist by your own counsel was to the effect that Evans was dead or dying when the ligature was applied, was it not?'

'Yes.'

'And that was the conclusion of the pathologist.'

'Yes, eventually.'

'You killed Evans – there is no qualifying that, is there?'

'I hit Evans with the axe. If he died from axe blows, I killed him.'

Obsessed with the details of his crimes, Ian Brady demonstrated no understanding of their meaning. When Myra took the stand, on the eleventh day, she tied herself to him.

'Could you tell us, Miss Hindley, what were your feelings for Ian Brady?'

'I became very fond of him. I loved him. I still do love him.'

Godfrey Heilpern asked whether she shared Brady's beliefs on religion.

'Yes,' she replied.

'On politics?'

'Yes.'

'On sex?'

'Yes.'

'On people in general?'

'Yes.'

'The same literary tastes?' the lawyer concluded.

'Not quite . . . I didn't have any enjoyment from pornography.'

Her replies, rapped out as a staccato 'yes' or 'no' in a flat Gorton accent, made her appear hard and calculating, as though she were reluctant to elaborate

for fear of betraying a secret. She had agreed with Ian
that he would 'do the talking'. Any chance there may
have been of winning the jury round evaporated long
before the tape was played.

Myra had heard that recording twice now, studied
the transcript, and constructed a story to fit. When
Lesley Ann was being undressed Myra was 'downstairs'; when the girl was being forced to kneel, naked,
in an attitude of prayer, she was 'looking out the window'; when she was being strangled, Myra was 'running
a bath'. She was asked, under cross-examination, why
she told the girl to 'shut up' and said she'd 'get a slap'
if she didn't. Myra agreed this was 'unforgivable' and
'cruel'. But words of contrition, uttered alongside
obvious lies, rang hollow.

Myra did not deal with any of this in her letters to
Nellie. Her loyalty to Ian forbade it. 'He's not concerned
about his future, just mine. It's the same with me: I'm
not interested in my future, just him. However, we'll have
to wait and see what happens. I believe in one thing,
though, that no matter how black things look, some day
we can begin again together. I know what we've done
and what we haven't done. You know too, no matter
what happens.'

But as the trial wore on, shorn of credibility, Myra
wrote less and less. She and Ian stuck rigidly to their
strategy of lying. They had two aims: to protect
their secrets, and to get her a shorter sentence than
him. Patricia Cairns told me that they were already

planning for the future. 'The idea was that she would do a few years and be released. She would go to places, experience things and let him know what they were like. He would live his life through her until, after many years, he was released.'

Recalled to the witness box on the twelfth day of the trial, Ian did all he could to play down the significance of the photographs. It wasn't a system, as the police alleged, simply a coincidence that there were 'landscape shots' in the vicinity of the two graves. What's more, the police pictures taken to match his own were completely inaccurate. The trial transcript shows that the judge struggled to take in what he was saying.

'You are saying they are not exactly the same spot?'

The court was looking at two photographs of Lesley Ann Downey's grave: one taken by Ian, the other by Detective Constable Ray Gelder.

Ian remained quite calm. 'I am just going on what I can see. There is boulders all over this and there is no boulders at all on that. This is sandy and this is dark.'

The Attorney General cut in. 'You know it is the identical spot. You know it was a deliberately taken photograph of the grave of Lesley Ann Downey, do you not?'

'No,' Ian replied.

'And a number of photographs similarly taken. We will see them before the end of the cross-examination. Those are photographs of this cemetery of your making on the moorland, are they not?'

'Those photographs are snapshots,' Ian replied, as though mystified by the suggestion that he had recorded where the bodies lay buried.

The cross-examination moved on. The purpose of the trial was to establish the defendants' guilt or innocence, not to prove that there was a system for recording where bodies were buried. Nor was its aim to establish what had happened to the other missing children. Everyone knew about Pauline Reade and Keith Bennett, but their names were not mentioned by the prosecution. Keith's mother, Winnie Johnson, sat watching in the public gallery; she was sure they had killed her son. Detective Chief Inspector Mounsey came up to her, teased her for being cross with him, said he understood, and that they would find her son's body. Winnie recalled the meeting with regret in her voice. 'He was the only one who seemed bothered. Soon afterwards he died, and I'm still waiting.'

In his summing-up, Mr Fenton-Atkinson drew attention to a slip made by Brady in the witness box. When asked what happened after he finished photographing Lesley Ann Downey, he'd replied, 'We all got dressed and went downstairs.' The judge told the jury, 'This, possibly, casts a flood of light on the nature of the activities that were going on.'

Rather than crumble as the verdict and sentencing drew near, Ian and Myra's relationship hardened under the force of opprobrium. Myra found a poem in the prison library she hoped might sustain Ian as he faced up to years of separation from her, Wordsworth's *Tintern Abbey*.

> Five years have past; five summers, with the length
> Of five long winters; and again I hear
> These waters, rolling from their mountain springs
> With a soft inland murmur. Once again
> Do I behold these steep and lofty cliffs,
> That on a wild and secluded scene impress
> Thoughts of more deep seclusion; and connect
> The landscape with the quiet of the sky.

In their hearts, neither of them had left the moor. They could not accept that they would never go back.

On the final morning of the trial, sitting in the back of the prison van, Myra scrawled a note to Nellie. 'I don't know what the verdict will be yet but I do know that I will be convicted of something, like harbouring Ian after he and Smith killed Evans. Once you know what the verdicts and sentences are you must not let them affect your life as they will mine. I've just started crying and don't want anyone to see me.'

Myra stood shoulder to shoulder with Ian to hear the verdict. The clerk of the court asked the foreman of the jury whether she had murdered Edward Evans: 'Guilty.' Lesley Ann Downey: 'Guilty.' A feeling of numbness spread through her. She hardly heard the words 'not guilty' to the murder of John Kilbride, and 'guilty' to harbouring Brady after the boy's death. Ian was found guilty of all three murders. The clerk asked him whether he had anything to say. 'No,' he replied, 'except the revolvers were bought in June '64.' Rather than plead innocence, Ian had pointed out a mistake made by the prosecution.

'And you, Myra Hindley?'

'No.'

The judge turned to pass sentence. His words indicate regret at the abolition of hanging.

'Ian Brady, these were three calculated, cruel, cold-blooded murders. In your case I pass the only sentences which the law now allows, which is three concurrent sentences of life imprisonment. Put him down.'

As Ian was led below, the judge shifted his gaze to Myra.

'In your case, Hindley, you have been found guilty of two equally horrible murders, and in the third as an accessory after the fact. On the murders the sentence is two concurrent sentences of life imprisonment. And on the charge of being an accessory after the fact to the death of Kilbride, a concurrent sentence of seven years' imprisonment. Put her down.'

Chapter Four

The cubicle was three feet across, three feet deep and six feet high. There was a slatted wooden bench to sit on; it vibrated in time with the van's large diesel engine. Myra was heading south, towards London. She told Nellie that she could not bear the thought of Ian being carried away, in the opposite direction, to Durham.

The prison gates showed black through the small rectangular window behind her head; a great stone griffin loomed out of the brickwork. The van slowed, and she heard a door slam as a warder came round the back to let her out. Myra emerged, squinting, into the light. The redbrick walls of Holloway towered above her. Each narrow wing, isolated in the middle of a large gravel yard, stretched cell upon cell into the sky. Where Risley had offered the hope, however remote, of freedom, this place looked like the end of the road.

Myra was led into a room beside the gate where she was told to strip, put on a blue dressing gown and sit in a curtained cubicle. A few minutes later the nurse came and checked her over for nits and any obvious diseases. A prison officer handed over a small pile of clothes: black shoes, grey skirt, grey cardigan. Which colour blouse would she like? There were three to choose from: blue and white, pink and white or green and white. Myra went with the blue. The rhythm of the admission was faster than at Risley. It was a huge place, used to turning prisoners round fast.

The reception officer told Myra that she was on E-wing, maximum security, and pointed at a bundle of bedding for her to pick up. She was led through the railings and across the courtyard. Myra read recognition in the eyes of the women she passed. Some glanced away immediately, others stared with open curiosity or contempt. There would be no hiding here.

In her cell, Myra threw herself onto the cot and stared at the ceiling. Light reflected down off the magnolia paint. It really wasn't too depressing. She thought of Ian and imagined holding him again. Other prisoners were given 'conjugal rights'; they would get the same, wouldn't they?

I asked Patricia Cairns, who left her convent in Salford for life as a prison officer, what the atmosphere on Myra's wing was like. 'It was quiet. They put Myra there to make up the numbers rather than because she was an immediate risk. There were a couple of child killers, a pair of Russian spies, and Bunty Gee, who was in for treason. They all got on OK. They had to – they were in for long stretches.'

Ian and Myra worked at their love. They wrote to one another every day and started the same German course, exchanging hints and comparing marks. It was a link back to what had mattered during the killings, and a way of preserving their relationship for the future. Myra was a more diligent student: she sat her O level before Ian and got an A grade. He wrote to tell her he was proud.

Ian and Myra were furious when their respective governors refused them permission for inter-prison visits. They took it in turns to bombard the Home Secretary with 'petitions'. These were declined with metronomic efficiency. In desperation, Myra asked Nellie to lobby on her behalf. 'Now, you remember I drafted a letter for you, some weeks ago. For you to copy, more or less, and send to the HO? I want you to look it up and take points from it, and write to Lord Stonham, the Home Office, SW1, and tell him I've asked you to confirm that Neddy and I lived together for over 4 years.'

Ian continued to assure Myra that she would be out in a few years. It would make sense to start saving now so there was 'something to fall back on'. Once again, she had to turn to Nellie for assistance. 'Take out a policy for half a crown a week. It's not much but it'll mount up over time.' Nellie did as she was asked. The man from the United and Friendly called at her house. The policy document, grand and reassuring, offered Myra hope of a future. It's hard to tell, looking at it, when the payments stopped.

Myra wrote to Nellie every week, and on the back of each letter she added a page in bold capitals to Gran. The fiction, dreamt up to 'protect' her, that Myra was 'living in Scotland' had long evaporated. But Ellen never cut her granddaughter off. Instead, she offered un-questioning love, and knitted her clothes – a cardigan, a jumper, a scarf. Myra's letters to her harked back to a simpler time when they'd lived alone together.

Although Holloway was housed in Victorian build-ings, its morals were those of sixties London. Myra had never seen women holding hands before, or kiss-ing. Some had ragged-out pages from porn mags on their walls. At night, lovers in different wings called to one another through the bars. A film crew from the BBC's *Everyman* series came to make a documentary about Holloway. They recorded a prison officer walk-ing past Myra's cell. As I watched the film I marvelled at the free access the director had been given. There were open displays of physical affection between inmates; prison officers looked on and made no attempt to stop filming. Myra saw the documentary at a special screening for inmates in the prison gym the week before transmission.

She described all this to Ian as an observer, not yet part of the place. He sent her new messages, in their secret code, about harming children. Sadistic sex was still the fire that burned at the heart of their relationship, and it needed fuel to survive. The descriptions weren't explicit; the slightest allusion to a shared secret was often enough to recall an experience. There were a lot of references to photographs.

They continued to share the same solicitor, Robert Fitzpatrick. The lawyer from Hyde served them as he would any other client. He worked doggedly to recover their negatives and the tartan album. Myra wrote to let Nellie know how his campaign was going. As the months dragged by this commentary increased in urgency; the pictures were very important to her and Ian. 'The material he had in his head was losing its power,' Professor Malcolm MacCulloch explained. 'The fantasies that sadists like Ian Brady use tend to lose strength over time so they escalate the content of what they're fantasizing. They're being more violent, more obscene or distressing to their victims in fantasy. The request for pictures is driven by the fact that he has remembered material which is important to him, which will reinvigorate him.'

Just before Christmas, a letter arrived from Ian. He had a cold, and was confined to bed. She thought back to Risley, where they had been able to celebrate together and share half a bottle of port wine. There was no alcohol in here. Ian's mother, Peggy, tried to make up for this by sending her chocolate liqueurs – whisky, rum, cherry brandy.

Ian told Myra that she must agree to see the police, who had booked a visit for 27 January 1967. They wanted to ask her about the other missing children. The detectives had allowed Myra enough time to 'cool down' – a common strategy. Myra wrote to Nellie to say she was only agreeing to the visit so that it would look good on her prison record. 'Once the police have been, I'm not going to see them again. They can leave us alone for the rest of our sentence, and I'll tell them that when they come. Remember the record you brought down one week, "It's All Over Now Baby Blue?" Can you get me another copy of it some time and keep it for me?' I read these last words with astonishment. The Joan Baez record had been Ian's gift to her on the morning of Edward Evans's murder. Her request for a new copy suggests that she was still caught up in reliving, and savouring, the murders with Ian.

In 1968 the Attorney General finally gave in and agreed to hand over the pictures. Robert Fitzpatrick delivered the tartan album, and negatives, to Nellie for safe keeping. There were around 200 images. Ian was very clear about which ones he wanted. 'I told Neddy you were having those 3 of me developed, and he's pleased, for he feels you will get them done quicker than his mam. Post them direct to him, right away. Put his number 605217 HMP Old Evet Durham.' Myra told Nellie that once she'd done this the rest of the pictures could be destroyed. Just a week later Myra wrote again. 'Have you sent the slides to Neddy yet?' But Nellie had stalled; it seemed as though she'd suspected what the pictures were. Time after time Myra's letters sidled up to the issue with chatty descriptions of prison life before the inevitable question about the slides.

Professor Malcolm MacCulloch was clear about the reason for Ian Brady's persistence. 'The only reason I can think of is that they portray, or remind him of, burial sites. He wants them so he can relive the murders, and enjoy possession of the bodies.'

'So,' I said, 'the letters between them might tell us which pictures he was after, and where the last body is buried.'

'They might do. But remember, Myra Hindley and Ian Brady were very, very good at this.'

Two weeks after this conversation I was sitting opposite Superintendent Tony Brett in his sparse office at Leigh police station.

'We have asked the Home Office to pull all the letters between Myra Hindley and Ian Brady for us,' the detective told me. 'They were copied and are held at a store in Staffordshire.'

'How hopeful are you?'

'If the letters can be decoded we might get the information we need to find the final missing body. At the very least they'll tell us more about the way they operated. That may help us in the long run. It's got to be done.'

* * *

Over time, Myra's questions to Nellie about life 'at home' became more detailed. Have you been re-housed yet? How is little Mikie (a nephew)? Tell me about the kids in their Whit clothes. Her references to Ian became more desperate. 'I've been in prison for three years now, Mam, and haven't seen Neddy for two and a half of them, which I think is awful, think-ing how many other prisoners have been granted this privilege.' It was as if the rope to one anchor was slipping through her fingers, and she was grasping at another.

Lord Longford came to see her for the first time in 1968. She asked him to lobby the Home Office for inter-prison visits with Ian. Incredibly, the serving cabinet member agreed. Myra's solicitor in later years, Andrew McCooey, says that Longford agreed to help her out of religious conviction rather than because he believed her claims of innocence.

'Frank was extremely sharp,' McCooey told me. 'He was alive to what was going on but believed that no one was beyond redemption – not even Myra Hindley.'

Lord Longford told Myra about his conversion to Catholicism and suggested she try praying. She wrote to Nellie, 'I doubt I'll "see the light" again, but who knows?'

Myra's tastes altered along with her friends. In prison she had the time to read, and study, in a way that would not have been possible had she remained free. 'I hate Radio 1,' she wrote. 'The third programme has all the best classical music, study and good plays and poetry readings.'

For all these superficial changes, Myra remained bound to Ian by their shared secret. But then his demands for the slides became threatening, and in her letters home she stopped calling him Neddy. 'He keeps asking why he hasn't received them yet. In his last letter he said he'll have to send someone round for them.' Slowly, the bonds were being broken.

Chapter Five

The first six hundred pages of Myra Hindley's autobiography were delivered, in instalments, to the house of her most trusted supporter, David Astor, in the mid-eighties. They were checked for spelling mistakes, typed up and numbered by his secretary, Pat Hepburn. The former editor of the *Observer* newspaper read the completed pages with a growing feeling of dismay. 'I tried to suggest changes, persuade her to be more honest, but she just couldn't do it.' In the end, of course, Astor told her to abandon the project and ordered Pat Hepburn to destroy the handwritten original manuscript. But Myra Hindley kept a complete copy of her work, and several years before she died it was parcelled up and sent out of prison for safe keeping. She didn't want it to fall into the hands of a tabloid newspaper.

When I pulled the last section out of its brown manila envelope I found, at the back, a handwritten addition of more than two hundred pages. The words were laid down with a passion and honesty missing from the earlier chapters. Myra was able to achieve this tone because she was no longer writing about the murders. It was the story of a love affair that Ian Brady viewed as a supreme act of betrayal.

In 1970, Myra's friend and fellow inmate Carole O'Callaghan returned from a visit to the dentist in a state of high excitement – she'd just seen Myra's type! Myra did not get over-excited as Carole was always picking out potential lovers for her. Just what, she asked, made Carole think she knew what her type was? No, no, came the breathless reply, this one was really lovely. Her name was Trish Cairns – she was an officer!

Around this time, the prison governor, Dorothy Wing, decided that keeping the inmates of E-wing – child killers, spies, traitors – locked up together with no outside contact was a bad idea. It would be better to integrate them, mix them with a better class of criminal, in the hope of rehabilitation. It was the first time, Myra recorded in her autobiography, that she had left E-wing in four years. Her group of women were sitting on a bench in the prison 'centre', outside the canteen, waiting to be called in for their pay. The other inmates, many of them short-termers, treated them circumspectly. Carole O'Callaghan and Myra Hindley did not look like the sort to mess with.

They were waiting for F-wing to finish, watching people they had never seen before, when the door to

A-wing opened and a lithe, brown-haired young officer emerged. As soon as she saw her Myra knew she was the one. She felt Carole tense up with mirth at her side. 'There she is!' she said in a loud stage whisper as the officer passed within a few feet of them. The women either side of them collapsed in a heap of giggles. Myra wrote that the officer turned and stared, and 'something happened' deep inside Myra. Just like with Ian, it was love at first sight.

Myra's cell faced the main gate. She took to standing on her bed when the warders changed shifts, at 7.45, 12.15, 1.30, 5.15 and 9.15, in the hope of catching a glimpse of her. The young officer always walked briskly, and looked happy. Myra and Carole talked about nothing but how attractive she was, and what she could do to meet her. In the end, it happened by chance.

Myra felt a rising sense of excitement. She had not been into a library since 1965. Heads turned as she and five other E-wing inmates passed by. She was walking beside her 'special' friend, Alice. They ignored the glances thrown in their direction by the other prisoners. Acknowledging them would have eroded respect, and invited trouble. The E-wing escort chose a key from the ring at her waist, slid it into the gate and pulled. The heavy iron door swung open to reveal the object of Myra's desires.

The escorting officer, Myra noted in her autobiography, laid a hand on her head and said, 'This one's Cat A.'

'I know,' replied the officer. She turned, and led the group inside.

Over three decades later, Patricia Cairns's recollection of this meeting remained bright in her mind. 'She stood out, straight-backed and calm, not like the others. They were chatting away. She would think that was beneath her. She was very dignified. And she was very bonny in those days as weii.'

'What was she wearing?' I asked.

She laughed. 'They were allowed their own clothes by this stage. She was wearing black trousers, a turquoise and black blouse that came down to six inches above her knees, and a cardigan.'

Patricia Cairns recognized Myra's name but said she had very little idea of her crimes. During the Moors murders trial she was living in an enclosed Carmelite convent in Salford. By the time a crisis of faith prompted her to leave, Myra and Ian were behind bars. Her first job was at a borstal, Bulwood Hall. She had just started work at Holloway when she met Myra.

There was a limit to the number of prisoners allowed into the library. As one left, another came in. When Alice's turn arrived, Myra tried it on. She was teaching her friend to read; could they go in together to choose some books she'd like? Patricia gave Myra an 'old-fashioned' look and let her in. Myra scooped up a few titles for teaching and got lost in finding books for herself. Even though the library was small –

it was in a cell – it offered a wider choice of reading material than she had seen for years. She became so absorbed that she almost forgot about Trisha. She was pulled back to the present by the officer's voice at her shoulder: they'd better go back to the wing or they'd think she'd lost her. Myra apologized, took the books to the front of the room, and had them stamped. She was reading with a purpose other than entertainment. There were rumours that male lifers were to be allowed to study for an Open University degree, and she wanted to do the same.

Back on the wing, Myra was distracted from her books by thoughts of Trisha. She was attractive. More than that, there seemed to be a warmth about her. But there was no point even thinking about it: Myra was an inmate, Trisha Cairns a warder.

It was several days before they met again. Trisha stood stern-faced in the doorway: what was that girl doing in her bed? Alice lay sprawled across the mattress watching Myra, naked after a bath, apply 'intimate' body lotion. Myra looked up and replied that where she came from, when you were on top of the bedspread you were on, not in, the bed. The officer did not back down: she was from the same place, and she said the girl was in the bed. In order to avoid a fight, Alice pulled herself up and ambled over to the wash stand. She did her best to imbue the act of brushing her teeth with insolence. Myra held the officer's gaze and asked her where she was from.

Crown Point, Denton came the reply. Myra smiled –
the place next to the sewage works? The officer
ignored the dig, and said that she knew Gorton
Monastery. She'd taught Sunday School there when
she was a nun. A bell rang. The officer said goodnight,
pulled the door to, and turned the key. Myra lay back
on her bed. A nun?

The following week Trisha was on reception. She
noticed in the prison records that Myra's friend Alice
had been transferred to Styal prison. Trisha's duty, as
third officer, was to escort women to their wings. Most
of the runs back and forth did not go near the area for
'high-risk' inmates – E-wing had the smallest popu-
lation. But the inmate on reception duty that evening
was a neighbour of Myra's.

At the end of her shift, Trisha walked the woman
back and stood in the corridor, waiting while she went
to get some water for the night. She had the feeling of
being watched through a spy-hole. Nothing unusual in
that – prisoners didn't have much to do. It was less
common, however, for them to start banging on the
door. She heard Carole's voice, demanding that she
open up. Trisha hesitated and asked, impatiently, what
she wanted. There was every reason to be suspicious.
Carole said she had something for her – it was from
Myra. Trisha glanced quickly up and down the
corridor, pulled at her keys and opened the door.
Carole was standing there, holding out a letter in her
right hand. Trisha took it, stuffed it into her uniform

pocket, and went back to her duties. Myra watched through the bars of her cell as Trisha made her way out of the wing. In the letter she'd told Trisha how much she loved her, and spent hours watching the prison gate just so that she could see her come and go. As she peered into the darkness Carole boomed, with mock sonority, 'It is consummated!' Myra ignored her, and lay back on her bunk.

That night was hell for Myra. If Trisha reported her she'd be up before the governor and was certain to be punished, but even worse was the possibility of rejection. Ian's spell had been broken; she wanted someone else, someone who would make her happy now. From her letters, and her autobiography, it is clear that this was a turning point for Myra. She had come to realize that she was never going to see Ian again. Unlike him, she could no longer find nourishment in the crimes of the past. She needed new experiences, and love, in the present.

Where was everyone? asked Trisha the next day. The E-wing duty officer, Stevenson, looked up from her book and replied that they'd all gone to see a film in the hall – except Myra. Oh, said Trisha, she'd come in to practise her table tennis for the prison tournament. Stevenson said she'd go and find Myra, see if she fancied a game.

Myra was in the ironing room. She didn't recognize Trisha at first, dressed carefully in jeans, an olive green suede jacket and matching Chelsea boots. She felt suddenly awkward in her black bell-bottoms and nylon housecoat – a more fashionable version of Gran's. She considered changing, but didn't want to be seen to be trying too hard. When Stevenson left them Trisha thrust out a record-shaped package at Myra. She took it, tore off the paper and read the title: Rachmaninov's 'Rhapsody on a Theme of Paganini'. They walked down to the music room and sat in silence as notes filled the air. Trisha passed her a card showing Dalí's *Christ of St John on the Cross*. On the back were the words 'The feeling is mutual.'

Myra was the happiest she had been for years.

They were interrupted when the door swung open and Carole walked in. A look of glee spread over her face. Oh sorry! Had she interrupted something? Myra cut her off and asked if she wanted to join them for a game of table tennis.

Myra and Trisha discovered that they had more in common than working-class, Catholic, Manchester backgrounds. Like Myra, Trisha came from a home dominated by a violent, hard-drinking father. She had entered the Carmelite convent in Salford to escape home as well as to dedicate her life to God. They worked out that they must have attended mass at the monastery together. Myra still went there for a year after she met Ian. In Myra's letters home now there were no more expressions of frustration at not being allowed to see Ian, no more complaints about the small number of letters she received, and fewer requests for information about life 'at home'. She seemed, for the moment at least, to have found something to keep her genuinely happy inside.

One night, Myra heard a knocking on her cell door. She got up off her bed and there was a rose bud, wet with dew, in the centre of the spy-hole. She took it, and found Trisha staring at her. Myra seized the initiative and told her to put her ear to the spy-hole. Trisha did as she was told. In her autobiography, Myra recorded that she whispered, 'I love you!' The spy-hole fell shut and Myra wondered if she'd gone too far. She banged on the door. 'Are you there? Did you hear me?'

'Yes, I heard. And I love you too. It's hopeless, but I can't help it.'

I found it hard to understand how anyone could fall in love with a person convicted of multiple child murder. Trisha Cairns explained that it was both because she was living in an enclosed order during Myra and Ian's trial, and that the nature of prison life meant people's crimes were rarely discussed. Inmates were taken at face value. What's more, Trisha told me, Myra did not rush to discuss her past. 'She told me after a few months. I was upset when I found out it was children. But it was beyond my control by then. I was just in love with her.'

Security at Holloway was lax, and it did not take long for them to work out a way of meeting every day. They set up arrangements using a warder's trusty, or 'red-band', called Pat to carry their letters. There was no shortage of private places: the craft room, where Myra 'worked' on a large tapestry; the prison chapel, where she practised piano; the room in the tower, where she made tea for the prison officers; even her cell on E-wing, where Trisha 'dropped in' to visit colleagues. They got even more time together when Trisha was made Myra's legal aid officer. But it never felt like enough. 'Some people like the risk of situations like that,' Patricia Cairns told me, 'but it wasn't like that. I found it very worrying. But my feelings were so strong it was beyond my control. It was overpowering.'

The relationship gave Myra a reason to cut off all ties with her 'one-time God'. Patricia Cairns said that she began to dread getting Ian Brady's letters and having to fake love in her replies. 'She had been struggling to reply to his letters for about a month before we met. His grip was loosening and her world view had broadened. Do you know that she used to get 150 Christmas cards a year – peers of the realm, religious leaders, prison inspectors, artists? How many people can you say that about? But she needed a push to get rid of him. I was a sort of replacement.'

Although Myra Hindley was physically attracted to Patricia Cairns, the relationship went far beyond sex. She had enjoyed other physical affairs, but none had threatened her bond with Ian. Myra recorded in her unpublished autobiography that Trisha was the love of her life; she had 'led her by the hand out of the wasteland'.

As her love for Trisha deepened, so the letters to Nellie, demanding that she supply the pictures to Ian, became increasingly urgent. 'Ian's going on about slides and photos again . . . he thinks of little else . . . you promised to write and let me know about the slides and photos . . . he'll keep on for years . . . I'm so sick of the whole thing . . . don't make things difficult for me, love . . . I'm sorry (in more ways than one) to have to mention the slides and photos yet again . . . post the things . . . try to do this for me, love, and let me know when it's been done.' But Nellie refused to send the pictures. Finally, on 11 May 1972, Myra wrote the words that finally changed her mother's mind: 'I have decided to bring our relationship (mine and Ian's) to a close.' Nellie sent a total of five pictures to Ian Brady. After that, the letters home from Myra, although still frequent, were no longer edgy.

Professor Malcolm MacCulloch told me that supplying the pictures was the only hope Myra had of achieving a clean break. 'She's spent all these years together with Ian Brady, corresponding about what they've done. She knows he has got to have closure. If she's going to cast him aside he has got to have what he needs. That's why things happened in the order that they did.'

Myra sat down to write her final letter to Ian. The

words did not come easily, even though she was clear about the decision and had committed herself to Trisha. They had shared so much. She forced herself to go on, posted the letter, and waited for the reply.

'He was furious,' Patricia Cairns told me. 'He was blazing that she should reject him.'

'Do you think he realized that you had replaced him?' I asked.

She paused before replying. 'He must have picked up signs in her letters. It's hard to fake emotion convincingly.'

Ian Brady refused to accept that the relationship was over. He no longer had someone to share his secrets, a lover who might one day be free to send back sounds and smells from the outside world to sustain him. In the end, the social skills which he needed Myra for during the murders carried her away from him. Myra asked the governor to return all of his letters unopened, then demonstrated to Trisha that there would be no turning back. 'She burned all his correspondence,' Patricia Cairns told me. 'At the bottom of E-wing there was a gate on the left-hand side that led out to a brazier for inmates. I helped her. It took a few weeks.'

The prison governor, Dorothy Wing, was impressed with Myra's decision to cut off Ian Brady. It seemed as though there might be some hope of rehabilitation. She took a keen personal interest in the development of her prisoners. When she felt they were 'ready' to be reintroduced to the outside world she took them on trips: up the river to Kew; down the river to Greenwich; a day out at Crufts; an evening at the Royal Tournament. It was against all the rules, but she was a determined maverick.

Mrs Wing lived in a house by the prison gates with her cairn terrier Piper. On Tuesday, 12 September 1972, she was finishing off her early-afternoon cup of tea when the small dog began to whine. He needed to go for a walk. 'I suppose if it hadn't been for him wagging his tail at me, this might not have happened,' she later told the *Daily Mail*. She decided to take Myra out with her. They were gone for two hours. It was the first time Myra had felt grass and smelt fresh air since 1965. The papers were tipped off, and reporters only missed them coming back through the prison gates by a few minutes. The story headed the evening news and was splashed on the front pages of the tabloids the following morning. The Home Secretary, Robert Carr, issued an official rebuke: there were to be no more of Mrs Wing's excursions. That weekend Myra wrote home to Nellie, 'I spent the two most enjoyable hours for many years, and certainly the quickest two. I'll tell you all about it when I see you. I feel terribly sorry for all the publicity the governor has had to contend with today, and that such a kind and thoughtful gesture has been abused.'

I visited the newspaper library at Colindale to see if I could learn why the story had gained such momentum. Every page of national newspaper print is stored here, much of it on microfilm. The first roll I loaded onto the viewer gave me the answer: Lord Longford. The former cabinet minister had begun a campaign for Myra to be paroled; he said she was 'a good girl, and a devout Catholic'. The 'walk in the park' was seen as evidence of her being prepared for release. Neither the families of the victims nor the newspapers were willing to countenance this possibility, however. The former Chief Constable of Lancashire, Bill Palfrey, told the *Daily Mail*, 'I think some of our do-gooders are living in cloud cuckoo land. I have always believed in the death penalty and I would have said this was a case where it should have been imposed.' Myra did not understand that, by allowing Lord Longford to campaign on her behalf, she was fanning the flames of controversy. Her judgement was impaired by a desperate desire for freedom, for a life outside with the woman she loved.

Myra and Patricia's relationship continued for the next three years. A former assistant governor of E-wing, who did not want to be named, told me that it was an open secret among the prison management. There was a lot of sympathy for the pair: many of the officers were gay and involved in relationships either with one another or with inmates. But Myra found the situation deeply frustrating. She wanted a complete life with Trisha. The snatched moments they shared together over more than three years began to feel like footholds on an impossibly steep climb.

It was as she was contemplating the abyss beneath that a friend, Maxine Croft, came up with a solution: why didn't they escape? What was she on about? demanded Myra. Maxine was in for fraud; she'd been caught carrying a large sum of used notes in Holland. Myra liked her, but thought she was dippy. That's what I would do in your position, explained Maxine. You'll die in here otherwise. The idea began to take hold in Myra's mind. But where would they go? she asked. Abroad, replied Maxine. She could get hold of passports, visas, cash. Some people on the outside owed her one. She had taken the drop for the fraud and had refused to grass up the other members of her gang. It was a mad idea, but it nagged away at Myra. It seemed like the only chance she and Trisha had of living together. The more she thought about freedom, the more impossible the idea of a life without it felt.

'She just came out with it,' Patricia Cairns told me. ' "I want to escape." "So do I," I replied. "No, I mean it," she said. "I'm going to be stuck in this place until I die. I want you to think about it." ' At first, Trisha Cairns said, the idea seemed like pure fantasy.

'But she was depressed at the time. What I did was to keep her going. I had no intention of springing her. In my mind I was pretending to go along with it.'

Myra, however, was determined to go through with the escape and went over the details again and again. Over time, it slowly became real. They would flee over

Holloway's perimeter wall using a ladder, drive to Heathrow in a hired car and take the 'very convenient' eleven p.m. flight to Rio. Once there they would book themselves into a hotel and make enquiries about missionary work. Myra began to make practical arrangements, and asked Maxine for help. 'I was annoyed because involving Maxine made it real,' Trisha said. 'It had turned from a fantasy I was happy to go along with into a reality.'

Maxine and Trisha met in a small office off the warders' rest room to press the master key to the prison into a bar of Camay soap. They'd never done anything like it before, and bodged the job. The only thing for it was to try again the following evening with plaster of Paris. Maxine had agreed with the forger that the package containing the impressions would be 'dropped' in a left-luggage office at Euston station. The locker slip would be sent, for collection, to a garage in Kilburn. A few days later, Trisha caught the tube to Euston to meet Maxine, who was on day-release.

'It went wrong because the IRA were active at the time and they'd closed the left-luggage office.'

'Because of the letter bomber Shane Paul O'Doherty?' I asked.

'That's the one!' A flash of anger showed in her eye. 'I interviewed him once.'

'Well, give him a punch from me next time you see him!'

Maxine and Trisha discussed what to do, and decided to post the package to the garage direct. They walked down the hill to the post office opposite King's Cross. Maxine, who was on her way to meet her girl-friend, also a prison officer, promised to call the forger. Trisha made the mistake of taking her at her word.

The garage owner, George, did not know what to make of the package when it arrived. He was worried: the IRA bombs seemed to be everywhere; one had even injured the Home Secretary, Reggie Maudling. George asked the customer he was serving what he thought. The man bent down, felt the weight of the parcel and ripped it open. Inside were the impressions of Holloway prison's master keys and a note. The man asked George who this Maxine was. It turned out that he was an off-duty detective inspector.

The following day Myra walked into her cell to find Maxine sitting on the bunk, white as a sheet: Scotland Yard were coming to see her that afternoon! Myra got a message to Trisha, who was on escort duty at Croydon Crown Court, asking to meet her in the chapel that evening. But the net was closing in. When Trisha tried the chapel door from the officers' side, she found it had been security locked. Maxine must have started talking. Myra told her, through the door, to get rid of all the incriminating evidence in her flat.

Trisha rushed to Earls Court and cleared everything out: the luggage she'd bought for their escape, the literature from the Brazilian Embassy, and all the letters Myra had written to her over the past three years. She'd just finished when, at ten p.m., the police arrived to search her flat. They missed it the first time, but when they came back the following day detectives found Myra's new driving licence. Trisha had completely forgotten about it.

Maxine told the police that Trisha had threatened to get some 'heavies' she knew to hurt her mother unless she helped organize the escape. Trisha was charged with 'conspiring with persons unknown to effect the escape of a prisoner', and bailed. The other officers had a whip-round to help raise the £2,000 she needed for a bond. The police questioned Myra before charging her too. Civilian workmen arrived to change the prison locks. This had a profound effect on Myra, and a deep depression began to set in.

The only good thing about being back in court was that Myra got to see Trisha, but the case did not go well for either of them. What's more, they had to see Maxine every day. Maxine's co-operation with the police earned her some reprieve. The judge, Mr Melford Stephenson, said that he felt sorry for the way she'd been manipulated and sentenced her to eighteen months (this was later quashed on appeal). He was a good deal less sympathetic towards Trisha, describing her piety as 'brittle', and gave her six years. An escorting officer tried to stop Myra as she reached out across the dock for Trisha. 'I almost crushed her hand as I held it for the last time.'

The attempt at escape shows that Myra Hindley was desperate for freedom from the moment her relationship with Ian Brady ended. And that the feelings she had for the woman who replaced him, Patricia Cairns, were overwhelming. Once again, she was blinded by the force of her emotions.

Ian Brady, Professor Malcolm MacCulloch told me, watched every twist and turn of the court case from his prison cell.

'Her disloyalty devastated him,' he said.

'But they hadn't seen one another for years,' I replied.

'He called her "my girl" to the day she died. And she was.'

'How do you mean?' I asked.

'He always had a hold over her. Her failure to admit to their surviving secrets meant he could reveal them, and damage her, whenever he liked. She was trapped by her lies.'

And Ian Brady would get his revenge. It was only a matter of time.

Chapter Six

Myra's despair at the loss of Trisha was alleviated by a piece of good news: she was to be allowed to study for an Open University degree. Books were a way of reaching out beyond the walls of Holloway. She told Nellie in a letter home, 'I'll be the first woman in prison to do it, right from scratch. So to speak. It'll be nice to make "history" in a more pleasant way.' A BBC news reporter did a stand-up outside the prison about the lifers' degree scheme. It was all about Myra; no one was interested in the men, even if they were murderers. The implication was that the decision offered her a glint of freedom.

Myra worked hard and tried to smother her distress at losing Trisha. But prisoners transferred from Styal prison, where Trisha was being held, brought news. Most of the inmates were kind to her – it was a good job she'd been well liked as an officer – but the staff were harsh. She was being kept in 'Bleak House', the punishment block, just because of who she was. The only way to communicate with other inmates was through the pipes running along the back of the cell wall. The prisoner in the adjoining cell was a woman she'd guarded at Bulwood Hall Borstal. Months later came the news that Trisha had been moved to the block for short-term prisoners – the worst place to be for a long-term inmate, let alone Myra Hindley's girlfriend. Anyone who wanted to show that they were 'hard' could have a go at her, safe in the knowledge that they'd soon be beyond reach.

'Did you hear from Myra?' I asked Trisha Cairns.

'I hardly got any news. She did send me letters, got them smuggled through. I read them then destroyed them straight away. It was dangerous though, and we used a code right from the start.'

The authorities refused to allow the women to write openly to each other, and it became increasingly dangerous to use couriers: there was always the risk that a letter might be sold and end up in the *Sun*. Trisha Cairns served four years and one week. When she was finally released the former lovers were denied permission to see one another.

Myra was faithful to Trisha during the initial pain of separation, but she knew that they had very little prospect of ever being together again. It was only a matter of time before she took another sexual partner. Trisha was just going to have to get used to it.

'Weren't you jealous of Myra having other relationships?' I asked.

Trisha replied, without faltering, 'She couldn't have coped without someone else by then. It's a question of depth anyway – what we had endured.'

Myra increasingly turned to her family for emotional support. One by one they came to see her in Holloway, relatives like Nanna Hindley, who had wanted nothing to do with her while she was loyal to Ian Brady. Myra's happiest moment came when, after years of beatings from her hard-drinking husband, Maureen finally left David Smith. Mo wrote to Holloway begging for reconciliation. In her reply, Myra said that the letter had brought forth 'sweet tears of joy', and she enclosed a precious 'V.O.' (visiting order).

A month later, Myra was sitting at a table in the visiting area, waiting for Maureen. She watched her come in, glance anxiously round and walk forwards – straight past her table. Myra caught her arm.

'Moby, it's me!'

Maureen gasped, and put her hand over her mouth. She hadn't recognized her sister with brown hair. She looked so different! Myra had stopped using any dye, had had it cut straight across her shoulders, just like Joan Baez.

Each new reconciliation and visit was recorded with delight in letters home. These documents are a record of Myra Hindley's shifting feelings. Shortly after her capture, and while she remained in love with Ian Brady, she was cool and manipulative. When she fell in love with Patricia Cairns her tone softened but remained full of confidence. Now that 'the love of her life' had gone from her day-to-day existence there was a needy, almost desperate tone. Her focus settled on Manchester. She hated it when the members of her family forgot about her. In the middle of February 1975 she wrote to Nellie: 'I haven't heard anything from home for ages. If I wasn't so worried and anxious I'd feel very annoyed . . . no visit and no letter.'

When a letter did eventually arrive the wait for the next one seemed interminable, and Myra often became depressed. 'Do try to drop me a line occasionally, mam, it makes such a difference to life in here to receive letters regularly. I've been in prison 10 years this year, as you know, and things don't get any better. I'm weary of it all, and often wish it would just quietly end, with no bother.'

Myra's reaction to Nellie's letters and visits was euphoric. She allowed herself to imagine what things would be like when she was released, able again to play a part in life outside. I found repeated descriptions in Myra's letters home of how she would care for Nellie, and make things up to her. 'I'm living for the day when I'll be able to look after you.' It seemed as though she could not survive without at least the flickering hope of freedom. The candle might spit and gutter, but if it went out completely she would no longer be able to survive.

Lord Frank Longford continued to see Myra regularly. He was pleased that she had maintained her faith, and introduced her to David Astor. Sir John Trevelyan, the Chief Inspector of Prisons, also became a friend, as did his daughter Sarah Boyle, a young GP who had recently returned from Australia.

'I wasn't really aware how sensitive the case was because I'd been living abroad,' she told me.

'How did you come to see her?'

'The people visiting her, including my father, were predominantly older men, or members of her family. It was felt that it would be good for her to have contact with someone her own age who had a life outside.'

As Myra was allowed just a handful of visits a month, most friendships had to be sustained by writing. The volume of correspondence was huge. She only kept the letters that moved her or were relevant to her campaign for freedom; the rest were burned to prevent them being sold to newspapers by unscrupulous warders. Nevertheless, it took me several weeks to sort through a mound of boxes stuffed with carrier bags, containing carefully labelled envelopes.

Her two most enduring correspondents were David Astor and Frank Longford, but there was a marked difference in the tone and content of their letters. Longford wrote on whatever material fell to hand – House of Lords paper, that of charities he chaired; Astor always used the same restrained, cream-coloured personal stationery. Where Longford was passionate, ungrammatical and campaigning in tone, Astor's carefully formed words spoke of a more politically astute mind. Myra was encouraged to apply for parole. The decision to pursue her freedom ensured that she stayed in the papers. Ann West, the mother of Lesley Ann Downey, accused her supporters of being 'dirty old men'. Myra was enraged by the ensuing banner headlines and attacked the 'vulturous, scabrous pigs' who wrote them. 'Why can't they leave me alone?' she asked Nellie.

I was driving across the rolling Wiltshire Downs, heading for London. On the passenger seat next to me was a package that had arrived in the morning post. I reached over, pulled out a cassette box, flipped it open and slipped the tape into the stereo. I thought there must be some mistake as a clear, pitch-perfect voice filled the car with the words of Joan Baez's 'Prison Trilogy' – the story of three criminals mistreated by the penal system. It was several seconds before I realized that this was Myra Hindley's winning entry to the 1976 Koestler Prize, an arts competition for prisoners. The song ended on a lilting refrain about razing all prisons to the ground.

I pulled in, rewound the tape and listened again as I read the accompanying judges' notes, scrawled in a spidery hand. 'Very well put across – with some sensitive touches which gave it a strange beauty. Words and tuning excellent.' They did not understand, or ignored, Myra's calculated choice of a song that portrayed the criminal as a victim. I ejected the tape, pulled back onto the road and accelerated away.

Every prisoner who came through the gates of Holloway knew it as 'Myra Hindley's nick'. She could feel their eyes on her. Most people just wanted to do their time in peace – get on and get out; there was nothing to be gained by trouble – but not everyone was capable of such rational detachment.

Josie O'Dwyer, a striking young woman who dressed like a man, had a volatile temper. She got on with the child killer Mary Bell but deeply disliked Myra Hindley. Antipathy turned to violence on the tenth anniversary of the Moors murders trial when the *News of the World* re-examined the case in detail. Trisha Cairns told me that the governor had been warned, and she told the warders on E-wing to cut the feature out. But, somehow, it 'found' its way to Josie.

She came at Myra on the landing, grabbed her hair, kicked her in the face, stamped on her leg and tried to heave her body over the railings onto the concrete floor twenty feet below. Blood gushed from her split skin, but Myra did not offer any resistance; she just hung limply on to the metalwork as the blows rained down. Her close friend Janie Jones, recognizing that her life was in danger, leapt onto Josie, grabbed the hand that was holding Myra's hair and stamped on her foot. Josie let go, and Myra slumped to the ground, moaning. Her nose was smashed and the cartilage in her knee torn.

Myra spent six weeks in the prison hospital wing. Her injuries were beyond Holloway's medical staff, and specialists had to be brought in. After careful assessment she was spirited out of the prison for a series of operations. Despite severe warnings from the governor, a warder leaked the story to the *Sun*.

Myra wrote a letter to Nellie from her hospital bed on 12 December 1976, cancelling their Christmas visit. She did not want her niece, Sharon, to see the state she was in. The torn knee cartilage had been removed and her nose rebuilt. 'The centre of my nose wasn't just knocked right, as it appeared to have been, but the whole nose was twisted in all directions. So first the surgeon put it back in the centre, then he took out "the hump" (my request) which we all have (our family, I mean).' The distinctive shape of her nose, the deep shadow it cast, is central to the power of her arrest photograph. It was a trait directly inherited from Bob Hindley. She told Nellie the surgery had left her with 'huge black eyes, but I'll be better soon'.

The decision was taken that she'd be better off in Durham prison. She had been at Holloway for eleven years and had fallen deeply in love there. Despite what had happened, and the knowledge that she'd always be at risk among so many short-termers, leaving was a wrench.

Myra's supporters, Frank Longford and David

Astor, wanted the parole board to consider her for release. Their campaign stirred the interest of the BBC's *Brass Tacks* current affairs programme, which was based in Manchester. Shortly after the move to Durham Myra got a letter: would she help to arrange a televised debate on her case for freedom? The idea was to have four people arguing for her, and four against. In the end, Myra was seduced by the BBC producer's promise to examine the 'role of the press'. In a letter to Nellie she stated that the programme would 'ascertain how much "decision makers" are influenced by public opinion (which is prostituted by the press). The producer has made it clear that the showing of the programme will necessarily depend on my willingness.'

The BBC library tape shows an earnest presenter in a flared suit. The camera jerks around the bare studio in a self-conscious display of 'gritty' realism. Maureen sits in silhouette, an outline of beehive hair and dark glasses projected against the studio wall. Janie Jones and Sarah Boyle argue calmly on Myra's behalf, but struggle to defeat the simple argument that she murdered three children and should not be released after serving little more than a decade. Maureen, her fag-roughened Gorton voice tense with nervousness, sounds aggressive. She loses a slanging match with Ann West, who bellows, 'It was Myra Hindley's voice on that tape, not Ian Brady's. And my daughter was begging for her life!'

Myra heard the parole decision on the radio. Merlyn Rees, the Home Secretary, told the House of Commons that her case had been rejected and would not be reconsidered for another three years. 'I just couldn't believe that the decision could be so savage and callous,' she told Nellie. 'I feel spiritually battered and shattered, but I'll pull myself together because we have to keep each other going. As long as you're alive and waiting for me out there, I'll struggle along somehow.'

Myra got ever closer to Nellie; a continual stream of mundane detail sustained her. Were her workmates kind? Which shops did she go to? When her mother replied that a street had been redeveloped or a cinema closed, it became harder to remember where she was from. She got Nellie to tell her what the new buildings looked like, and where they stood in relation to the old ones. Gorton was the only place she had known, and she needed it, 'otherwise I'll die in here'.

But it wasn't only Nellie who mattered to Myra. Each member of her family represented a tie to the outside world, to where she came from, to what she was. One message delivered to her by the prison chaplain – Mo was ill and had been taken in for 'some tests' – provoked near panic. She sent Mo a get well card, and Nellie a fiver so that she could afford the bus fare to and from the hospital. But before either letter could arrive, tragedy struck. The governor called Myra in to ask whether she wanted to go and say goodbye to her sister, but she arrived at the hospital half an hour after they switched the life-support off. No one had thought to tell Maureen's husband, Bill, that Myra was on the way. A few days later, she wrote to Nellie, 'It's the worst pain I've ever felt . . . but it must be worse for you.' Mo's death made Myra question her faith, but she concluded, 'If we have no faith in God, how can we take comfort knowing that Maureen is in heaven with God?'

In the agony of loss, Myra Hindley poured out page after grief-riven page to Nellie. The letters stood in stark contrast to those she had written immediately after her arrest. I travelled to Cardiff to discuss them with Malcolm MacCulloch.

'Do you think Maureen's death made her reflect on the suffering she'd inflicted on others?' I asked him.

He leant back in his chair and looked out of the window at the garden before replying, 'She did not think of it in those terms. She retained the immunity to violence that allowed her to carry out the crimes in the first place.'

With Maureen gone, Nellie became more dependent on Myra. She was always complaining about how little money there was. Myra asked Lord Longford and David Astor for help – they were rich men – but she could go begging only so often. It was not worth jeopardizing the friendship she had with them, and losing their support. These relationships had a profound effect on Myra's world view, according to

her friend and regular visitor Dr Sarah Boyle. 'Her
friendships were windows on the world!' she
exclaimed. I looked quizzically at her. 'They allowed
her to look outside. Gave her intellectual stimulation.'

Another form of escape was Myra's Open
University degree course. I found her essays, carefully
folded, in their original brown envelopes. They looked
as though they had been taken out and re-read several
times. In March 1981 she wrote nine neat pages of
comment on the banquet scene in *Macbeth*: 'This is
the point in the play, so to speak, when his past catches
up with him and he is faced not merely with Banquo's
ghost, but with all the consequences of his past
actions.' There are ticks and encouraging comments
on every page. At the end the tutor has circled a large
A and written, 'Very good indeed. A pleasure to read.'

Myra's efforts to escape her past only encouraged
newspapers to pursue it. In July 1982, a reporter working for the *Sunday Times*, Linda Melvern, called
round to see her mother. There was an unpaid gas bill
on the table, and the journalist offered to help. Nellie,
who was desperate, agreed, and let her take the tartan
album. When she discovered what had happened,
Myra was apoplectic with rage. 'She'll keep that album
over my dead body, and for her claims that she paid
you for it – that'll go on the score sheet too, the— just
as well I can't swear.' Losing control of the tartan
album made Myra feel deeply insecure. The more
people who saw it, the greater the risk that it would

give up its secrets. She had yet to admit to any of the murders she'd been convicted of, let alone reveal that there were any more victims buried on Saddleworth Moor.

The following year life became easier for Myra with her transfer to Cookham Wood prison at Rochester, in Kent. The regime was gentler, and the buildings newer. But her letters to Nellie remained full of longing for home.

I asked Malcolm MacCulloch what he thought her state of mind was at this time. 'She needed to get out,' he replied. 'The relationship with her family had replaced the obsession with Brady, and she wanted to go home. She thought that the best way of achieving that was to stick to the plan she'd made with Brady: stay silent. The trouble was, he knew the plan and wanted revenge for her betrayal.'

Ian Brady had developed a relationship with the chief reporter of *Today* newspaper, Fred Harrison, and started feeding him lines designed to damage Myra Hindley. Once he was sure of his man, Brady handed him a scoop: there were another two children buried on Saddleworth Moor.

Chapter Seven

Myra was desperate. Her only hope lay in undermining the story. She wrote a letter to the *Observer*, David Astor's old paper. To her relief, they printed it in full. I found a draft, written in blue biro, complete with crossings-out and underlinings, among a bundle of legal documents. 'Ever since I broke off contact with Ian Brady, 13 years ago,' she wrote, 'he has been implying that he could implicate me in "other matters". I have always denied this. If he does have information about other killings then I wish he would tell what he knows to the police, and not just to journalists and psychiatrists, to end the speculation.' But the damage was done. Four days later the Home Secretary announced that the parole board would not reconsider her case for another five years. It looked as though the decision had been influenced by Brady's 'revelations', but Myra still thought that confirming his story would make matters worse.

Friends like Sarah Boyle risked ridicule by remaining loyal to her. 'My husband, Jimmy, said she was lying. I got very cross with him because I felt he was being unjust and cynical.' But Jimmy Boyle knew about criminals: he had been Scotland's most feared gangster. He met Sarah, who was a prison psychiatrist, at Barlinnie Gaol's special unit. He was doing life for the murder of a rival, Babs MacKinchie. Jimmy arrived at the unit as the most feared and uncontrollable prisoner in the Scottish prison system. He had led riots and dirty protests, and had even demolished part of a prison wing. Then an artist in residence handed him something that was to change his life – a chisel. Jimmy found that he could sculpt, very well. On his release he became a celebrated artist and wrote an autobiography, *A Sense of Freedom*.

Jimmy and Sarah visited Myra in prison. I was astonished to read, in a letter to Nellie, that they asked Myra to be godmother to their first child, Susie. Today, Sarah Boyle lives in a large Georgian house in the prosperous Inverleith area of Edinburgh. The garden is full of Jimmy's sculptures, but he has moved to France.

'Jimmy said she should tell the truth, that it had worked for him. She said, "I am, Jimmy, I am."'

'What did he reply?'

'"Come off it, hen! I've been there." But she stuck to her guns, and I believed her.'

Trapped by lies, Myra Hindley tried to make her

story ring true through repetition. In a letter to Nellie she wrote, 'Two friends of mine went to read the trial transcripts. One of them, who has known me for fifteen years, said she's absolutely stunned that I was convicted on no evidence at all, while it's obvious Smith set me up so he wouldn't go down with Brady.'

But Brady's claim wouldn't go away. The families of the missing children demanded the reopening of the case. They were supported by the parents of the victims who had been found. Both were sure that exposing the full horror of the crimes would ensure Myra Hindley's death behind bars. The police issued a statement saying that the case had never been closed. The families' response, Myra told Nellie, was furious: 'Mrs pain in the neck West got back on her bandwagon and threatened to dig up the moor herself if the police didn't. She seems to feed on such publicity with a somewhat masochistic compulsion.'

The details of the murders were repeatedly reprinted in every national newspaper. Myra railed to Nellie, 'What on earth is amiss when they have to start scraping the bottom of a twenty-year-old barrel for news when there is so much happening out there? Anyway, my precious one, for your sake more than mine, I hope they don't print any garbage. I hate them. God forgive me, but I do.'

Myra's exaggerated indignation reminded me of the words she had written to Nellie while on remand at Risley in 1965. It was the same tactic: denying an allegation in the hope that it would never be proven. The increasingly desperate tone of Myra's protestations suggest that Nellie might have voiced the same thought. But Myra's resolve began to weaken when she got the news that Fred Harrison was writing a book.

The police were compelled to revisit the case. The head of Greater Manchester CID, Superintendent Peter Topping, and his deputy, DI Geoff Knupfer, went to see Myra Hindley on the off chance that she might help. 'We were there on a flyer, really,' Knupfer told me. 'We didn't expect her to give us anything.' The detectives told her that there had been 'a lot of pressure' since Brady's revelations for them to reactivate the investigation into the disappearance of Pauline Reade and Keith Bennett. At last, Myra decided to abandon the strategy she had maintained for the past twenty years and agreed to help. The police moved quickly in case she changed her mind, but Myra had finally realized that the best way out of the current situation, and to make people forget that she had lied for so long, was to help find the missing bodies. However, according to Patricia Cairns, there is no doubt that given the choice she would have kept silent about the murders of Pauline Reade and Keith Bennett. 'She only came clean because she had to. She needed to get in first. She wanted to stop him taking control. She told me that the effort of going through with it nearly killed her.'

Myra was determined that any help she gave should improve her chances of release rather than damage her image still further. She knew how sensitive the Home Office was to the demands of public opinion. There was no mention to the police of a system for recording where bodies were buried, or her role in creating it. She did, however, agree to return to the moor to try to find the missing children. The police blocked the A635 and threw a cordon of armed officers round the moor. Myra was told that she'd be going in by helicopter, with a bodyguard. She was advised to wear a pair of cords, a couple of pairs of socks, and two thick sweaters.

The deputy governor came to see Myra the night before with some 'news'. She wasn't going to like this, but there would be two prison officers going along as escorts and she'd have to be cuffed to one of them, 'for her own safety', at all times. Myra was furious, and demanded to know who was behind the decision. 'Head office,' came the answer – probably a government minister. 'The idiot' who made the decision had clearly never set foot on Saddleworth Moor; she could see herself and the escort floundering from tussock to tussock, slipping hand in hand down peat crevices.

They woke Myra at four in the morning and introduced her to her bodyguard, Detective Inspector Roy Rainford. The firearms officer had arrived with a selection of different-sized wellingtons, waterproof trousers, balaclavas and bulletproof vests for her and the prison officers. He told them they had to keep their balaclavas pulled down at all times. The police wanted to make it as difficult as possible for the press, or an assassin, to pick Myra out. Myra told the officer that she wasn't worried, whatever happened happened. The policeman gave her a look which said that he was worried, it was his job. Once they were dressed, Myra was handcuffed to 'Speedy', the junior of the two prison officers.

They sat three abreast on the back seat and waited for the prison gates to open. Roy Rainford told them to duck their heads, and the car accelerated at high speed towards the waiting helicopter. There was just one photographer's car, a Jaguar, waiting outside the gate. The Metropolitan Police helicopter was surrounded by armed officers. Myra and 'Speedy' went up the steps crabwise, their arms twisting in the cuffs, and settled down in the back of the machine. In her confusion, Myra put the ear-muffs on back to front; Rainford turned round, gently lifted them off her head and put them back the right way round. Myra felt comfortable with him. The helicopter lifted off and slipped over the green fields of Kent towards Saddleworth Moor. Myra noticed that 'Speedy', who hated flying, had gone very pale. The officer lit a cigarette to calm her nerves, and handed one to Myra. A convoy on the ground followed the helicopter north, in case of emergency; police records show that they had checked out the accident facilities in every hospital along the route. They stopped twice to refuel, the second time just twenty miles from their destination.

Before long the moor appeared through the clouds, covered in patches of snow. They were so high up that it appeared featureless – not the beautiful landscape Myra had known so intimately. Still, she felt a thrill of excitement to be returning to a place that lived on inside her. The winds were so strong that the pilot had to circle several times before bringing the machine down.

On the ground they were led across the uneven turf to the police command centre. Myra held her wrist up to her solicitor, Michael Fisher, in exasperation. Could he do something about the handcuffs? What about calling the lifer unit at the Home Office? A man who had been watching stepped forward and introduced himself as Commander John Metcalfe, the Home Office liaison officer. He said he knew about the order and it couldn't be changed. Peter Topping, who'd been up all night, took the commander into an adjoining room for 'a chat'. When they came back, the cuffs were removed.

Myra told Topping that their best chance lay in starting at the lay-by where she and Ian Brady parked the night Keith Bennett died. But the whole operation was considered so risky that every detail had been worked out beforehand, and the superintendent was reluctant to change his plan. They drove her down a water board track to where Shiny Brook poured into the reservoir. It was a route she had never taken before.

Topping's decision, which he later admitted was a mistake, is understandable. He was under severe pressure. A junior Home Office minister, David Mellor, had given away what they were doing on Radio 4's *Today* programme. His revelation robbed the police of the element of surprise over the press. It was only a matter of time before hired helicopters carrying photographers with long lenses appeared in the sky above them.

The walk up Shiny Brook from the water board track is treacherous, especially in wet weather. At the start you have to climb over large boulders to join a narrow path above the roaring water – one slip, and you're in. Further up, where Myra and Ian shot guns, the stream cuts back and forth across the valley floor. The only way to make your way up is to jump across the water. It is difficult for a fit person, never mind a sedentary, middle-aged life-sentence prisoner.

It was not long before the press helicopters arrived. The police machine held position in the sky above, trying to give the search party some cover, but every so often one of the newspapers' helicopters broke through and the police had to form a protective circle around Myra. What if it was a man with a gun rather than a camera? In the distance, a helicopter touched down and two journalists sprang out. They were pursued across the moor by police officers. Another photographer was discovered, shivering and close to hypothermia, in a bush. He was in no state to take a picture. John Kilbride's father, Pat, walked up to a police road-block brandishing a kitchen knife. As he was escorted by a couple of reporters, the police suspected he'd been put up to it and turned him back gently rather than arrest him. He repeated the scene, over a pint, in front of the cameras a short while later. 'You see what I've got here? I'd like to fucking kill her!' he bellowed. I watched the BBC library tape with discomfort: the journalists in the background looked far too eager for this display of grief.

Myra struggled to orientate herself. She was looking for a gully close to the waterfall, but was confused by the direction from which they had approached Shiny Brook. The snow on the ground didn't help. One after the other the two dog handlers accompanying the party fell into the stream. Then 'Speedy' twisted her knee. Peter Topping called for a stretcher to carry her off the moor, but the ground was so rough that first the front, then the rear stretcher bearer stumbled, dumping 'Speedy' among the tussocks.

After lunch, Topping agreed to approach Shiny Brook from the lay-by. But by then Myra was hobbling on a strapped ankle, sleet had begun to fall, and the press helicopters had returned. She was doing her best to find the right gully, but did not make any mention of marker photographs. After reading her account of this visit I found it hard to accept that Myra had forgotten about the pictures. It seemed more likely that she did not mention them because they tied her directly to the murder of Keith Bennett, and its subsequent celebration. This could only worsen her chances of release.

Back at Cookham Wood Myra spent all night sitting up with her 'very close friend' Noreen, from New Zealand. They agreed that the 'hate-inciting gutter press' might leave her alone if she managed to find the missing children. But she hadn't formally admitted to taking part in their murders yet. Her manoeuvring was getting in the way of the truth.

Over the next eight weeks Myra turned the story over and over in her mind, and in February 1987 she finally agreed to give Peter Topping a formal confession. The details were worked out with the help of a former prison governor, and clergyman, Peter Timms. It was agreed that he would attend to support her. The confession was tape-recorded over three days at Cookham Wood. Her solicitor, Michael Fisher, read a statement from Myra to the press outside, saying that she had made the decision to 'tell the truth' in response to a letter from the mother of Keith Bennett, Winnie Johnson. Again, it is hard to accept this as the driving force behind her decision as there had been many heart-rending letters over the years. The difference now was that Myra had been cornered by Ian Brady.

During the interview Topping asked Myra a direct question: did Ian Brady use photographs to mark graves? As far as she knew, came the reply, he didn't. The police officers felt that every word she uttered was carefully chosen, the desire for freedom at the forefront of her mind.

'She was always in the other room, or over the hill,' Geoff Knupfer said. 'She was never there when things happened.'

'Did you feel that she was shaping her story?' I asked him.

'Definitely. She never told a direct lie, and was always very helpful, but there was no doubt that she had an agenda.'

Many of Myra's friends cut her off when they realized she had been lying to them about her role in the murders. They had accepted her promise that she was innocent. 'It was a betrayal,' Sarah Boyle told me. 'I felt devastated by it. It was very, very difficult because I had trusted what she'd told me and I'd put my own name and reputation on the line to support her, as had many other people.' Her friend from Holloway Janie Jones was also outraged at the deception, and spent the next year writing a book, *The Devil and Miss Jones*. Myra could live with this, but she was devastated when Maureen's husband Bill cut off all contact with her niece, Sharon. She kept dozens of pictures of the little girl and wrote to her every week. 'I cannot bear it,' Myra told Nellie, 'but I thank God your feelings towards me haven't changed.'

Peter Topping rang Myra at the end of each day's digging to tell her what his men had done, in the hope of unlocking some hidden memory. He was dispirited when he called Cookham Wood late on the evening of 7 July. Frustrated by a lack of progress, the press, lacking anything to report, had turned on him. On the table lay a copy of the *Manchester Evening News*: STOP THIS FARCE NOW.

The detective told her they were looking on Hollin Brown Knoll. Geoff Knupfer sat and watched the conversation. He didn't expect anything to come of it, but you never could tell. 'He asked her what she could see from the graveside. It was a chance thing. She said, "Nothing, except the body, and the dark outline of the hills against the sky." We knew we were on to something straight away.' There was only one place on the knoll where you could see the distant Pennine ridge. The following day Topping and his team found the grave of Pauline Reade. 'I have to admit,' Knupfer told me, with a gentle smile, 'that we took a certain amount of pleasure from the apology in the *Manchester Evening News*.'

Chapter Eight

Myra told me that she watched the funeral on the news. The service was held at the monastery church in Gorton. Joan Reade, driven half-mad by the agony of unresolved grief, scattered soil on the coffin as it was lowered into the ground. Topping and his team stood around, looking awkward. Frank Longford gave an interview to demand Myra's release as she had 'done the right thing'.

A few days later Topping went to see Myra at Cookham Wood. He wanted her to help find the body of Keith Bennett. She still did not tell him that she and Ian had taken marker photographs of his grave. Had Topping been able to read the first draft of her autobiography, written two years earlier, he would have found a clue, for there Myra described an incident that occurred before any of the murders. She and Ian had been to midnight mass at St James's Protestant Church in Gorton. He staggered out of the front door, took a swig from a whisky bottle and relieved himself on a grave. 'Little did I realize then that his graves would be marked by photographs and not head-stones,' Myra wrote.

After Topping's investigation she completed another draft of the autobiography. Here she admitted being less than frank with the detective superintendent and his deputy, Geoff Knupfer, during an interview. The policemen produced pictures of her and Ian standing, grinning, on the rocks at Hollin Brown Knoll. Myra wanted to help, to take the credit for finding the missing children, but did not want to admit the depth of her complicity as this would under-mine her case for release. In the autobiography she wrote, 'I wanted them to know, without saying in so many words, which grave was in which area.' So she was not completely open about the meaning of the pictures, even though 'they were taken to indicate there was a grave'. Instead, she suggested Topping get the pictures blown up – her way of saying that they mattered. The enlargement would reveal the expiry date on the tax disc, April 1964, by which time two children were dead, John Kilbride and Pauline Reade. As the picture was clearly not of John Kilbride's grave, 'it had to be marking the location of Pauline Reade's grave, which, in turn, meant that Keith Bennett's grave was in the Hoe Grain/Shiny Brook area [where similar "landscapes" were taken]'. But at the time Topping and Knupfer had no chance of working out what she meant. Nevertheless, Geoff Knupfer did go through the tartan album in a fruitless search for clues. He also looked at his predecessors' claims about a system.

'There was some mention of a system at the original trial,' Knupfer told me. 'But we felt it was all pretty tenuous stuff. The only picture you could be sure about was John Kilbride's.'

In the second draft of her autobiography Myra Hindley writes in detail about the pictures taken at Shiny Brook. 'We visited this place several times before Keith Bennett was taken there, and often packed a picnic lunch, cooling a bottle of wine in the stream on top of what I called the plateau of the moor,' Myra wrote. There are some pictures of her standing by the waterfall, others of her with Carol and David Waterhouse from Wardlebrook Avenue. 'The police on the original case returned the slides after about 18 months. Ian had them in prison, where he had permission to view them through a hand-size projector.'

I took the autobiography to Birmingham University, and sipped bad instant coffee while Professor John Hunter and his assistant, Barrie Simpson, read it from cover to cover. When Simpson had finished he re-read the passages dealing with marker pictures. The former head of the West Midlands Police murder squad was emphatic: 'This is it. This is the confirmation that they marked Keith's grave, and they took him to Shiny Brook. The police have got to act on this.'

Several weeks later, in the basement of a small west London independent production company's premises, DC Gail Jazmik and DS Fiona Robertshaw read the newly discovered text. I was cutting a film for Channel 4 along the corridor, and popped in to see them every couple of hours. At the end of the day they got to the section about marker photographs.

'Can I take a copy of these pages?' Fiona Robertshaw asked, pinching four sheets between her fingers.

'Of course.'

Topping decided to take Myra back to the moor. Not only had she helped to find Pauline, but she had also confessed to her role in the killings. This time they would be able to openly discuss burial sites, not 'places of interest to Ian Brady'. But first Topping had to persuade the Home Office, which had taken a battering from the press over the last visit and was anxious to avoid a repeat. Topping got his way, and he smuggled Myra onto the moor at 5.40 one morning without any journalists spotting her. But the reason for the reporters' failure also hampered the search: mist. Even officers who had spent months searching Hoe Grain struggled to work out where they were. Myra could not be certain about any locations.

Ian Brady observed events closely from his cell at Ashworth Special Hospital. His former psychiatrist, Malcolm MacCulloch, told me that he was worried about losing control. 'So, almost as a retaliation, in order to recoup power and omnipotence about what had happened, he assisted as well and Peter Topping was able to go and speak to him.' Topping decided to accept Ian Brady's offer of 'help' and got the Home Secretary's permission to take him to Saddleworth. Brady appeared confident of success, and strode so fast over the tussock grass that Topping had to grab hold of his arm for support. But when they reached Eagle's Head rock, which has a clear view of a vast expanse of moorland, he acted confused. It was all different. Topping asked what he meant. Brady replied, improbably, that the rock sheep pens had moved.

I pored over Topping's notes at Greater Manchester Police headquarters. They state that two days after the visit to the moor he went to Ashworth Special Hospital. Brady got out the pictures procured by Myra. Surprised, Topping asked why Brady was showing them to him. Brady replied, only so that he could see how the landscape had changed. A few days later Topping rang Brady: there was no other meaning to those pictures, was there? Oh no, came the reply, of course not! Brady knew that Myra had not admitted to helping mark all the graves, that it conflicted with her story and her campaign for freedom.

I pointed the notes out to DC Gail Jazmik. The blood drained from her face.

Professor Malcolm MacCulloch smiled wryly when

I asked him about Ian Brady's return to the moor.

'It is possible that Ian Brady was on the moor and checked the site without letting on. So he has got his last body still in place, and I think that would be entirely consistent with what we know [about him].'

'And would it be very important for him to have that control?' I asked.

'Yes, absolutely. The final control is the possession of the body.'

'He's the winner?'

'Yes. "I know you don't know, you want to know, and I'm not going to tell you."'

The press had been friendly since the discovery of Pauline Reade, but it was only a matter of time before they turned again. Peter Topping and Geoff Knupfer decided to call off the search for Keith Bennett. 'We'd done everything we could,' Knupfer told me. 'There was no way forward.'

Shortly afterwards a letter bearing a Manchester postmark arrived for Myra. The handwriting looked like Winnie Johnson's. She slit the envelope open and began to read. 'Dear Ms Hindley, My name is Alan Bennett, Keith's brother . . .' Myra understood now why the letters she had received from 'Mrs Johnson' had sounded so calm, while her public statements were filled with anger. The letter asked whether she might be willing to help. Myra wrote back and invited Alan to correspond with her.

In his next letter Alan told her that he had begun to

search Saddleworth Moor with his brothers, and a team of volunteers. He said his family felt as though they had been abandoned by the authorities. When he called Peter Topping, who had left the police to write a book based on Myra Hindley's taped confession, he was told to speak to his 'publicity agent'. He later discovered that Topping's team had kept no record of their search.

At first, Alan and Myra's exchanges were cautious. She half expected her letters to appear in the *Sun*, but it never happened. Finally, she asked him to come and see her. He hesitated before deciding that she was his only hope. 'It was a very difficult thing to go through,' Alan told me. 'But what choice did I have? There was no other way of finding Keith. I wrote to Brady as well. At first it seemed as if he wanted to help. But I soon realized that he was just playing games.'

'How do you mean?'

'Look at this letter here.' Alan held out a sheet of paper covered in neat blue copperplate. 'He says that trying to tell me where Keith's grave is would be like "describing colours to a blind man". He's getting off on it.'

Myra's decision to 'co-operate' with the police had not improved her prospects of release. An opportunity to stem the flow of negative headlines arose in 1989 when she was told that she'd passed her Open University degree. The certificate was awarded to her at a specially arranged ceremony. It was one of the proudest days of her life. David Astor rang up his former picture editor on the *Observer* for advice on how to get photographs of the ceremony into all the nationals. The answer was simple: the Camera Press agency, 'totally reliable and very efficient'.

David Astor and his wife cropped the pictures themselves, to exclude 'irrelevant figures', before handing them over. The result, he wrote to Myra, was not all that he had hoped for: 'They interpreted the issue of the pictures as the launch of a new campaign to get you out. I think they would have said this whatever we did.' Reading Astor's words I could not help but feel that, however crudely expressed, the tabloids had understood the situation correctly. The following year, her parole application was turned down.

Five Home Secretaries in succession ruled that Myra Hindley should die behind bars. She was certain that this was because her face was never out of the papers, and raged about them in letters home to Nellie. At Durham it had been: 'Myra and Rose West in Love'; at Cookham Wood the governor allowed inmates to have a go on a pony to maintain their awareness of the outside world. The *Sun* front page: 'Trot in Hell'. Then she was moved to Highpoint in Suffolk, or 'Hi-de-Highpoint': a 'holiday camp' with 'luxury rooms'. Her arrest photograph stared out of every new story.

In order to try to lower the temperature, Myra even cut off Frank Longford, refusing to send him invitations to visit. In a letter to me she wrote: 'It is a task even beyond Hercules to gag Frank Longford . . . if the dangerous dogs act was still in force I'd take it upon myself to muzzle him.'

Alan Bennett asked Myra whether she might consider hypnotherapy as a way of unlocking the 'secret' of where Keith lay buried. He had a doctor, Una Maguire, lined up to do the work. Myra agreed; the Home Office dithered. Only after a lengthy campaign, behind closed doors, did they finally relent. But before going ahead Myra 'sought medical advice' and wrote to tell Alan that her doctors had advised her it was 'unsafe'. Knowing Myra, I could not imagine her ever going through with hypnotherapy. She was such a controlled figure that letting go would have been extremely difficult. Especially as she might have revealed the true depth of her complicity.

But Myra knew that the case would stay in the public eye as long as it remained unsolved. In 1998 she decided to have one last go, without incriminating herself, at telling the police where the final missing victim of the Moors murders lay buried. She sent Alan Bennett a visiting order to come and see her at Highpoint prison. As they sat in the segregation block's small beige meeting room she agreed to meet detectives, with him, to go through the police copy of the tartan album. 'You never know, I might remember something.'

As Alan walked out of the prison gate a smartly dressed man crossed the car park towards him.

'Hello, Mr Bennett. Dick Saxty of the *Sun*.'

Alan refused to speak to him, and failed to see the photographer on the other side of the road. He was on the front page the following day: 'Evil Myra murdered his little brother . . . yet he's gone to jail to give her a *hug*.'

Undeterred, Alan met the police, and they agreed to the visit. Myra wrote to Sarah Boyle to tell her about it. 'She said she was looking forward to it,' Sarah said. 'She seemed ready to help.' Myra also called me to ask whether I could advise Alan Bennett on how to deal with the press. The plan was for him to come in with the detectives. She seemed optimistic: 'I have seen the pictures before, but I am hopeful. It's definitely worth doing.'

Alan and I met at his bedsit in Longsight and roughed out a statement. It explained that he was visiting Myra Hindley so that he could find, and bury, his murdered brother. But two days before the visit was to take place Alan got a call from Sergeant Alan Kibble to cancel – Superintendent Montgomery had a 'family crisis'. A few days later Myra Hindley was rushed to West Suffolk Hospital after suffering a cerebral aneurysm. To Alan Bennett's dismay, the visit was never rearranged. 'I suspect now they were worried about the press. The focus was always on her getting out, and I think someone warned them off.

They were so paranoid they even suggested I shave my beard off to avoid being recognized.' Alan stared through the net curtains, towards the school he and Keith had attended. The campaign to keep Myra Hindley behind bars had also hindered the search for Keith Bennett.

It took Myra Hindley six months to recover from the operation to save her life, and the deep depression it precipitated. She cut off contact with Alan and passed a message through her priest, Michael Teader, to say that she 'couldn't cope' with seeing him any longer.

Chapter Nine

I laid the magazine down. Myra Hindley's arrest photograph was splashed across the cover of the *New Statesman* above the words LORD CHIEF JUSTICE GIVES HINDLEY HOPE OF FREEDOM. Lord Woolf, Britain's most senior judge, had spoken about the adoption of the European Convention on Human Rights. He believed that judges would now take over the Home Secretary's role in deciding how long lifers should serve.

Woolf was due to hear Myra Hindley's case in the House of Lords towards the end of 2002. It seemed as though Myra's strategy of withholding the whole truth might be about to pay off. David Astor called me to say that he had begun planning what would happen when she got out. There was a convent in New York that had agreed to take her, and Myra had accepted; all they had to do was 'get the tabloids off her back'. Did I think a press conference might do the trick? I told him that I didn't think so.

There was a leaflet about the convent among her papers. It spoke of a reflective life and showed nuns at prayer. Tucked inside were photographs of the building where they lived, a white 1930s stucco-fronted house near the sea. It stood on a large plot surrounded by similar buildings, and looked in good order. I struggled to imagine her there, and asked Patricia Cairns how deep she thought Myra's faith really was. 'I never sensed it was 100 per cent genuine,' she replied, 'but I don't know. She returned to the faith to please me, and even when we were separated she kept it up. But she read the spiritual works of a number of people like the Dalai Lama and Khalil Gibran. I'd say she was spiritual but not religious.'

The *Sun* found out about the plan – MYRA TO BE NUN. The sisters took fright and David Astor had to start all over again. He asked Terry Waite, the Archbishop of Canterbury's former special envoy to the Middle East, to help. The court case was approaching rapidly and they did not have much time.

During the House of Lords hearing her advocate, Edward Fitzgerald, called Myra every evening to tell her how things were going. The Law Lords were giving him a hard time, but he thought he was winning the argument. I watched the hearing from the public benches a couple of metres behind Fitzgerald. The feeling among the spectating lawyers seemed to be that his optimism was well founded. The judgment was due in the New Year.

I was about to go into a meeting in London on Friday, 15 November 2002 when my mobile rang.

'Duncan, it's Gail Jazmik. The boss asked me to let you know she's been taken ill.'

'Is it serious?'

'Yes.'

Father Michael Teader sat by Myra's side as the ambulance rushed her the ten miles to Bury St Edmunds Hospital. The doctors said there was nothing they could do. Father Michael summoned a nun, Sister Bridget, who was close to Myra. He thought she would want her there.

'Yeah, won't be long now, she's on the way out,' the uniformed policewoman barked into her radio.

'Do you mind!' snapped Sister Bridget. She was holding Myra's hand; Father Michael held the other.

Myra Hindley slipped away at lunchtime, taking all that she knew with her.

Chapter Ten

'Duncan, we've heard back from the cryptologist about the letters and notebooks.'

Superintendent Tony Brett sat with his back to the window, staring at me. To his right were DC Gail Jazmik and DS Fiona Robertshaw. Their faces remained impassive as he spoke. The press officer, DC Andy Meekes, flicked nervously at his notepad with a pen. Brett did not sound like a man with good news.

'There is a code,' he said.

'What does it say?'

'That's the problem. The messages are unclear to anyone other than Myra Hindley and Ian Brady.'

'In what way?'

'If I were to say to you, remember the day we went to Blackpool? It sounds innocuous, but if that were the day we had killed someone you'd know instantly what I meant.'

The police faced a difficult situation. Myra Hindley

had taken the secret to her grave, and Ian Brady was clearly not going to help.

'We're going to do his room, see if we can find the pictures, and see if they are markers.'

'When?' I asked him.

'We need to speak to our lawyers. You can be sure that Brady will take legal action. Everything's got to be watertight.'

I felt a sense of excitement as I walked out of Leigh police station imagining detectives pushing their way into Brady's room at Ashworth Special Hospital and seizing the pictures that show where Keith Bennett is buried. His family would, at last, be able to lay him to rest.

I called Alan, and he invited me round to his bedsit for a cup of tea.

'It's great news,' he said. 'For years there has been no progress, and now this.'

We sat in silence for a couple of minutes. Suddenly, Alan stubbed out his roll-up and stood up.

'I've got something I want you to hear.'

He walked over to the large stereo system next to the window and slipped a cassette into the tape deck. From the speakers emerged the sound of a middle-aged lady speaking, and the giggling of excited children. Then a high, clear voice filled the room. It was several moments before I realized that I was listening to Keith Bennett singing 'Jerusalem'.

And did the countenance Divine
Shine forth upon our clouded hills?
And was Jerusalem builded here
Among these dark Satanic Mills?

As the hymn ended, Blake's words were replaced with the applause of proud adults.

Alan clicked off the tape.

'My Auntie Jean recorded that the Christmas before he died. Towards the end of each year, I drive up to the moor, park up, and listen to it. It makes me feel close to him.'

Brett told me that he intended to carry out a search within days. But three weeks after the meeting at Leigh there was still no news. He called me as I was walking, in the rain, up to Birmingham New Street station.

'Duncan, there's a problem.' He sounded angry.

'What?'

'Treasury Counsel says because Brady can't be charged with the murder of Keith Bennett we can't have a warrant to search his cell.'

Only recently, of course, had Greater Manchester Police sought to charge Myra Hindley with the murders for which she had never been tried. Treasury Counsel, the government's legal service, would not proceed with this attempt to keep her behind bars because of an earlier court decision. The families of Pauline Reade and Keith Bennett had demanded a new trial in the mid-eighties. The Director of Public Prosecutions refused then on the grounds that it would be a waste of taxpayers' money. To try to reverse that decision would have been ruled an 'abuse of process' – and the same applied to Brady now. After being denied permission to raid Brady's cell Tony Brett did hire a firm that analyses images for the security services to study his photographs. But they ran up against the same problem as GCHQ: the coded messages in the pictures were too oblique. There was nothing that said 'X marks the spot'. I realized that Greater Manchester Police would definitely not resume a search of the moor without information that pinpointed the exact location of Keith Bennett's grave.

The family of Keith Bennett and forensic archaeologists working on the case were exasperated by the police's insistence on precise information. 'I just don't agree with their strategy,' Professor John Hunter told me. He remained determined to find Keith Bennett and was certain that the body lay buried by Shiny Brook. 'They know which area he's in and should get on and clear it. It's politics: they took a battering from the press last time they searched and don't want the same again.'

I returned to Saddleworth Moor for a final time and took the path to Shiny Brook. It was a grey day, and Professor Malcolm MacCulloch's words seemed to hang in the wind: 'Final control is possession of the body. "I know you don't know, you want to know, and I'm not going to tell you." '

I now understood that the struggle over Myra Hindley's freedom had obscured the truth. In order to try to present a favourable image and win release she failed to admit complicity in recording the murders; and in order to respond to the demands of public opinion successive Home Secretaries focused on keeping her inside rather than on the needs of justice. Manchester's most senior detective was only assigned to the case, after fifteen years of inactivity, to make sure Myra Hindley died behind bars rather than to find Keith Bennett. By playing to the gallery, Myra Hindley and the forces of law and order unwittingly conspired to hand Ian Brady what he wanted – the perfect murder.

I climbed back into my car to drive home, and tried to put out of my mind the stretch of windblown cotton grass where Keith Bennett still lies.

Conclusion

It should not have been necessary for me to write this book. The forces of law and order, rather than a journalist, should have discovered the truth behind the Moors murders. I firmly believe that, had they been told to go looking, detectives would have found much of the material that has fallen into my hands over the past few years. Why does this matter? After all, Myra Hindley is dead and Ian Brady will never be free. The answer is that a family remains trapped by suffering, a great city continues to live under a dark shadow, and Ian Brady still has his perfect murder. It is a matter of national shame.

On Thursday, 7 October 1965, Superintendent Bob Talbot's knock on the back door at 16 Wardlebrook Avenue set in motion the mechanism that deals with all major crime. The police investigate, a case is put before a court and the guilty are, more often than not, convicted. The recovery of the bodies of Lesley Ann

Downey and John Kilbride was necessary to this process. There was evidence directly linking the accused to their disappearance: a tape, photographs, and Ian Brady's notebook. Although Keith Bennett and Pauline Reade were also believed to be victims they did not need to be found in order to secure a conviction.

The legal system functioned as it is meant to. A well-constructed prosecution case, and the offensive behaviour of the accused, ensured guilty verdicts. There were glimpses in court of what lay behind the killings: references to de Sade, Hitler, pornography, and a system for marking where bodies lay buried. It was clear that Myra Hindley had been 'normal' before she met Ian Brady – the judge said so – and that something had turned her from a 'good Catholic girl' into a 'monster'. But these facts only emerged as the defence and prosecution vied with each other to establish guilt or innocence. Neither side was interested in cause, in what had brought them all to Court Number 2, Chester Assizes.

It was only thirty-six years later, with the death of Myra Hindley and the discovery of her private papers, that an explanation for the Moors murders emerged. In large part, this account is told from Myra's point of view. But that is its strength, as it leads us to an understanding of the woman and her actions. The account is far too comprehensive, and full of detail, to be the work of an outright liar. It stands up to comparison with contemporaneous sources. Where there is deception, it is by omission.

There may be even more to be learned about the Moors murders, but what has emerged over the past few years is of real value. We now know, as Professor Malcolm MacCulloch said, that the murders were the result of an appalling 'concatenation of circumstances'. A young woman with a tough personality, taught to hand out and receive violence from an early age, became obsessed with a sexually sadistic psychopath. They found common cause in their dislocation from the working class and set out to establish their superiority through murder. Myra told me that she and Ian Brady were 'separated by a chasm from the rest of the world'. On their side of this divide they built a home, and in that home they kept their possessions – the perfect murders. The killings were what defined them; they were something to be treasured and remembered. Ian Brady's marker pictures and the tartan album were an affirmation, and celebration, of what they had achieved together. When Judge Fenton-Atkinson sentenced them to life he may have glimpsed these facts, but they did not really concern him. What mattered was that Ian Brady and Myra Hindley had killed, and must pay the price.

The year after she was sent to Holloway prison the police did interview Myra Hindley to see if she'd 'cooled off' and might tell them the truth. What they found was a woman still in love with her accomplice and, although physically separated, still as one with him. The officers returned north to Manchester and the case, although still open, was put back on the shelf. The Moors murderers were behind bars – what else was there to do? I wonder what photographic officer Ray Gelder, who first suspected there was a system for marking bodies, must have thought when he learned that the tartan album had been returned to the Moors murderers. Almost every police officer was sure that there were more bodies.

During the first five years of their imprisonment, we now know, Myra Hindley and Ian Brady exchanged sexually sadistic fantasies. They wrote to each other incessantly, in a secret code, about the photographs in the tartan album. The Prison Service meticulously copied all of these letters and put them into storage. But it was only when I pointed out their contents to Greater Manchester Police that GCHQ was called in to try to decode them. No one had thought to do so before because the job of the Prison Service was to keep the Moors murderers behind bars, not to try to close the case.

It is now clear, from Myra Hindley's papers, that a fundamental shift took place when she fell in love with Patricia Cairns. The bond with Ian Brady was broken and she became desperate for her freedom. In retrospect, this may have offered an opportunity to get at the truth. An adviser to Greater Manchester Police in the 1980s, and professor of forensic archaeology at the

Smithsonian Institution in Washington, Bruno Frohlich, told me how the authorities in the United States might have approached the situation. 'We cut deals,' he said. 'You give us the body, we'll consider your request for freedom. It works.' But there was no question of talking to Myra Hindley at this stage, never mind cutting a deal. It wasn't worth the political cost for any Home Secretary to be seen to engage with her. The overriding priority was to keep her behind bars.

Myra Hindley, in her desperation to be released, did not mention either Keith Bennett or Pauline Reade during the first twenty years of her sentence. Only when the case was revisited following Ian Brady's revelation that there were another two bodies on Saddleworth Moor did she agree to talk to the officer in charge of the inquiry, Superintendent Peter Topping. But we have now learned that this co-operation was partial, her words hemmed in by the need not to say anything that might harm her chances of release. It was a vague description of the view from Pauline Reade's graveside – 'the dark outline of the hills against the sky' – that led to the recovery of the teenager's body.

During the subsequent search for Keith Bennett, Myra Hindley did hint at the existence of a photographic marker system to Peter Topping, but her words were so convoluted as to be meaningless. The superintendent's work was further hampered by the debate surrounding her campaign for freedom, the press hectoring on the one hand, politicians grandstanding on the other. The interests of the Bennett family were not at the forefront of reporters' or government ministers' minds.

The decision to abandon the search for Keith Bennett left his family quite alone. In desperation they spent a decade digging over miles of moorland. Alan Bennett contacted both Ian Brady and Myra Hindley for help. Brady taunted him, Hindley appeared to co-operate. But, once again, her help was partial. Although she had described the existence of a marker system in her unpublished autobiography, she did not disclose its existence to Alan. Instead, she offered to look at Ian Brady's photographs, with the police, 'in case' she 'remembered something'.

What could have proved a decisive meeting never took place. When Alan Bennett was snapped by a *Sun* photographer outside Highpoint prison, the newspaper's front page the next day lambasted him for going to see her, portrayed him as a fool. 'It's just a story to them,' he told me, 'but it's our life.' Alan believes that a consequence of the paper's action was to frighten the police off. It reminded them of the hammering they had taken from the press during the search in the mid-eighties.

Myra Hindley was deeply frustrated by the police's decision. I believe that she wanted to help find the body, but needed to do so without incriminating herself further. She sent a series of maps, through me, to the forensic archaeologist Professor John Hunter. But these drawings were vague, always lacking enough detail to lead to the body. She could not put herself by the graveside in case it compromised her case for release.

After the failure of John Hunter's search, Myra Hindley focused on her legal campaign and took her case for freedom to the highest court in the land, the House of Lords. Frightened that she might succeed, the Home Secretary, David Blunkett, ordered Greater Manchester Police to assign a team of officers to the case. Again, Detective Superintendent Tony Brett's brief was not to find Keith Bennett. But Brett was a Mancunian, and he responded the way most Mancunians in his situation would: 'If we can find Keith Bennett, we will.' But after spending months trying to work out which of the pictures in the tartan album might be the marker, no 'X marks the spot' had materialized so no full-scale search was started. The police have now fed all the new information into a review of the case by Bramshill Police Academy.

There is a sharp divide between experts who have worked on the case. The police, and the Home Office, want certainty before conducting another search. Professor John Hunter, who works for police forces all over the world, says that such certainty cannot be found. The peat of Saddleworth Moor, he explains, lies like a blanket on top of the underlying rock. Over time, that blanket slips. A photograph in the tartan album that would have provided pinpoint accuracy forty years ago might now be several metres out. The professor says that the only answer is for the area around Shiny Brook to be cleared. But this action would need to be taken in the knowledge that it might fail, and that's a risk the authorities are not prepared to take.

Alan Bennett has waited patiently since a new police team was assigned to the case, hoping that a fresh search might be sanctioned. But it seems, once again, that the work will be left to him and his family. As I was writing this conclusion, a text message came through from him: 'Going to see the police and if nothing happens hope to start digging again.'

It is wrong, over forty years after his murder, that Keith Bennett's family are left to scrabble for his remains in the peat of Saddleworth Moor. Greater Manchester Police, and the Home Office, can be forgiven for their failure to see through the Moors murderers' lies, but they could not be forgiven for in-action now that they know the truth. Do they really want Ian Brady to retain possession of the perfect murder?

Index